TECHNOLOGY TOOLS FOR TEACHERS

A Microsoft® Office Tutorial

STEVEN C. MILLS
University of Kansas

M. D. ROBLYER
University of Maryland University College

Merrill
Prentice Hall

Upper Saddle River, New Jersey
Columbus, Ohio

Dedication

For Diane Mills and Eddy Mills,
Kyle and Jessika Hill,
Bill and Kimberly Langwell.

For Bill and Paige Wiencke:
The high-touch part of my high-tech life.

Library of Congress Cataloging-in-Publication Data

Mills, Steven C.
Technology tools for teachers: a Microsoft Office tutorial / by Steven C. Mills, M.D. Roblyer.
   p. cm.
  Includes bibliographical references and index.
    ISBN 0-13-029381-4
    1. Education—Data processing. 2. Microsoft Office. I. Roblyer, M.D. II. Title.
LB1028.43 .M553 2003
005.369—dc21   2002075307

Vice President and Publisher: Jeffery W. Johnston
Executive Editor: Debra A. Stollenwerk
Editorial Assistant: Mary Morrill
Development Editor: Kim Lundy
Production Editor: Sheryl Glicker Langner
Production Coordination: Lea Baranowski, Carlisle Publishers Service
Design Coordinator: Diane C. Lorenzo
Cover Designer: Linda Sorrells-Smith
Cover Art: Linda Bronson
Production Manager: Pam Bennett
Director of Marketing: Ann Castel Davis
Marketing Manager: Krista Groshong
Marketing Coordinator: Tyra Cooper

This book was set by in Century Book by Carlisle Communications, Ltd. It was printed and bound by Courier Kendallville, Inc. The cover was printed by Phoenix Color Corp.

Pearson Education Ltd.
Pearson Education Australia Pty. Limited
Pearson Education Singapore Pte. Ltd.
Pearson Education North Asia Ltd.
Pearson Education Canada, Ltd.
Pearson Educación de Mexico, S.A. de C. V.
Pearson Education—Japan
Pearson Education Malaysia Pte. Ltd.
Pearson Education, *Upper Saddle River, New Jersey*

10 9 8 7 6 5 4 3 2 1
ISBN: 0-13-029381-4

PREFACE

NOTES FOR THE PROFESSOR

We shall not fail or falter; we shall not weaken or tire... Give us the tools and we will finish the job.

Sir Winston Churchill, BBC radio broadcast, February 9, 1941

Churchill's sentiment seems as applicable for today's teachers as it was for the British people in 1941. Like them, teachers are dedicated, tireless, and committed workers in one of the noblest of callings. Like them, teachers are faced with a daunting task, and yet our very survival depends on their success in accomplishing it. But how the "tools" they are given have changed in the last 60 years! Who could have predicted that in the post-World War II era, we would become an Information Society in which technologies like word processing and e-mail would help re-define the nature of work and make fundamental changes in the way we relate to each other, to our jobs, and to the world itself?

This textbook was written as an acknowledgement of the importance to teachers and students of learning to use information tools that have become an essential part of the fabric of our modern society. Modern teachers are faced with the task of integrating these tools into their everyday work and, by their example and instruction, teaching their students to do the same. It is for this reason we feel that teaching teachers how to exploit the power of these tools is a crucial part of their preparation for the classroom.

This book was designed to help current and future teachers use a common and widely-used set of software tools, the Microsoft® *Office* suite, to gain the following insights and skills related to these software tools:

- **Software skills are a learning continuum**—The learning activities in each section are designed to take learners from low level of knowledge with each component to a fairly high level of skill. The chapter tutorials make it easy for beginners to learn the basics, but also show them how to build on this foundation. End-of-chapter exercises demonstrate how they can use Microsoft® *Office* Help and other features to increase their expertise with these powerful technologies.
- **Software tools can empower teachers**—As teachers learn the features of the software packages in Microsoft® *Office*, the examples they work through show them how the tools they are learning can enhance both their productivity and their teaching methods. The exercises not only teach them technical "how to" skills, they demonstrate that software tools are a fundamental part of every educator's "teaching toolkit."
- **Integrating software tools enables other technology integration**—Microsoft® *Office* is rapidly becoming the common denominator of classroom technology; many teachers have only this suite of programs available to them. Learning to use word processing, spreadsheets, presentation software, e-mail, and planning tools—all powerful resources in themselves— provides teachers with both the motivation and enabling skills to learn about the broader scope of technology tools available to teachers: instructional software, the Internet, multimedia/hypermedia, and content area tools.

Who Will Find This Book Useful

Educational Computing in Elementary/Secondary Education, Using Technology/ Computers in the Classroom, Instructional Design/Multimedia Authoring for Teachers Common software and communications applications including word processing, multimedia presentations, spreadsheets, e-mail, and the World Wide Web are now used in most teacher preparation courses in instructional technology as well as most K–12 classrooms. The authors of this book made several assumptions that were relevant for the publication of this book:

- Most universities now offer one or more teacher preparation courses in instructional technology, all or a portion of which is lab-based.
- The current focus of these teacher preparation courses in instructional technology is computer technology and not necessarily educational media or instructional design issues.
- There is an emphasis on curriculum integration of technology as opposed to only teacher use or productivity, suggesting the emergence of a generation of educators who will utilize the potential of computer-based technologies in the teaching/learning process.

This book is designed to support a hands-on approach to learning how to use software tools and integrate them into classroom activities. The methodology used by the book is to blend step-by-step lesson tutorials with technology application and integration activities. Each chapter demonstrates not only how to use particular features of the Microsoft® *Office* software productivity tools, but also provides examples of how to apply new skills in using these tools for classroom teaching and learning. This book should be useful in several educational contexts:

- **As a primary instructional text.** It can support basic instructional technology courses for preservice teachers and workshops and graduate courses for inservice teachers.
- **As a supplemental instructional text.** For courses that cover integration strategies for all technologies, this text can provide in-depth coverage of the software tools portion of integration.
- **As a reference.** In K–12 school libraries/media centers and university and college of education libraries and media centers, it can provide a handy way to look up specific skills and information related to the use of Microsoft® *Office* software tools in education.

Cognitive Tools for Technology Integration

The chapters in the book include tutorials and exercises that demonstrate features of Microsoft® *Word*, Microsoft® *Excel*, Microsoft® *PowerPoint*®, Microsoft® *Outlook*®, that can be used as cognitive tools to support and facilitate teaching and learning in 21st century classrooms. While this book is intended to tutor students in the use of software productivity tools, it is also very much about applying the technology skills acquired through the tutorials to create interesting and engaging learning experiences for the classroom. This book includes many features that will equip preservice and inservice teachers for integrating technology in the classroom:

- **Lesson procedures:** A list of the tutorial steps at the beginning of each chapter provides an advance organizer for the lesson content and instructional activities.

- **New terms:** New words for students to learn so they can "talk the talk" as well as "walk the walk." This feature supports or reinforces the chapter content and instructional activities.
- **Chapter overview of the lesson content and titles:** Each chapter starts with a short overview of the chapter contents and a list of the lessons in the chapter. This feature provides an advance organizer for the chapter instructional activities
- **Lesson tutorials:** Each chapter contains step-by-step lessons that teach the various features of the program as well as how to integrate these features into classroom teaching and learning.
- **Post-lesson exercises:** After each lesson are practice exercises to reinforce and support the technology skills described and demonstrated in the lesson.
- **Post-chapter exercises:** After each chapter are four sets of exercises:

   Set 1: Reviewing Terms and Concepts—Fill in items to review terms and concepts.
   Set 2: Expanding Your Skills—More activities to expand on skills learned in the chapter.
   Set 3: Use Microsoft® Help—Topics to look up on the Microsoft® *Office* Help Menu to get additional information on any topic and apply to the learning activities in the chapter.
   Set 4: Create Your Own Lesson—Ideas and activities for designing and developing a lesson that applies the features of the program to classroom teaching and learning.

- **Alignment with national technology standards:** The tutorial lessons presented in each section are aligned with the ISTE Standards for Students (NETS·S).
- **Lesson scenarios:** At the start of each section (for each productivity tool), a new case study or scenario is introduced. The chapters and lessons in the section are then presented from the point of view of a classroom teacher learning and applying the tool to teaching and learning in the context of his/her school and classroom.
- **Windows and Mac compatibility:** When differences occur between the Macintosh® and Windows® versions of an *Office*® task, a set of instructions specific to the Macintosh® version immediately follow the instructions for the current task.
- **Compatibility with most versions of Microsoft®** *Office:* The lessons are designed to be compatible with the latest releases of Microsoft® *Office* including Microsoft® *Office XP* for Windows® and Microsoft® *Office 2001* and *Outlook*® *2001* for Macintosh® as well as most earlier versions of these products.

The following ancillaries assist the instructor in helping students learn these technology tools and in evaluating their progress in integrating these technology tools to classroom instruction:

- **Lesson Plans ePortfolio:** The Lesson Plans ePortfolio is a database students use in conjunction with some of the practice exercises in this book. As students progress through the tutorials and exercises in the book, they will build a portfolio of technology-based learning activities that integrate technology into instruction. The Lesson Plans ePortfolio may be installed on the student computer from the T3 CD and both Windows and Mac versions are contained on the CD.
- **T3 Practice Files CD:** The T3 Practice CD that accompanies this book contains practice files and completed solutions to use in conjunction with some of the tutorials and exercises in this book. The files on the T3 Practice CD may be installed on the student computer or disk.

Acknowledgments

The year 2001 has given us a new appreciation for the freedom and opportunity we enjoy as Americans. We are reminded that writing a textbook is one of those extraordinary opportunities that occur because of the high value our country places on education for all its citizens. We acknowledge both our gratitude for this opportunity and our debt to so many people who make it possible for us to take advantage of it.

Our thanks go to the staff at Merrill/Prentice Hall who guided the development of this work with patience and competence. Debbie Stollenwerk, Heather Doyle Fraser, Kim Lundy, and Lea Baranowski (Carlisle Publishers Services) are, as usual, a pleasure to work with and a constant source of fresh ideas and good-natured encouragement. We are grateful to our families and friends who supported and sustained us during the long labor of writing and rewriting, creating, and revising. Steven C. Mills is grateful to his wife, Diane Mills, who has always encouraged him to write, and for her support and understanding and that of their son, Eddy Mills, for their sacrifice during the long hours spent writing this book, to Cynthia Huebner for assistance with indexing and proofing, and to Tim Zeigler, Eddy's science teacher, and the many teachers who have provided information as well as inspiration for the learning activities presented in this book. M.D. Roblyer is especially grateful for the support of her husband, Bill Wiencke, and daughter, Paige Wiencke, and friends Sherry Alter and Paul Belt, Herb and Marilyn Comet, Barbara Hansen, Jon and Sharon Marshall, Mary Ann Myers, Sharon Milner, Gwen McAlpine, and Paul Zimmer. Finally, we acknowledge the contributions of those who are with us now only in memory: Dorothy J. Mills, S. L. Roblyer, Catherine Pryor Roblyer, and Raymond and Marjorie Wiencke. We appreciate the suggestions provided by those who reviewed the text: Lee Allen, Southern Methodist University; Michael Blocher, Northern Arizona University; Kim Foreman, San Francisco State University; Mary Juliano, SSJ, Caldwell College; Virginia Jewell, Clark County Appalachian School System.

NOTES FOR THE TEACHER AS LEARNER

Why This Book Was Written

You thought teaching was already difficult. Then came the Information Age! Now nearly everyone you know is trading disks of lesson plans, doing *PowerPoint*® presentations, keeping their grades on spreadsheets, and surfing the Internet. It's time to begin learning new skills and start using a whole new set of tools, but you are suddenly overwhelmed. After all, you never wanted to be a techno-whiz!

Yet there is good news! First, this book will take you, the beginner, on a step-by-step tour through the landscape of this new territory you soon will own yourself. Second, once you learn these tools, you will be ecstatic about the ways they enhance your work. Some examples are:

- **Better productivity:** The nickname for the programs you will learn in this book is "productivity tools." Once you have learned them, it will be faster for you to get organized, produce instructional materials, or accomplish paperwork tasks (e.g., create handouts or calculate grades). This saves valuable time that you can use to focus on working with your students or designing new learning activities for them.
- **Improved appearance:** You will be able to produce high-quality materials that resemble the work of professional designers. In fact, these tools are frequently the same ones used by professional designers. The quality of classroom products is limited only by the talents and skills of teachers and students using the tools. Students appreciate working with professional-looking materials, and they also find it rewarding and challenging to produce attractive products of their own.
- **Improved accuracy:** You will find it easier to keep more precise, accurate records of events and student accomplishments. More accurate information supports better instructional decisions about curriculum and student activities.
- **Support for sharing:** These tools let you take advantage of instructional materials, handouts, and products that teachers have created—and you can share your own with them.
- **Enhanced instruction, more visual learning:** Many teachers find that software tools help them teach better by giving more visual explanations and examples. For example, a *PowerPoint*® presentation provides pictures and videos along with text, and a spreadsheet helps students see how modifying one number has an impact on changing totals, averages, and other summary data.
- **Enhanced instruction, multimedia methods:** *PowerPoint*® is a multimedia tool that allows teachers to include many sensory modes. You can use pictures, sounds, movies, and text to illustrate concepts and give examples.
- **Enhanced instruction, group learning:** All the capabilities described above let people create products that can be revised easily at any time and that promote interaction among students. They have the effect of helping to change teaching strategies from largely individualized to more group-based and from

mostly directed models to primarily student-centered ones. For example, they can allow input from several people at once and can encourage many creative, cooperative group-learning activities.

Each chapter will show you examples of how you can incorporate your new skills into your teaching. You will find that even though it takes some hard work to acquire each of these new skills, you will have made a good investment of your time and effort.

What You Need to Use This Book

You will need three resources to take advantage of this book. Two of these resources are materials, and one is the set of skills you must bring to this work.

1. **Computer requirements:** You will need the following:

   - A personal computer (a Windows® PC or a Macintosh®)
   - Microsoft® Windows® 95, 98 or later operating system, or Microsoft® Windows® NT Workstation operating system 4.0 or later
   - 128 megabytes (MB) of memory is recommended
   - A printer
   - A CD-ROM drive
   - A color monitor
   - A keyboard and a mouse

2. **Software:** Although you can use any software tools, this book uses Microsoft® *Office*, a specific collection of programs that is widely used by teachers.

3. **Prerequisite skills:** Know your computer system! Be able to identify and understand the use of each of the following components:

   - **Capabilities of the system you are using:** How many disk drives are there? How much memory is on the hard disk drive? How much Random Access Memory (RAM) is inside the computer? What is the version of the operating system? What is the size/kind of monitor? What type of printer is connected, and how fast does it print? Is there a CD-ROM, DVD, or zip drive?
   - **Basic how-to operations:** Turn on/off all the devices of the system; use each of the keys on your keyboard; use a mouse; use the Microsoft Windows® desktop, including the icons for programs, files, and folders or subdirectories and how to use them.
   - **Types of computer media:** Diskettes, zip disks, CD-ROMs, and DVDs and how much memory each contains.
   - **Disk how-to operations:** Insert a blank disk into the drive; initialize/format it; rename a disk; move items from a disk to a hard drive or from one disk to another; copy a disk; remove a disk from a disk drive; correctly handle and store disks.

What You Will Learn: The Microsoft® *Office* Suite

Microsoft® *Office* is not one program but a set or suite of programs providing a number of functions that operate similarly and easily in order to share data or information with one another. This book will help you learn four of these programs:

- **Microsoft® *Word*:** *Word* is a word processing program that lets you use, create, and publish documents that contain text, such as letters or reports. A word processing program allows you to create form letters that can be merged with a mailing list.

- **Microsoft® *Excel:*** *Excel* is a spreadsheet program that lets you create and publish documents that use numbers and calculations, such as grade books or budgets. A spreadsheet also allows you to format information in rows and columns and to display data as graphs or charts.
- **Microsoft® *PowerPoint®*:** *PowerPoint®* is a presentation program that lets you produce sets of slides with text or graphics information that can be displayed on a computer screen as a slide show or projected on a larger screen using a projection device for a large-group presentation.
- **Microsoft® *Outlook®*:** *Outlook®* is a messaging and collaboration program that lets you communicate with other people using e-mail and organize and share information on your desktop. *Outlook®* includes functions such as e-mail, contact information storage, calendaring, and project management.

The lessons in this tutorial textbook are designed to work with the current releases of Microsoft® *Office* and *Outlook®* for Windows and Macintosh®. The latest releases of the *Office* suite are Microsoft® *Office XP* for Windows® and Microsoft® *Office 2001* and *Outlook® 2001* for Macintosh®. The lessons are designed to be compatible with the latest release as well as most earlier versions of these products. The sections of this book are aligned with the *Office Standard for Students and Teachers* suite, which includes *Word, Excel, PowerPoint®,* and *Outlook®*. (See Appendix B.)

Components in Each Part and Each Chapter

Chapter 1 contains introductory tips on how to learn more efficiently. Following it are parts for each of these four Microsoft® *Office* tools. Within each part you will find chapters to help you learn various skills in using the software. Each of these chapters has a common structure:

- **New Terms:** New words for you to learn related to the lessons in the chapter
- **Chapter Overview:** The lesson content and titles in the chapter
- **Lesson Tutorials:** Each chapter contains two or three tutorial lessons to teach you various features of the program as well as how to integrate these features into classroom teaching and learning. The T3 Practice CD that accompanies this book contains practice files and completed solutions to use in conjunction with some of the tutorials and exercises in this book. Look for the T3 Practice CD icon to indicate that you need supporting files from the T3 Practice CD.
- **Postlesson exercises:** After each lesson are more practice exercises, Follow-up Practice Projects, to reinforce and support the technology skills demonstrated in the lesson. The T3 Practice CD also contains a Lesson Plans ePortfolio that you may install on your computer. The Lesson Plans ePortfolio is a database to use in conjunction with some of the practice exercises in this book. As you progress through the tutorials and exercises in the book, you will build a portfolio of technology-based learning activities that integrate technology into instruction. Look for the Lesson Plans ePortfolio icon to indicate that the practice exercise includes ideas and activities you can use to add lesson plans to the Lesson Plans ePortfolio.
- **Postchapter exercises:** After each chapter are four sets of exercises:

  Set 1: Reviewing Terms and Concepts: Fill-in items to review terms and concepts

  Set 2: Expanding Your Skills: Activities to expand on skills you learned in the chapter

Set 3: Use Microsoft® Help: Topics for you to look up on the Microsoft® *Office* Help Menu to get additional information on any topic and help with troubleshooting procedures when you encounter problems

Set 4: Create Your Own Lesson: Opportunities for you to develop and describe a lesson that makes effective use of software features. You can use these ideas to create additional lesson plans and add them to the Lesson Plans ePortfolio

Using This Book

Integrating technology in the classroom is not so much about technology—it is about teaching and learning! Before you can integrate technology into your teaching, however, you need to be proficient in the tools for teaching that computer technology makes available. While this book is intended to tutor you in the use of some of these technology tools, it is also very much about applying your new technology skills to creating interesting and engaging learning experiences for your students. The tutorials and practice exercises in this book are loaded with instructional activities and lesson plan examples that will enable you to quickly add the various technology tools presented in this book to your teaching toolbox.

Managing Files

Know the location of your files

It is helpful if you understand how to manage files on the computer hardware platform you are using. When you open or save files, it is important that you know the location of the file. Files may be located on the hard disk of your computer, on a CD-ROM in the CD drive of your computer, or on a floppy disk in the floppy disk drive of your computer. Since different users of this book will use different hardware and software configurations, the instructions in the lessons do not provide references to specific locations of your files. You have to supply this information.

Know the drive names on your computer

On a computer using the Windows® operating system, the hard disk is usually called the C: drive while on a Macintosh® it is called by its assigned name or label such as Mac HD or Mac Hard Disk. The CD-ROM drive (we call it the CD) may be assigned some other drive letter such as D: or E: on a computer using the Windows® operating system, while on a Macintosh® the CD pops up on the Desktop when you insert it into the CD drive and it is called by its assigned name or label. The floppy disk drive (we just call it the disk) is usually assigned drive letter A: on a computer using the Windows® operating system, while on a Macintosh® the disk pops up on the Desktop when you insert it into the disk drive and it is called by its assigned name or label.

Know how folders work

Files are stored in folders. Folders are sometimes called subdirectories on computers using the Windows® operating system. Folders are areas of computer storage where collections of files are stored. Some folders are built into the file structure of your computer operating system (e.g., the Desktop folder or Programs folder) while other folders can be created and named by the user (e.g., My Word Documents folder).

Know how to use folders

The default folder for a program is the folder in which a program automatically or first looks to locate a file. Most computers using the Windows® operating system will have a folder named My Documents. The My Documents folder is usually located on the Desktop or hard drive of your computer. Macintosh® users may want to create a folder on the Desktop named Documents or My Documents. Microsoft® *Office* applications generally default to the My Documents folder under Windows®. To use this book, you should know how to locate files in a folder on the hard disk, CD drive, or disk drive of your computer.

Conventions Used in This Book

Several conventions are used in this text to standardize the explanation of how to perform the tutorial steps of a program operation or function. A more extensive explanation of the common features among the programs in the Microsoft® *Office* suite is included in the appendices.

- The first step for selecting a command from the Menu Bar in the tutorial steps is expressed by stating the Menu command followed by the option from the drop-down menu. For example, to open a file, saying "select Open from the File menu" would simply be expressed as **File | Open.**
- **CAPS** and bold print are used for keyboard keys to be pressed. For example, "press **DELETE.**"
- When the tutorial steps refer to the ENTER key, you should press the RETURN key on the Macintosh®.
- User interactions required to perform the tutorial steps including menu commands, icons, buttons, and folders to be clicked are listed in **bold** print.
- Text to be typed or input appears in **bold** print.
- For some tasks, screen captures (replicas of the screen display) are provided to assist the learner in visualizing the corresponding task. All screen shots are from the Windows® version of the program. Some differences in the look of the screen captures in the text and your screen may occur. These differences do not necessarily mean that you have performed the task incorrectly but may be due to differences in versions of the program or differences in hardware platforms.
- When a concept is taught and differences occur between the Macintosh® and Windows® versions of the task, a set of instructions specific to the Macintosh® version appears in the margin, not within the windows instructions. If the differences are slight, a parenthetical notation is inserted within the text of a tutorial step.

Differences in Microsoft® *Office XP*

This text is designed to work with most versions of Microsoft® *Office*. The latest version of Microsoft® *Office*, which is called *XP*, provides several new features. Although all the basic commands and menu functions have remained essentially the same as in previous versions, these new features sometimes provide a little different look to the *Office*® interface. The learning tasks and procedures in this text generally will not refer to these features since all users of this text may not be using the *XP* version of Microsoft® *Office*. A more complete discussion of all the products and versions in the Microsoft® *Office* suite is included in the appendices.

If you are using Microsoft® *Office XP*, some of the new features that may result in differences in the look of the *Office*® interface on your computer and what is shown in the text include the following:

- **Office Task Panes:** Many common tasks are organized in panes that pop up or display on the right side of your document window. Your document continues to be displayed, and you can work in your document or you can work in the Task Pane. The Task Pane replaces several features that were formerly performed using Wizards that were layered over your document window. Additionally, the Task Pane provides enhanced processing capability while you work in your document. For example, you can quickly create new documents or open files using the Task Pane. You can close the task pane at any time once it pops up on the screen. Task Panes vary per *Office*® program.

- **Clipboard gallery:** When multiple items have been copied to the clipboard, a clipboard gallery is displayed in the Task Pane.
- **Enhanced interface:** Microsoft® *Office XP* uses softer colors to create a cleaner, simpler look.
- **More convenient access to Help:** In *Office*® *XP* the Answer Wizard is less obtrusive. When you enter a question about an Office program in the Ask a Question box on the Menu Bar, you can see a list of choices and read a Help topic whether or not you are running the Office Assistant.
- **Smart Tags to control paste options and automatic changes:** When you change or paste information in your document, in-place buttons called Smart Tags allow you to adjust how information is formatted when it is pasted to a new document or a new location in the same document. For example, when you paste text from Microsoft® *Word* into Microsoft® *PowerPoint*® or even from one location in a *Word* document to another location in the same document, a button appears next to the text. You may click the button to see a list of choices for fine-tuning the formatting of the pasted text, or you may ignore the Smart Tag and it will disappear when you begin another operation. Smart Tags and their associated choices vary per *Office* program.

Credits

Microsoft®, Windows®, *Outlook*®, *PowerPoint*®, *Exchange, Internet Explorer*®, *Office XP*®, and *FrontPage*® are registered trademarks of Microsoft Corporation in the United States and/or other countries. Microsoft® *Office, Word, Excel, Access, Publisher*®, and other Microsoft® products and their features and various versions mentioned in this text are products of Microsoft Corporation.

Mac® and Macintosh® are registered trademarks of Apple Computer, Inc.

All screen captures used in this text are reprinted by permission from Microsoft Corporation.

National Educational Technology Standards for Students, copyright © 2000, International Society for Technology in Education (ISTE). All rights reserved.

BRIEF CONTENTS

CONTENTS

CHAPTER 3   DOCUMENT LAYOUT AND GRAPHICS EFFECTS USING *WORD*   33

CHAPTER 4   CONSTRUCTING INTERACTIVE FORMS AND WEB DOCUMENTS WITH *WORD*   49

PART 2   INTEGRATING TECHNOLOGY IN THE CLASSROOM WITH MICROSOFT® *EXCEL*   61

CHAPTER 5   NAVIGATING, UPDATING, AND FORMATTING WORKSHEETS IN *EXCEL*   65

PART 3   INTEGRATING TECHNOLOGY IN THE CLASSROOM WITH MICROSOFT® *POWERPOINT*®   125

CHAPTER 8   DESIGNING PRESENTATIONS AND HANDOUTS USING *POWERPOINT*®   131

TECHNOLOGY TOOLS FOR TEACHERS: INTRODUCTION

Learning Activities

Technology Tools for Teachers
Ten Tips for Tackling Technology
Start-up Techniques
Technology Standards for Students

NEW TERMS

electronic spreadsheet	*Office*® Assistant	Windows®
e-mail	presentation	word processing
ISTE	shortcut	
NETS	technology standards	

OVERVIEW

Bob Harris is District Technology Coordinator for Rockville Independent School District. Although Bob considers himself an educator and instructional leader, like many school district technology departments he has no staff other than himself. He is responsible for providing computer and technology support for all the schools in the district. Therefore, he spends most of his time providing technical support for the district network and solving computer hardware and software problems. Little of his time is available for providing leadership in the instructional use of computers and the integration of technology in classrooms. Bob primarily functions as a network administrator, computer programmer, and computer technician.

Since Bob has so little time to devote to technology integration in classrooms, he has devised a simple plan for strengthening the educational and instructional use of technology in classrooms. All of the classrooms in Rockville ISD have at least one computer, and some even more. Additionally, several computer labs are distributed

throughout the district. Most of the computers in his district use the Windows®
operating system, although some computers labs are equipped with Macintosh®
computers. All have Microsoft® *Office* installed on them. Because of limitated
time and the availability of a common software platform in the district, Bob focuses the application of educational technology in classrooms to teaching teachers to use *Office*®.

Bob reviews several current textbooks used in technology integration courses
in teacher preparation programs and then reviews the features of Microsoft® *Office*.
He discovers that *Office*® programs have potential as productivity tools and as
agents for creating and implementing teaching and learning activities in the classroom.

As Bob discovered for the teachers in his school district, other teachers you will
meet throughout this book are also discovering that the productivity tools in Mi-
crosoft® *Office* offer them the opportunity to begin integrating technology in their
classrooms. As these teachers learn to use the various programs in *Office*®, they are
finding ways to use these productivity tools to develop interesting and engaging
learning activities.

TECHNOLOGY TOOLS FOR TEACHERS

Word processing is a software tool that facilitates written communication. With
word processing teachers can save time on their own work and help each other
by sharing written documents. They can word process anything they type or
write by hand. Likewise, word processing supports a variety of teaching and
learning activities by allowing students to become more involved in critical
thinking activities as they think about what their words really mean, use an ex-
tended vocabulary, and elaborate, reorganize, and refine written composition
(Morrison, Lowther, & DeMeulle, 1999). Word processing makes it faster and easier for students to complete their work of writing, editing, and illustrating stories
and reports or keeping classroom notes and logs. Word processing allows a class
or group of students to produce a group poem, letter, or story, each student
adding and/or changing lines or producing new sections (Roblyer, 2003). Word
processed exercises can allow students to combine sentences, add or correct
punctuation, write sentences for spelling or vocabulary words, or identify parts
of speech. Students and teachers can save work on disk and take it from one
classroom to another or send it through e-mail or a computer network, making it
easier to integrate writing into interdisciplinary and thematic learning activities
or to form collaborative writing teams.

    Electronic spreadsheets are computerized ledger sheets organized in rows
and columns in which a user can automatically perform calculations or other operations on numeric or text data. Teachers can use electronic spreadsheets to prepare classroom instructional materials or perform calculations they would
otherwise do manually. For example, they can keep grade or attendance records or
prepare budgets on spreadsheets. The act of creating spreadsheets causes learners
to engage in a variety of mental processes, including generating rules and relationships and organizing information (Jonassen, 2000). The role of spreadsheets in the
classroom has focused primarily on mathematics and science, but teachers may integrate spreadsheets into classroom instruction through demonstrations of concepts, creation of student worksheet products, support for problem-solving and
decision-making, storing and analyzing data, and projections and simulations
(Roblyer, 2003).

    Presentation software provides the capability to combine and present the re-
sults of word processing and electronic spreadsheet products. Movie clips, sounds,
music, graphics, animation, and hyperlinks can be added to the presentation to cre-

ate a nonlinear presentation that stimulates more of the senses (Forcier & Descy, 2002). Presentations are often used for whole classes of students or even to enhance large-group lectures (Roblyer, 2003). They also are useful for organizing and enhancing the communication of information in the classroom. Further, teachers may use multimedia presentations to reinforce classroom instruction and to prepare and provide handouts and notes to students. For example, they may use presentations to introduce and overview a unit of instruction or provide a structure or sequence of learning activities for students to follow. The construction of presentations cause learners to engage in both creative thinking skills and a number of complex thinking skills, including designing, organizing, problem solving, and decision making (Jonassen, 2000). While teachers will find presentations effective for communicating information in classroom lectures and discussions, students will develop communication skills and reinforce learning when they are required to design and develop presentations that explain a learning activity or project in which they participated.

E-mail programs send written messages electronically between computers connected by a local area network or by the Internet. E-mail allows teachers, students, and resource experts to send and receive messages to and from one another, which is especially useful for collaborations when teachers, students, or experts are separated by distance or time. Through e-mail collaborations with students in other schools, experts, or people in other communities around the world, students become aware of the global nature of information and discover the importance of connecting with others in acquiring knowledge and information (Morrison, Lowther, & DeMeulle, 1999).

Planning and organizing tools help teachers and students organize their time and plan their activities (Roblyer, 2003). Calendaring or scheduling programs provide the capability of planning and managing appointments on a daily, weekly, or monthly schedule. Scheduling programs often have the capability of providing reminders of activities prior to their occurrence. Project management tools help in coordinating projects and activities by tracking the specific details or tasks of a project, progress in completing the project, and the time required to complete individual tasks and/or the whole project.

TEN TIPS FOR TACKLING TECHNOLOGY

1: Learn a Little Every Day, Make the Anxiety Go Away

Software tools have many, many features to make your life easier, but you will learn them over time, rather than all at once. Even experienced technology users say they learn something new nearly every time they sit down to work at a computer. Therefore, do not become overwhelmed at the number of things you do not know yet or worry that you are learning too slowly. Instead, congratulate yourself each day on what you *have* learned. One way to do this is to check off the beginning-of-the-chapter learning activities as you learn them. Review them every day to remind yourself of the good progress you are making.

2: Keep Trying—Everything Is Easier Once You Know How

You may sometimes become frustrated because a software feature does not work as you think it should. Although software can have "bugs" or "glitches" (errors in how the program functions) usually it works exactly as the person who designed it intended. The difficult part is understanding how the designer thought it should work! Once you understand it, it will be as natural for you to continue doing it that way as if you designed it yourself.

3: Have a Human Helper Handy

Like working crossword puzzles, some people like to figure out computer tasks for themselves. Most of us, though, prefer to take our more thorny technical problems to an expert. Identify others whom you can call on when you become frustrated while learning these new concepts, but try not to rely on them too much. Develop your own problem solving and troubleshooting abilities, but remember that a little human help once in a while may be just the boost you need.

4: Arrange Your Work Space Comfortably

A comfortable work environment will help you learn better, enjoy what you are doing, and prevent discomfort or fatigue. Place your monitor on a surface so that the screen is at or below eye level. With your feet comfortably resting on the floor, sit as straight as you can in a chair that supports your back and has arms to support your forearms as you type. Have a well-lighted area but reduce glare on your monitor. Take frequent breaks to rest your eyes and your hands.

5: Refrain from Turning Off the Computer

Unless you become so frustrated that you hit the computer with a blunt object, it is difficult to do any lasting damage to it. Refrain from correcting problems by turning off the computer and turning it on again, which is the tendency of many novice computer users. Although turning off the computer will not necessarily damage the computer, it may cause you to lose some of your work. Unless the computer "freezes up" so you cannot make the mouse or keyboard respond, quit the program as described in this book, rather than turning off the machine.

6: Save, Save, and Save Your Work

Learn that your work must be saved to disk frequently. If the computer "freezes up" or the electricity goes off, you will lose any work you have not saved. As a rule of thumb, save everything unless you do not mind doing it over again. Even if you saved your document, new information that you added or changes that you made are not saved until you resave the document. The authors of this text recommend saving every few minutes or after entering a few lines or items.

7: Back It Up If It Is Important

A corollary to the "save, save, save" rule is to keep copies of important work in more than one place. Multiple copies are insurance in case something happens to the hard disk or the disk medium on which the file is stored. Most users work from and store on the hard drive, saving every minute or two to a specified location. But before you end any work session, put a copy of your important work on a floppy or zip disk, a CD-ROM, or, if none of these is handy, on another location on the hard drive.

8: Recognize that Software Tools Have Differences and Similarities

The Microsoft® *Office* software tools you learn in this book have many features in common with other software packages, but procedures do differ from program to program. Also, software manufacturers tend to update their software every so often, resulting in a changed appearance on the screen (e.g., the menus) and clicks and keystrokes for carrying out procedures. If you look at your learning in terms of concepts, rather than sequenced steps, you will find that what you learn in this book will transfer easily to other tools you learn in the future.

9: Know Your Computer

Computer systems differ from one machine to the next and from one "platform" (e.g., Windows® vs. Macintosh®) to the next. The system that is "better" is a source of continual and probably pointless debate. Simply know the system on which you are working, whatever it is. Determine that you have enough computer memory to support Microsoft® *Office*, and know the correct procedures to keep track of where you are saving your work.

10: Have Patience and a Pioneering Attitude

Finally, the attitude you adopt as you learn these new and powerful tools is very important. Learning will become easier as you go. Do not feel unique or "stupid" if you become frustrated; even computer experts feel frustrated now and then. The traveling on your journey learning computers is as important as the destination. Although you may not want to become one, you may find there is a techno-wiz in yourself. Enjoy the trip!

START-UP TECHNIQUES

How to Start a Program in Microsoft® *Office*

Microsoft® *Office* is a suite of programs or software tools. Each program in the suite provides a different function for formating and organizing information. For example, *Word* creates and formats text, *Excel* creates and formats numbers and text and performs calculations, and *PowerPoint®* creates text and graphic presentations. *Office®* also provides tools for sending e-mail, scheduling, and managing tasks. You can choose from three different ways to start a program in *Office®* on a computer using the Windows® operating system:

Macintosh®: Locate and double click the icon for Microsoft® *Word*. If the Microsoft® *Office* Manager is installed on your computer, click on the *Office®* Manager icon and highlight and select Microsoft® *Word* from the drop-down menu.

❶ If you have an icon for a program or document on your desktop, you can double-click on the icon. The program (e.g., *Word, Excel, PowerPoint®*) will open, and if the icon represents a document, double-clicking on it starts the program and opens the document in one step. For that reason the icon is called a shortcut (Macintosh® calls it an alias).

❷ **Windows® only:** Click the **Start** button (see example to the right) located on the Taskbar to access the menu of programs. Move your cursor up to **Programs.** After you click **Programs** or when the list of programs appears, select the program you want (e.g., Microsoft *Word*) by clicking once on its name. Once the program opens, you can open a blank document or an existing file.

❸ **Windows® only:** When you install Microsoft® *Office*, one of the options is to install a *Office®* Shortcut Bar. The Shortcut Bar is positioned at the top, bottom, or side of the Windows® screen and includes an icon for each program. To open a specific program, click the shortcut icon for that program. Once the program opens, you can open a blank document or an existing file.

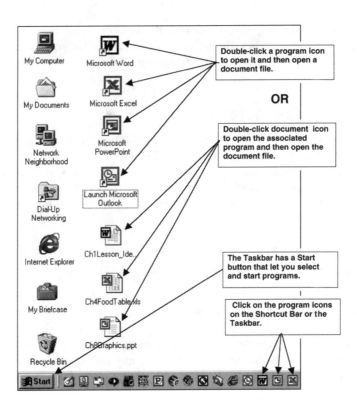

The Windows® screen capture[1] (above) illustrates options for starting Microsoft® *Office* programs.

Getting to Know the *Office*® Assistant

When you start a Microsoft® *Office* program, you notice immediately an animated "creature" that looks like an animated paper clip standing on a sheet of paper. Other computers may have one that looks like a robot, a cat, or another type of animated creature. It is called the Office Assistant and helps you if you need it. If you click on the **Assistant,** a list of Help topics appears. If the list does not include the information you need, type in your request (for example, "How do I do a header?") and select **Search.**

Sometimes a light bulb will appear near the Office Assistant to let you know it has a tip to help you with your current document. Click on the light bulb to get the tip. If you find the Office Assistant distracting (or even annoying), you can "hide" it. Place your cursor on the **Assistant** and right-click your mouse. On the pop-up menu that appears, click **Hide.** You can bring it back whenever you wish by selecting **Help | Show the Office Assistant** on the **Menu Bar.**

TECHNOLOGY STANDARDS FOR STUDENTS

Guidelines and Indicators for Integrating Computer Technology in the Classroom

Standards reflect shared values by identifying and describing those things that are important for a student to know and do. The National Educational Technology Standards

---

[1]Screen captures of Microsoft® Windows® are reprinted by permission from Microsoft® Corporation.

(NETS) is an ongoing initiative of the International Society for Technology in Education (ISTE), a professional organization for educators who use technology. The primary goal of the NETS project is to recommend national standards for educational uses of technology that facilitate school improvement in the United States (ISTE, 2001).

The NETS project has currently defined standards for students (NETS·S), teachers (NETS·T), and school administrators (TSSA). The NETS·S is comprised of 14 indicators that are organized into 6 categories. These standards are useful for teachers in planning classroom learning activities to develop recognized technology skills and proficiency in their students.

National Educational Technology Standards for Students

The technology foundation standards for students are divided into six categories with 14 indicators for the categories. Standards within each category are to be introduced, reinforced, and mastered by students. Teachers can use these standards as guidelines for planning technology-based activities in which students achieve success in learning, communication, and life skills.

1. Basic operations and concepts

   - Students demonstrate a sound understanding of the nature and operation of technology systems.
   - Students are proficient in the use of technology.

2. Social, ethical, and human issues

   - Students understand the ethical, cultural, and societal issues related to technology.
   - Students practice responsible use of technology systems, information, and software.
   - Students develop positive attitudes toward technology uses that support lifelong learning, collaboration, personal pursuits, and productivity.

3. Technology productivity tools

   - Students use technology tools to enhance learning, increase productivity, and promote creativity.
   - Students use productivity tools to collaborate in constructing technology-enhanced models, prepare publications, and produce other creative works.

4. Technology communications tools

   - Students use telecommunications to collaborate, publish, and interact with peers, experts, and other audiences.
   - Students use a variety of media and formats to communicate information and ideas effectively to multiple audiences.

5. Technology research tools

   - Students use technology to locate, evaluate, and collect information from a variety of sources.
   - Students use technology tools to process data and report results.
   - Students evaluate and select new information resources and technological innovations based on the appropriateness for specific tasks.

6. Technology problem-solving and decision-making tools

    • Students use technology resources for solving problems and making in-formed decisions.
    • Students employ technology in the development of strategies for solving problems in the real world.[2]

The text will provide annotations at the beginning of each part that reference the NETS·S for the corresponding Microsoft® *Office* program. All the NETS·S will be addressed by the learning activities in this book.

EXERCISES TO REVIEW AND EXPAND YOUR SKILLS

Set 1: **Reviewing Terms and Concepts**—For each question below, provide a term on the blank that matches the description.

_____ **1.** An icon that represents and allows a user to open a program or document.

_____ **2.** A software tool that performs calculations and may be used to calculate grades, maintain attendance records, or prepare budgets.

_____ **3.** A software tool for storing and revising text information and may be used by students to write, edit, and illustrate stories and reports or keep classroom notes and logs.

_____ **4.** A software tool often used for organizing and enhancing the communication of information in the classroom and to support or reinforce group lectures.

_____ **5.** Definitions and descriptions of technology-related skills that are important for students to know and do, published by ISTE.

Set 2: **Expanding Your Skills**—Insert the **T3 Practice CD** in the CD drive of your computer. Based on the computer hardware platform you are using, lo-cate and open either the **Macintosh® Lesson Plans** folder or the **Windows® Lesson Plans** folder by double-clicking on the folder icon or folder name. Next, double-click the **Lesson Plans ePortfolio** icon or file name inside the folder to open the portfolio file. Use the **Next** and **Previous** buttons to scroll through the sample lesson plans in the portfolio file. Click **Print** to print the sample lesson plan for each software tool—word pro-cessing, spreadsheet, and presentation—when the lesson plan is displayed on the screen. Press **Quit** to close and exit the **Lesson Plans ePortfolio.**

Set 3: **Use Microsoft® Help**—Microsoft® Windows® Help can provide additional information on any topic and help with troubleshooting procedures when you encounter problems. Click **Start,** located on the Taskbar at the bottom of the Windows® screen to access the menu of programs. Move your cursor up and select **Help.** In the **Windows® Help** dialog box, select the **Index** tab and in the **Type in the keyword to find** box, enter the following features to get further information and tips. Close the Windows® Help dialog box when you have completed the learning activity.

---

[2] Reprinted with permission from *National Educational Technology Standards for Students-Connecting Curriculum and Technology,* copyright ©2000, ISTE (International Society for Technology in Education). For a complete listing of these standards, see pages 7–8.

- **Shortcuts:** To start a program or open a file or folder without having to go to its permanent location in Windows®.
- **My Documents:** A desktop folder that provides a convenient place to store documents, graphics, or other files you want to access quickly. Review the topic on customizing the default settings for a workbook or worksheet.
- **Accessibility:** To find features, products, and services that make Microsoft® Windows® operating systems more accessible for people with disabilities.

Set 4: Create Your Own Lesson—Adding Lesson Plans to the Database— The following exercise is intended to prepare you for adding lesson plans you prepare to the **Lesson Plans ePortfolio** in subsequent chapters of this book. To add lesson plans to the **Lesson Plans ePortfolio,** you must install it on your hard drive (the file is too big to use on a floppy disk). You cannot add lesson plans to the **Lesson Plans ePortfolio** file on the CD.

Install the **Lesson Plans ePortfolio** on your hard drive by dragging or copying the **Macintosh® Lesson Plans folder** or **Windows® Lesson Plans folder** from the **T3 Practice Disk** to an appropriate location on your hard drive. Personalize the folder by renaming it (e.g., Mills Lesson Plans). **Do not rename the portfolio file**.

To open the portfolio and add lesson plans, double-click on the folder you just copied to your hard drive and then double-click the **Lesson Plans ePortfolio** icon or file listing. Practice adding a sample lesson plan to your lesson plan portfolio:

1. When the Lesson Plans ePortfolio update screen is displayed (see Figure 1-1), click **New** to start a new lesson plan. To move from field to field, use **TAB.** To start a new line within a field, press **ENTER.**

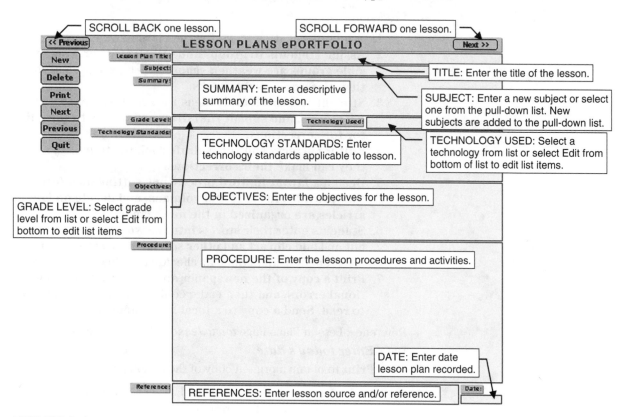

FIGURE 1–1
Lesson Plans ePortfolio Update Screen

2. Enter the following sample lesson information into the Lesson Plans ePortfolio Update Screen:

Lesson Plan Title: **Publishing a Student Newspaper Using Word Processing**

Subject: **Select Language Arts**

Summary: **Invite a reporter from a local newspaper to discuss how reporters work and how papers are put together. Students use Microsoft Word to create a class newspaper. The class newspaper reports on current assignments and homework, school events, and community affairs.**

Grade Level: **Select High School**

Technology Used: **Select Word Processing**

Technology Standards:

1. **Students use technology tools to enhance learning, increase productivity, and promote creativity.**
2. **Students use productivity tools to collaborate in constructing technology-enhanced models, prepare publications, and produce other creative works.**

Objectives:

1. **Exercise skills in basic typing.**
2. **Use formatting and desktop publishing features of Word.**
3. **Collect and research information and reports.**
4. **Structure a document using columns and insert graphics in documents.**
5. **Write and design creatively.**

Procedure:

1. **Students create a name for the class newspaper.**
2. **Assign students to groups and elect an editor. Some possible groups are weather, school sports, school activities, classroom assignments.**
3. **Students research topic ideas for articles, create ideas for stories, and submit first drafts of stories to the editor for corrections.**
4. **Editor corrects and sends draft back to students so that they can make their corrections.**
5. **Design a layout in word processing, setting up a format that provides for title and columns, and decide on how articles are organized in the newspaper.**
6. **Students enter their stories into the word processing layout and add clip art and other special effects; use automatic spelling and grammar checking to check for errors.**
7. **Print a copy of the newspaper and proofread for additional errors, and then make copies for the whole school to read. Send a copy to a local newspaper to evaluate.**

Reference: Lesson Plans Page *www.lessonplanspage.com*

Date: ***Enter today's date***

3. Click **Print** to obtain a printed copy of the lesson plan.

- To delete a Lesson Plan, with the Lesson Plan displayed on the screen, press the **Delete** button.

- The **Previous** button allows you to scroll backward through your lesson plans. The **Next** button allows you to scroll forward through your lesson plans.
- Make revisions to the text in any field (except the drop-down lists) by clicking in the field and editing the text.

4. Click **Quit** to exit the **Lesson Plans ePortfolio.**

In later chapters when exercises direct you to add a new lesson plan to the **Lesson Plans ePortfolio,** refer to these steps until you become familiar with using the lesson plans database.

INTEGRATING TECHNOLOGY IN THE CLASSROOM WITH MICROSOFT® *WORD*

OVERVIEW

Julia Rodriguez is a high school English teacher. She has been teaching for almost twenty years. Although she has never been particularly interested in computers, some of her colleagues were regularly using computers in their classrooms. So she decided to take advantage of a special purchase program sponsored by the district technology office and purchased a personal computer equipped with Microsoft® *Office*.

In an implementation workshop for teachers purchasing a new computer, Julia learned about word processing. She learned that the powerful text processing capabilities of word processing can assist her in classroom management tasks and the preparation of lessons. She was most excited about the possibility of using word processing in her classroom to facilitate student learning activities. Before the workshop was over, she was already thinking about ways she could integrate word processing into several of the reading and writing activities her students complete.

In Part I you will learn how to use the Microsoft® *Office* word processing application, *Word*, to create and modify text documents. Teachers can save time on their own work and help each other by sharing products. They can word process anything they type or write by hand. Many teachers keep files of templates or models that they use repeatedly with modifications each year. Roblyer (2003) provides examples of these:

- Beginning-of-the-year welcome letter
- Request for fee payments letter

- Fund-raising letter
- Periodic student progress letters
- Worksheets and exercises
- Student information sheets and handouts
- Annual reports for the school
- Lesson plans and notes
- Newsletter layouts
- Stationery

Roblyer (2003) also says that word processing also supports a variety of learning activities and makes possible others that would not have been feasible without it:

- **Writing processes.** Word processing makes it faster and easier for students to write, edit, and illustrate stories and reports and to keep classroom notes and logs.
- **Dynamic group projects.** A class or group of students can produce a group poem, letter, or story, with each student adding and/or changing lines or producing new sections.
- **Individual language, writing, and reading exercises.** Word processed exercises can allow students to combine sentences, add or correct punctuation, write sentences for spelling or vocabulary words, or identify parts of speech.
- **Writing across the curriculum.** By allowing students and teachers to save work on disk and take it from one classroom to another, word processing can integrate writing into interdisciplinary and thematic learning activities.

Technology Standards and Educational Best Practices for Technology

The lessons in this section assist learners in developing skills for the following International Society for Technology in Education (ISTE) National Educational Technology Standards for Students (NETS·S):

1. Basic operations and concepts

   - Students demonstrate a sound understanding of the nature and operation of technology systems.
   - Students are proficient in the use of technology.

2. Social, ethical, and human issues

   - Students practice responsible use of technology systems, information, and software.
   - Students develop positive attitudes toward technology uses that support lifelong learning, collaboration, personal pursuits, and productivity.

3. Technology productivity tools

   - Students use technology tools to enhance learning, increase productivity, and promote creativity.
   - Students use productivity tools to collaborate in constructing technology-enhanced models, prepare publications, and produce other creative works.

4. Technology research tools

   - Students use technology tools to process data and report results.
   - Students evaluate and select new information resources and technological innovations based on the appropriateness for specific tasks.

The chapters in Part 1: Integrating Technology in the Classroom with Microsoft® Word address indicators in four of the NETS·S standards. The tutorials and activities in Part 1 require you to open files from a CD, floppy disk, and/or a hard disk, use a keyboard and mouse, and manage files you create, save, or copy. Word is especially useful as both a productivity tool and research tool to process data and report results.

The tutorials and learning activities in Part 1 will provide learning experiences in which students create work products, such as a technical report, a newsletter, and even a Web page. Additionally, the chapters in Part 1 demonstrate how Microsoft® Word is a powerful technology integration resource in constructing and conducting curriculum-related learning activities. All learning activities in Part 1 are designed to promote responsible use of computer technology and help students develop positive attitudes about the use of technology to accommodate lifelong learning.

Chapters in Part 1

The step-by-step lessons in each chapter demonstrate the text and graphics processing features of Microsoft® Word. Each tutorial consists of guided practice that demonstrates how teachers and students can use Word features in classroom learning activities. For each chapter, use the practice files in the **WP folder** of the **T3 Practice CD** to complete the step-by-step lessons.

Several exercises follow each lesson, which may also include activities using files from the **T3 Practice CD** and the **Lesson Plans ePortfolio.** Complete these exercises to reinforce the learning activities demonstrated in the tutorial and expand your skills.

The tutorials in the following lessons do not include every feature of Microsoft® Word but are designed to address those features that will allow you to perform text and graphic processing tasks that support classroom instruction and student learning. The tutorials also provide activities that encourage you to investigate other features of Word not specifically included in these lessons.

Chapter 2: Inserting, Editing, and Formatting Text in Word

Chapter 3: Document Layout and Graphic Effects Using Word

Chapter 4: Constructing Interactive Forms and Web Documents with Word

INSERTING, EDITING, AND FORMATTING TEXT IN *WORD*

NEW TERMS

alignment	highlighting (selecting)	scroll bar
bulleted or numbered list	I-bar	toolbar
Close (a document)	justify	type size
cursor	Menu Bar	type style
exit (a program)	page break	Undo
file	Save/Save As	word wrap
font	ruler	

OVERVIEW

Microsoft® *Word* is a text processing tool. This chapter contains tutorial lessons consisting of step-by-step exercises to build skills in basic *Word* file operations, navigation of the *Word* window, and text formatting features.

Each tutorial consists of guided practice that demonstrates how teachers and students can use *Word* features in classroom learning activities. Practice files for the tutorials are located in the **WP folder** on the **T3 Practice CD.** Several exercises follow each lesson, including activities from the **Lesson Plans ePortfolio.** Complete these exercises to reinforce the learning activities demonstrated in the tutorial and to build your collection of technology-based lesson plans and ideas.

Lesson 2.1:   Managing and Navigating *Word* Documents
Lesson 2.2:   Inserting and Revising Text in a *Word* Document
Lesson 2.3:   Structuring and Organizing Text in a *Word* Document

LESSON 2.1: MANAGING AND NAVIGATING *WORD* DOCUMENTS

Lesson 2.1: Learning Activities

Opening the *Word* window
Opening an existing *Word* document
Using scroll bars, arrows, and boxes
Saving Documents
Making different versions of the same document
Saving in different formats to share documents
Previewing and printing a *Word* document
Exiting *Word*

Julia Rodriguez now has her new computer set up and running. Based on what she learned about Microsoft® *Office* in the implementation workshop, the first program Julia wants to learn is word processing with *Word*. She thinks that once she learns a few basics she can integrate *Word* with learning activities in her classes.

Since Julia has never used a computer before, one of her colleagues in the English department who uses computers in the classroom shared some of the files she uses for classroom learning activities. Julia is going to use these files and others she creates herself to learn how to use Microsoft® *Word* and to use the features of *Word* for teaching and learning in the classroom.

This chapter shows you how to use Microsoft® *Word* to open a document someone might give you on a disk, review the document, and put documents on a disk in ways that allow them to be shared easily among other teachers and students.

LESSON 2.1: TUTORIAL

Opening the *Word* Window

The *Word* program opens like other Microsoft® *Office* programs. Open it as follows below.

❶ Start the *Word* program by double-clicking on the *Word* icon or by selecting Microsoft *Word* from the Start programs menu on the Windows® screen.
❷ Click the **Minimize** button in the top right corner on the title bar of the active window. The *Word* window will minimize to a button on the Windows® taskbar.
❸ Maximize the *Word* window by clicking on the *Word* button on the Windows® taskbar.

FIGURE 2–1

The Microsoft® *Word* Window (with Standard, Formatting, and Drawing Toolbars activated)
Source: Screen captures of Microsoft® *Word* used in the chapters in Part 1 are reprinted by permission from Microsoft® Corporation.

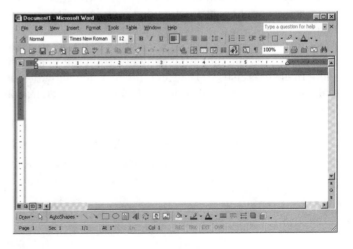

Opening an Existing *Word* Document

Open the file on the **T3 Practice CD** called **Ch2Lesson_Idea.doc** as follows:

❶ Place the **T3 Practice CD** in the CD Drive.

❷ Open the **WP Folder** on the **T3 Practice CD** either by double-clicking on it or by pointing at the **WP Folder** with the mouse, clicking on it once to highlight it, and then clicking **Open.**

❸ From the *Word* program window select **File | Open** to display the Open dialog box.

❹ In the **Open** dialog box the default working folder for *Word* displays. To select a file located on the CD drive, click the down arrow beside the **Look in** box. Then from the drop-down list select the CD drive by double-clicking on its name.

❺ From the file list double-click **Ch2Lesson_Idea.doc** to select and open this file. (The *.doc* file name extension may not appear on the file name based on the hardware platform and system settings of your computer.)

❻ The screen should look similar to the following example, except the document title. Notice especially the labeled parts of the *Word* screen, which you will be using in this chapter.

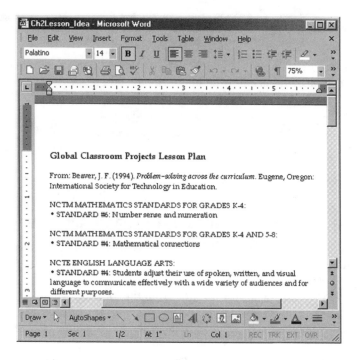

Using Scroll Bars, Arrows, and Boxes

Only part of the document appears on the screen. You need to scroll through the lesson to read all of it, as follows:

❶ Click on the side scroll box and drag it down, or click the down arrow repeatedly. The remainder of the lesson will scroll as you drag the bar.

❷ Click the double-down or up arrows at the bottom of the side scroll bar to move in the document down or up one page at a time.

Saving Documents

Saving stores a document onto a hard drive or disk. If someone gives you a document on disk, you can transfer, or save, the document to your computer hard drive or disk before returning it.

Use save *only* when you want to save your work or revisions to your document to the same file with the same file name.

1 Select **File | Save As.** Use Save As to save a document, even one on which you are currently working, to a new file with a new name or to a new location.

2 Choose between the default location or a new location on your computer where you will save the file. (*Word* usually saves files in a folder called **My Documents** on the hard drive. Unless it is changed by a user, Windows® displays the **My Documents** folder as the default working or active folder for saving files. For now the **My Documents** folder is a good place to store word processing documents, worksheets, presentations, databases, and other files.) To save to its default location, you would normally proceed to step 5. For our purposes here, save to another location; thus, proceed to step 3.

3 To save the document in a location other than the hard drive (e.g., your floppy disk drive), make sure a disk is in the drive. Then, click on the down arrow to the right of My Documents, and double-click a new location from the list.

> **Macintosh®**: Macintosh® may remember the last folder you selected, especially with **Open** or **Save As.** You should verify the folder in which you are opening or saving your file each time you perform these operations.

4 In the **File name** box, triple-click the name that appears and type *Global Lesson Plan* as a new name for the document.

5 Click **Save** then close the document by clicking **File | Close**.

Making Different Versions of the Same Document

Sometimes you want to make changes to a document and keep a copy of the original document as well.

> **Macintosh®**: In the Macintosh® **File | Save** dialog box, select an appropriate folder and click the **Save** button. You can also close the document by clicking on the ☐ in the upper left-hand corner of the document window.

1 Open **Global Lesson Plan.doc** from the location where you saved it.

2 Save it again under another name (e.g., **Global Lesson Mod.doc**). You can make changes to this file, and the other will remain as it was originally.

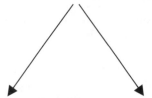

```
                Original lesson file: Ch2Lesson_Idea.doc




     Copy #1: Global Lesson Plan.doc     Copy #2: Global Lesson Mod.doc
```

Saving in Different Formats to Share Documents

You may want to share a document with someone who does not have the *Word* program. Through *Word* you can **save** it in one of several formats that can be used by other software programs.

❶ With the **Global Lesson Mod.doc** file still open, select **File | Save As**.
❷ Click the down arrow to the right of **Save as type** (**Format** on Macintosh®), and a drop-down list of file types or formats is displayed.

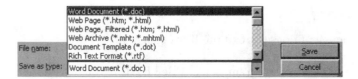

❸ Save the document in each of the formats below under a different name for each. Click on the file type, then rename the file and click save. (If you receive a message that the document contains features not compatible with the new format, continue by clicking **Yes** to save it in that format anyway.)

- **Text only** or **Text with Line Breaks:** Saves the words themselves, but removes most of the text formatting such as italics and bold and structural formatting such as tabs. (Suggested name: **Global Lesson Mod Text.txt**)
- **Rich Text Format:** Saves the words and some of the formatting (Suggested name: **Global Lesson Mod Rich.rtf**)

Word saves documents by default as *Word* document files. Such files should also be usable in the Macintosh® *Word* program.

Previewing and Printing a *Word* Document

You can see what your document will look like when it is printed before you actually print it. (Check with your instructor before actually printing.)

❶ Open **Global Lesson Mod.doc.**
❷ Preview the document by selecting **File | Print Preview** or clicking the **Print Preview** button.
❸ Print the document by first selecting **File | Print.** Then, in the **Print** dialog box, click **OK** (**PRINT** on Macintosh®).

If you use the **Menu Bar,** you may need to click the double down arrow at the bottom of the drop-down list to see more options.

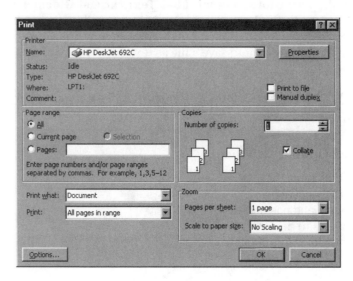

With permission you can try these print options from the Print dialog box:

Macintosh®: In the Print dialog box click on the **General** print options button and select **Microsoft Word** from the drop-down list. A new dialog box displays in which you select various printing options.

- Change the printer by clicking the arrow beside the **Name** box and selecting another printer name from the list.
- Print more than one copy of the document by clicking the up arrow beside **Number of copies.**
- Specify certain pages to print by clicking in the box beside **Pages** and typing the page numbers. For example, to print pages 5 and 7 of a 10–page document type **5, 7;** pages 5 through 7, **5–7;** and all pages after 5, **5–.**

Exiting *Word*

Closing a document does not exit the *Word* program.

Macintosh®: To exit the *Word* program, select **File | Quit.** If you have not already closed your document and have made modifications to it, you will be prompted to save the document in a file before exiting the program.

❶ To exit the *Word* program, select **File | Exit.** If you have not already closed your document and have made modifications to it, you will be prompted to save the document before exiting the program.

❷ You can also exit *Word* by clicking the **X** on the top right of the *Word* program window (not the **X** at the extreme right of the Menu Bar).

FOLLOW-UP PRACTICE PROJECTS

In the following lessons in this chapter and the remaining chapters of Part 1, you will use several practice files from the **T3 Practice CD.** The following projects allow you to practice the skills you learned in this lesson.

Insert the **T3 Practice CD,** open *Word,* and complete the projects below.

❶ From the **WP folder** of the **T3 Practice CD,** open the document named **Ch2Starter.doc** Save it to the hard drive of your computer or a personal disk then close it. Repeat the entire procedure with **Ch2StarterFormat.doc.**

❷ From the **WP folder** of the **T3 Practice CD,** open the document named **Ch3Newsletter.doc.** Save it to the hard drive of your computer or a personal disk and then close it.

❸ Expand your skills. Use the **Open** and **Save** procedures of *Word* to save each of the following document files on the hard drive of your computer or a personal disk, or use the Windows® or Macintosh® operating system to copy or drag each of the files to the hard drive of your computer or a personal disk: **Ch2Partsof-Speech.doc, Ch4Vocabex.doc, Ch4Spelling.doc, Ch4HomePage.doc.**

❹ Open the files **Global Lesson Mod Text.txt** and **Global Lesson Mode Rich.rtf** in *Word.* (They will display in separate *Word* windows.) How do these files look alike? How do they differ in appearance on your screen? When would you want to save a file as text or as rich text?

LESSON 2.2: INSERTING AND REVISING TEXT IN A *WORD* DOCUMENT

Lesson 2.2: Learning Activities

Positioning the cursor
Typing text in a document
Moving, copying and pasting text
Undoing changes to the text
Inserting blank lines in a document

Deleting or replacing text in a document
Aligning and justifying text

After just a little practice with word processing, Julia is ready to use *Word* for classroom instruction. Although she is still new to computers, she decides that a good way for her to learn more features of *Word* is to create a learning activity for one of her classes.

Julia wants to use *Word* to motivate student writing. She decides to create a *Word* document in which students can add their story endings to a series of statements or questions that prompts them to write something about themselves. In this lesson you will practice adding to a document by inserting text at each of the "story-starter prompts." This exercise is based on a lesson from Wresch (1990) entitled "Connecting Writing to Reading." This lesson describes a simple but powerful prompting strategy to motivate student writing. Although designed for high school students, this lesson may be adapted to any age level. The students read (or are read) a poem that focuses on self-reflection. Wresch's example is Walt Whitman's "Song of Myself." The teacher sets up a *Word* document to give prompts based on the reading and students add their own endings to describe themselves.

LESSON 2.2: TUTORIAL

Positioning the Cursor

Open *Word* and then open the file **Ch2Starter.doc,** which you stored previously from the **T3 Practice CD** to your hard disk or personal disk. Add endings to each prompt in the document.

❶ For each line, move the mouse pointer to the spot where text will be entered. For the first ending, move the mouse after the "I hear" prompt, but do not click.

❷ In a *Word* document the mouse pointer becomes a line called an I-bar. The I-bar indicates the location of the mouse, on screen, but you cannot yet type until you click there. To type, first click the mouse; you will then see a blinking bar, called a cursor, which means you can begin typing. **NOTE:** A common error for beginners is to forget to click on the spot where they want to type. Therefore, they see an I-bar but no cursor, and their typing appears in a place they did not intend.

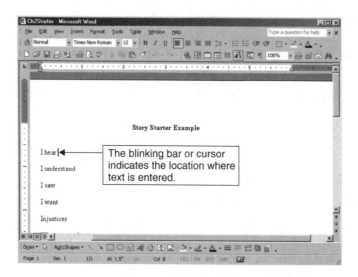

Typing Text in a Document

Enter the text below at the indicated line prompts. Do not press **ENTER** when you reach the end of a line. The line wraps automatically, by way of a feature called word wrap.

> **I hear my friends singing along with the radio. We listen to the radio in the car and in my room. Our favorite radio station is Hits 94.1. Sometimes we win tickets when the station has a contest.** [Press **ENTER.**]
>
> [Press **ENTER.**]
>
> **I understand that it's important to get a good education. My parents are always telling me that. I would like to graduate and go on to college. I want a degree in architecture so I can design houses and buildings.** [Press **ENTER.**]

Moving, Copying, and Pasting Text

You can cut and paste or copy and paste text from one place in a document to another place.

Macintosh®: Click and hold the mouse at the beginning of the text to be changed and drag it over the text. When it is enclosed in a shaded box it is selected or highlighted.

❶ In the "I hear" paragraph, select, or highlight the sentence, "Our favorite radio station is Hits 94.1." Select **Edit | Cut** to delete the block from this location.

❷ Click at the end of the first sentence after the word, "radio." Select **Edit | Paste**. The sentence appears in the new location.

❸ To move the sentence back to its original position, first select the sentence. Point at the highlighted text with the mouse; when the I-Bar has changed to an arrow, click and hold the mouse button down. Then drag the mouse pointer to the end of the sentence ending "in my room," and release the mouse button. The sentence is returned to its original location.

❹ To copy the sentence, first select it and then select **Edit | Copy**. Click at the end of the sentence ending "in my room," and select **Edit | Paste**. A duplicate of the sentence appears in the new location.

Undoing Changes to Text

Correct mistakes by selecting **Edit | Undo** or by clicking the **Undo** symbol on the **Standard Toolbar**. Each time you click **Undo**, you "undo" a step. You can delete the duplicate sentence by undoing the previous paste step. Click **Undo** once to clear the duplicate sentence.

Inserting Blank Lines in a Document

At the end of a line of text, use **ENTER** to move the cursor to a new line. (When typing running text, word wrap moves the cursor for you.)

❶ Type each line shown below after "I saw", pressing **ENTER** as indicated.

❷ Type the text shown below after "I want" but *do not* press **ENTER** after any of the lines until the end of the paragraph.

> **I saw many things when we went out West this summer. I saw:** [Press **ENTER**]
> **The Grand Canyon** [Press **ENTER**]
> **Yellowstone National Park** [Press **ENTER**]
> **Jackson Hole, Wyoming** [Press **ENTER**]
> **Animals I had never seen before, like roadrunners and bears**

I want to make a lot of money when I grow up. My family can't afford a lot of things I would like. For example, I want a new car for me, a swimming pool, and a digital video camera. I want to travel more. [Press **ENTER.**]

Deleting or Replacing Text in a Document

In addition to inserting text, there are three ways to change text: delete, replace, and reformat. Deleting and replacing are presented here and formatting later.

❶ Practice highlighting the paragraph that begins with "I understand." Then highlight or select the sentence "My parents are always telling me that." If you were to make changes while text is highlighted, the changes would apply only to the highlighted area.

❷ By selecting text and then pressing **DELETE,** the text disappears. You can also delete letters or words by placing the cursor to the left of the text to erase and pressing **DELETE** once for each letter or character to delete, or you can place the cursor to the right and press **BACKSPACE.**

Type the following paragraph, select the sentence "That isn't right," and delete it.

Injustices are all around us. One time the owner of a store hassled me because I was standing outside his music store. That isn't right. Adults shouldn't hassle teenagers just because they're standing around doing nothing.

❸ To replace text, select the text and then start typing. The new text replaces the old.

Type the following text after the prompt, "Who are you?" Select the text "I always do what my parents say," and type the text, "*I do what my parents say most of the time*" to replace it.

My character

I am a good person. I always do what my parents say, and I do all my schoolwork.

Aligning and Justifying Text

You can align, or justify, text at the left, in the center, at the right, or at the left and right (justified, or full). The text alignment buttons are located on the **Formatting Toolbar:**

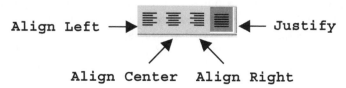

Alignment is usually performed to the line the cursor is on or to lines you have selected.

❶ Enter the following text two lines below the "My personality" paragraph.

❷ Center "My status" by clicking on that line and then clicking **Align Center** button.

❸ Center "My personality."

My status

I am 16 years old, and I am in the ninth grade in school.

❹ Save and close the document.

FOLLOW-UP PRACTICE PROJECTS

Perform each of the following projects for additional text formatting practice. Start *Word* and open the *Word* document, **Global Lesson Plan,** that you saved in Lesson 1. Perform each of the following practice exercises using this document. If you make a mistake on any of the operations, Undo the change to the text and Redo the operation. When you have completed the practice exercises, exit *Word*.

1. Insert a blank line to create a new paragraph. Position the cursor under the "F" in the word "Four" at the beginning of the last sentence of the paragraph that starts with the word "Despite." Press **ENTER** two times to make a new paragraph.
2. Select (highlight) the three paragraphs near the beginning of the document that begin with "NCTM" or "NCTE" and delete the paragraphs.
3. Select (highlight) the first paragraph of the document (begins with "From"), cut it, move it to the end of the document, and paste it. (Be sure to insert a blank line between your pasted text and the previous paragraph so they do not run together.)
4. Select all of the text in the document (**Edit | Select All**) and full-justify the text.
5. Replace all occurrences of the word "student" with "learner" and all occurrences of the word "students" with "learners."
6. Save the document as **Global Lesson Plan Revised.**

LESSON 2.3: STRUCTURING AND ORGANIZING TEXT IN A *WORD* DOCUMENT

Lesson 2.3: Learning Activities

Changing the margins of a document
Inserting page breaks in a document
Using indents and hanging indents
Setting tabs in a document
Creating bulleted lists in a document
Other text formatting features

The format of text can help enhance both the professional appearance and the readability of a document. In this lesson Julia will practice using more of the formatting and structuring features, or attributes, of *Word* to improve document appearance. She will continue the activity in the previous lesson by adding advanced formatting and document structuring features to the "story starter" document.

Text structure may be changed through the use of margins, tabs, indents, columns, and other features. For all, the first step is always to select the text to be reformatted and then reformat it.

In the following steps you will make the first page of this story starter document look like the second page by changing margins, aligning text, and setting tabs. Be sure to save your work as you go. You may also want to compare your work with the formatted examples on the second page of the document.

LESSON 2.3: TUTORIAL

Open the document named **Ch2StarterFormat.doc** you saved previously from the **T3 Practice CD** onto your own disk or hard drive.

Changing the Margins of a Document

New *Word* documents are automatically set for margins of 1" for Top and Bottom and 1.25" for Left and Right.

❶ To change margins for the whole document, select **File | Page Setup**. The **Page Setup** dialog box will resemble the one shown here. Click in the **Left** box and enter **1**"; do the same in the **Right** box. (You can also use the down arrows located on the right side of each field to decrease the margin value to 1".)

❷ Click the down arrow to the right of **Apply to** and select **Whole document**.

❸ Click **OK**.

Macintosh®: In the Page Setup dialog box click the **Page Attributes** button and select **Microsoft Word** from the drop-down list. Click the **Margins** button and enter **1**" for the Left and Right margins. Click **OK**.

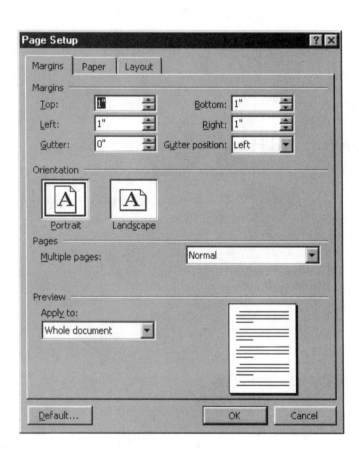

Inserting Page Breaks in a Document

Sometimes you want to force the page of a document to break at a certain point in the text and start a new page. You can press the **ENTER** key repeatedly to insert blank lines until you get to the end of a page. However, this series of blank lines does not maintain a "clean" page break, because the point at which your page break occurs may change if you insert or delete text before the blank lines (even pages before them).

❶ Move the cursor near the bottom of the first page and click in front of the "Story Starter Example (Formatted)" title for the second page. Select **Insert | Break**.

❷ In the **Break** dialog box, select the **Page Break** radio button.

❸ Click **OK**.

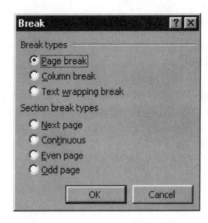

The unformatted example is on the first page and the formatted example is on the second page. In the following exercises you will be formatting the first page to look like the second page.

Using Indents and Hanging Indents

Different parts of documents can have different margins and indentions.

❶ Select the paragraph underneath the prompt "I hear." Click and drag the box at the bottom of the left margin marker on the **Ruler** to the right to the **0.5** position.

❷ Click and drag the right margin marker to the left to the **6"** position. The text indents as the margins are moved.

❸ Repeat step 1 for each of the paragraphs under the prompts "I understand", "I saw," "I want," and "Injustices."

❹ Change the text at the "Who are you?" prompt to a hanging indent. All lines after the first will begin at the indention. To do this, first select all text under the "Who are you?" prompt. Then, click and drag the top half of the bottom margin marker (above the box) to the 2" tab position. The second line of each paragraph highlighted will begin at the indent.

❺ To finish formatting these paragraphs, move the cursor immediately after the words "My character." Press **DELETE** to pull the following text up so that it is adjacent to "My character." Next, press **TAB** one time to align the first line of the paragraph with its other lines. Then, with the cursor in front of the words "My character," press **TAB** once. Your paragraph should be aligned as follows:

My character   I am a good person. I do what my parents say most of the time, and I do all my schoolwork.

❻ Repeat step 4 for the "My personality" and "My status" paragraphs.

Setting Tabs in a Document

You can set tabs by placing them in the **Ruler.** Set three tabs for the text under the last item, "My favorite things."

❶ Highlight the two lines of text underneath the prompt, "My favorite things."

❷ Click on the **Ruler** at the 2" and 4" tab positions. (The L displayed at each tab position indicates a left tab marker.)

❸ Align the text as shown below by clicking on the first letter of the text to be moved and then pressing **TAB**. The text will move to the tab position.

My favorite things
At home   At school   Else where
Sleeping and eating   Hanging out with friends   Listening to the radio

Creating Bulleted Lists in a Document

You can format text as a bulleted or numbered list.

❶ Select the list of items in the "I saw" prompt (after the first sentence).

❷ Click **Format I Bullets and Numbering**.

❸ In the **Bullets and Numbering** dialog box, click the **Bullets** tab, select a style, and click OK. (You can use the **Formatting Toolbar** and the **Bullets** button instead of the **Menu Bar,** too.)

Other Text Formatting Features

Review the following options available through the **Formatting Toolbar:**

Font	The selection of fonts, or kinds of type, available varies from computer to computer. They range from plain fonts, such as **Arial**, **Verdana**, and **Courier**, to fancy ones, such as **Old English**. Use the Font icon on the toolbar.
Size	Text size is measured in points (approximately 72 points per inch). Most documents are 10 point or 12 point. Some fancier fonts require a larger size to be clearly readable. Use the Font Size icon on the toolbar.
Style	A variety of style changes can make text stand out. The most common are **boldface**, *italics*, and underline. These can be selected from the Formatting Toolbar. Additionally, these formatting options can be selected from the **Format Font** option on the Menu bar, along with shadow, outline, subscript, superscript, and more.
Color	Add color to text by selecting **Font Color** on the Formatting Toolbar or by selecting the **Format I Font** from the Menu Bar and then **Font color**.

Now practice using some of these text formatting features to enhance the appearance of the document.

❶ Change the text for each of the prompt headings to bold and italic.

❷ Center and bold the page heading, "Story Starter Example," and set the font size to 14.

❸ Underline all headings in the document.

4 Change the color of the headings under "Who are you?" as follows: "My Character" to blue and bold, "My personality" to green and bold, and "My status" to red and bold.

5 Try some of the other format features from the Format menu. Select **Format | Font**. Notice that some of these options are available from the Formatting Toolbar. Try the ^{superscript}, _{subscript}, shadow, and outline options.

6 Strike through the text in the paragraph following the "Injustices" prompt. ~~Injustices are all around us. One time the owner of a store hassled me because I was standing outside his music store. That isn't right. Adults shouldn't hassle teenagers just because they're standing around doing nothing.~~

7 Save and close the document and exit *Word*.

Follow-up Practice Projects

In these practice projects you will construct a learning activity that helps students identify the parts of speech in a paragraph by giving each part of speech a different attribute, or appearance. Start *Word* and open **Ch2PartsofSpeech.doc** that you saved previously from the **T3 Practice CD** onto your own disk or hard drive. Perform each of the following practice exercises using this document. If you make a mistake on any of these operations, Undo the change to the text and Redo the operation. When you have completed the practice exercises, exit *Word*.

Students can practice identifying parts of speech in this paragraph by making the following style changes to make them stand out:

1 Bold each verb (**lived, filled, sit, eat, was, means**).

2 Italicize each noun (*hole, ground, hobbit, ends, worms, smell, nothing, hobbit-hole, comfort*).

3 Underline each adjective (<u>a</u>, <u>the</u>, <u>nasty</u>, <u>dirty</u>, <u>wet</u>, <u>oozy</u>, <u>dry</u>, <u>bare</u>, <u>sandy</u>).

4 Save the document using it's original file name (use **Save**, not Save As).

5 Insert a page break at the end of the document.

6 Copy the title and paragraph and paste it to the second page of the document. Use the text on the second page to perform the remainder of the practice exercises.

7 Set a left tab at 0.5" on the Ruler. Then tab and indent the first sentence of the paragraph. Position the cursor in the paragraph before setting the tab.

8 Change the font of the paragraph to a font of your choice and increase the font size.

9 Bold the title of the document and increase it to a larger font size than the text in the paragraph.

10 Change the color of the title to red and the text of the paragraph to blue.

11 Italicize the words "The Hobbit," a book title.

12 Create a bulleted list from the second sentence of the paragraph. To do so, click the "N" in "Not" at the beginning of the second sentence and press **ENTER**. Now click the "N" in "Nor" and press **ENTER**. Finally, position the cursor on the "I" in "It" and press **ENTER**. Select and format the two middle paragraphs (beginning with "Not" and ending with "eat:" as a bulleted list.

13 Rename the document to **Ch2PartsofSpeech Revised.doc** (using Save As) and print it. You will use this document again in a later exercise.

14 Develop a lesson idea or plan for the entire activity you just completed that is targeted for the grade level you teach or plan to teach. Add it to the **Lesson Plans ePortfolio**.

EXERCISES TO REVIEW AND EXPAND YOUR SKILLS

Set 1: Reviewing Terms and Concepts—For each question below, provide a term on the blank that matches the description.

_____ **1.** You must click on a document to get this before you can type.

_____ **2.** Choose this to "erase" a mistake without typing or retyping.

_____ **3.** Insert one of these to begin a new page without typing to the end of the first page.

_____ **4.** Use this to create a list of items within a *Word* document.

_____ **5.** You must do this before you format, delete, or align any text.

Set 2: Expanding Your Skills—Expand on the skills you learned in this chapter with these activities.

1. **Set Automatic Save.** *Word* can save your document automatically every few minutes, or however often you indicate. This helps protect you from losing changes to a document if the power goes off before you had a chance to execute save manually. With a document on the screen (blank or containing text), select **Tools | Options | Save**. Click in the check box beside **Save Autorecover info every,** enter a number in the minutes box, and click **OK**.

2. **Use Automatic Styles in the Style Box** (the leftmost button on the **Formatting Toolbar**). Highlight a heading in one of your documents, click **Style**, a style from the list of choices. Your heading is formatted automatically.

3. **Change Bullet Types.** If you want to change from the default bullet characters, select **Format | Bullets and Numbering** and then select the Bulleted tab. Click on one of the choices and then **OK**. If you do not like any of the options you see, choose one and then click **Customize** to get options for creating a new set with a different font, character, and other related settings.

Set 3: Use Microsoft® Help—The Microsoft® *Office* Help Menu can give additional information on any topic and help with troubleshooting procedures when you encounter problems. The **Help Menu** can be reached through **Help** on the **Menu Bar** in any *Office*® program and it contains information specific to the program in which you are working.

Look up the following features to get further information and tips, and then try out each of these features with one or more of the documents you used in this chapter.

- Look up **Save as** to learn the best way to save documents and when to use a fast save versus a full save.
- Look up **Styles** to learn about adding new styles to the list in the style box.
- Look up **Tab** to learn how to put a line of dots or other characters automatically between items and their page numbers in a table of contents.

Set 4: Create Your Own Lesson—After reviewing the lessons in this chapter, develop and describe a lesson targeted for the grade level you teach or plan to teach that makes effective use of each of the following *Word* features. Describe the document you or the students would need to create to carry out the lesson. Enter your lesson idea or plan into the **Lesson Plans ePortfolio.**

- Students write the ending to a story you give them in a *Word* document by inserting their ending text into the document.
- Students analyze a poem you give them in a *Word* document by inserting their remarks below each line (or group of lines) of the poem. They could use special formatting on their remarks to distinguish it from the poem text.
- Students record their observations of a science experiment using a *Word* document and bulleted lists, students record their impressions of a reading assignment using a *Word* document and bulleted lists.
- Students edit a written composition for incorrect grammar using text formatting features of *Word*, such as underlining or striking through incorrect grammar and replacing with corrected text.

DOCUMENT LAYOUT AND GRAPHICS EFFECTS USING *WORD*

NEW TERMS

AutoShapes	footer	TIF
BMP	GIF	table
bullet	grouping	tabs
clip art	header	text box
desktop publishing	indents	WordArt
EPS	JPEG	PICT

OVERVIEW

Although Microsoft® *Word* is primarily used for text-building purposes, it includes graphics and layout features that provide many functions common to graphics and desktop publishing programs. These functions allow you to improve the appearance, readability, and usability of documents. The tutorial lessons in this chapter demonstrate several operations that allow you to structure, organize, and enhance text and text style in documents as well as insert graphics and perform basic drawing functions in documents.

Each tutorial consists of guided practice that demonstrates how teachers and students can use Microsoft® *Word* features in classroom learning activities. Practice files for the tutorials are located in the **WP folder** on the **T3 Practice CD.** Several exercises follow each lesson, including activities from the **Lesson Plans ePortfolio.** Complete these exercises to reinforce the learning activities demonstrated in the tutorial and to build your collection of technology-based lesson plans and ideas.

Lesson 3.1:   Using Text Boxes, Images, and Headers and Footers in *Word*
Lesson 3.2:   Laying Out Text in Columns and Using Drawing Tools in *Word*
Lesson 3.3:   Using Tables in *Word* Documents

LESSON 3.1: USING TEXT BOXES, IMAGES, AND HEADERS AND FOOTERS IN *WORD*

Lesson 3.1: Learning Activities

Inserting and Double-Spacing Text in a New Document
Adding Numbering to a List of Items
Inserting a Text Box and Wrapping Text
Adding and Formating Text in a Text Box
Formating the Layout of a Text Box
Inserting Clip Art in a Document
Creating Headers and Footers in a Document

In this lesson Julia Rodriguez will explore several layout and graphics features of Microsoft® *Word* to see how technical writing can be enhanced and reinforced with layout and graphics effects. You will practice using several of the desktop publishing features in *Word* to enhance the appearance of a technical report.

LESSON 3.1: TUTORIAL

Inserting and Double-Spacing Text in a New Document

Open a new *Word* file (click **New Blank Document** on the **Standard Toolbar**), and name it **Ch3Report.doc.** Save your document as you complete each step.

❶ Enter the text shown below. Allow text to wrap except where noted to press the **ENTER** key (do not type the word "[**ENTER**]").

The World Wide Web

<u>Who Is the WWW?</u> [ENTER]
In October 1994, Tim Berners-Lee founded the World Wide Web
Consortium (W3C) at the Massachusetts Institute of Technology,
Laboratory for Computer Science (MIT/LCS). The W3C was created
to promote and manage the evolution of the Internet and to ensure
its interoperability. The W3C has more than 400 Member
organizations from around the world and is financed by its members
and by public funds. Membership in the W3C is available to any
organization. Along with MIT/LCS in the United States, the W3C is
jointly hosted at sites in France and Japan, and W3C offices are
located in 11 other countries. [ENTER]
<u>What Does the WWW Do?</u> [ENTER]
W3C activities and other work are organized into four domains:
[ENTER]
Architecture Domain to develop the underlying technologies of the
Web. [ENTER]
Technology and Society Domain to understand ethical and legal
issues from a new international perspective and in light of new
technology. [ENTER]
User Interface Domain to improve user interaction with the Web
including work on formats and languages. [ENTER]
Web Accessibility Initiative to pursue accessibility of the Web.
[ENTER]
The W3C has published more than 20 technical specifications for
the Web's infrastructure since its inception. Each specification not

only builds on its predecessor, but is designed to integrate with future specifications as well. [ENTER]

❷ Center and bold the title, and set the font size to **14.** Underline the subtitles. Press **TAB** at the beginning of paragraphs not used as a list.

❸ To double-space the text in the document, first select all the text in the document with **Edit | Select All.** Then select **Format | Paragraph,** click the down arrow by the **Line Spacing** field, click **Double** from the drop-down list, and click **OK.**

Add Numbering to a List of Items

Some of the items in the text would be better presented as a numbered list.

❶ Select the section referring to four types of domains: (beginning with the words "Architecture Domain" and ending with the words "accessibility of the Web").

❷ From the **Menu Bar** select **Format | Bullets and Numbering Numbered.** In the **Bullets and Numbering** dialog box select a **1.2.3.** format. You can also click the **Numbering** button from the **Formatting Toolbar.**

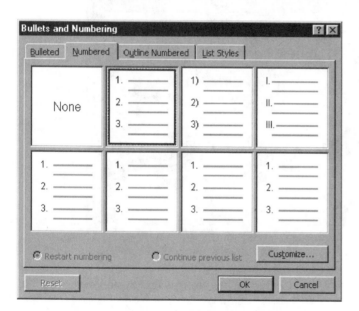

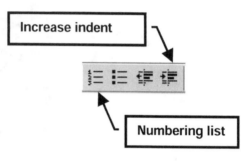

❸ After you have numbered the paragraphs in the list, click the **Decrease Indent** or **Increase Indent** (with the text still selected) to move the list left or right so that it aligns with the paragraph indent.

Inserting a Text Box and Wrapping Text

Text boxes can be used to draw attention to important information.

❶ With the cursor anywhere on the page where you want to insert the text box, select **Insert | Text Box** or click **Text Box** on the **Drawing Toolbar.** [The **Drawing Toolbar** is generally located at the bottom of the *Word* window (on the side on a Macintosh®). If the **Drawing Toolbar** is not displayed, select **View | Toolbars | Drawing** to display the **Drawing Toolbar.**] Click on a top corner of the list to place the box.

❷ Size the text box by clicking on a corner (hollow square called sizing handle) and dragging it to stretch the box the full vertical length of the bulleted list. The text does not wrap around the text box. (Use any of the other sizing handles to resize the box, if necessary. You may need to click again on the box border—after the cursor changes to a four directional arrow when passed over the border—to see the handles.)

❸ To wrap the text around the text box, select the text box by clicking on its border. Select **Format | Text Box** (or double-click on the outside border of the text box) and select **Layout.** Several wrapping styles are available:

- **In line with text:** Places the text box at the insertion point and text is above and below the text box.
- **Square:** Wraps text around all sides of the text box.
- **Tight:** Works like Square but conforms to the shape of text box, rather than wrapping around it as a square.
- **Behind text:** Places the text box behind the text.
- **In front of text:** Places the text box over the text.

Click **Tight,** click the **Right** radio button for **Horizontal alignment,** then click **OK.**

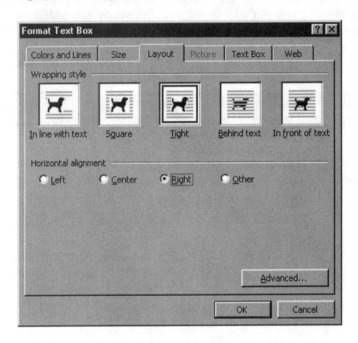

Your text box should be located in the bulleted list similar to the following example:

1. Architecture Domain to develop the underlying technologies of the Web.
2. Technology and Society Domain to understand ethical and legal issues from a new international perspective and in light of new technology.
3. User Interface Domain to improve user interaction with the Web including work on formats and languages.
4. Web Accessibility Initiative to pursue accessibility of the Web.

Adding and Formatting Text in a Text Box

You can insert and format text in a text box.

❶ Click inside the text box and enter the following text. Then, size the box to fit the text.

The WWW conducts its activities through five primary areas of work: technology, guidelines, tools, education and outreach, and research and development.

❷ Format the text in the text box by clicking on the border of the text box. With the text box selected, select **Bold** and change the **Font** to **Arial** and the **Font Size** to **10.**

Formatting the Layout of a Text Box

You can change the fill effects and lines of a text box.

❶ To add fill, in this case color, to the text box, select the text box, and then select **Format | Text Box.** Click the **Colors and Lines** tab and in the **Color** box under **Fill,** select a color.

❷ To change the line style of the text box, while the **Format Text Box** dialog box is on the screen, in the **Color** box under **Line,** select **Black** for the color of the line, select **1½ pt** in **Style,** and click **OK.**

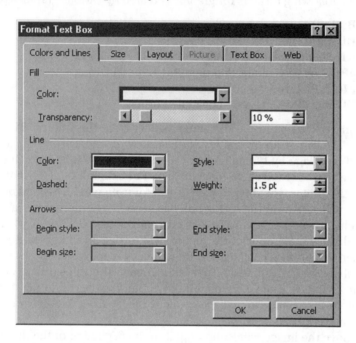

Your text box should be similar to the following example, or you may make a design you like better:

1. Architecture Domain to develop the underlying technologies of the Web.

2. Technology and Society Domain to understand ethical and legal issues from a new international perspective and in light of new technology.

3. User Interface Domain to improve user interaction with the Web including work on formats and languages.

4. Web Accessibility Initiative to pursue accessibility of the Web.

> The WWW conducts its activities through five primary areas of work: technology, guidelines, tools, education and outreach, and research and development.

Inserting Clip Art in a Document

You can insert five types of graphics or images into *Word* documents:

- **Clip Art:** These are prepared images (drawn, cartoon-like) and photos packaged within the *Word* program or that you buy from other sources.
- **Scanned:** With a digital scanner, you can scan in and save any image you see in a magazine or book and insert it in a *Word* document.

- **Digital:** You can use photos taken with a digital camera in *Word*.
- **Drawn:** *Word* provides several kinds of drawing tools that you can use to create your own graphics or to add features to prepared graphics or text.
- **WordArt:** This *Word* feature adds special effects to text; you can create curved or slanted text or other effects.

The Internet provides two more sources of ready-to-use images:

- **Web Pages:** Images on a Web page can be captured, saved, and used in a *Word* document. (You may need to obtain permission to download and use the image from the Web page owner.)
- **Design Gallery Live:** Microsoft® offers a huge collection of ready-made clip art and photos through links on its Web site.

Images are saved in many different formats by different graphics programs. *Word* can use all of the following formats for graphics created by various graphics programs:

BMP: Bitmap
EPS: Encapsulated PostScript
GIF: Graphics Interchange Format
JPEG or JPG: Joint Photographic Experts Group
PICT: Picture
TIFF or TIF: Tagged Image File Format

❶ To insert clip art in the document, select from the **Insert | Picture | Clip Art.** The *Word* Clip Art Gallery and a dialog box for inserting clip art displays.

❷ Find an image by typing search criteria in the box that says **Type one or more words** (**Search** on Macintosh®). For example, select what is entered and then enter **world wide web** or *web* or even **world.** Several different images will appear in the dialog box based on your search criteria. Select one by clicking on it, clicking **Insert clip** (or double-click the clip) and closing the dialog box. A copy of the picture will be displayed in your document.

❸ When the image is placed in the document, you may need to resize the image (probably make it smaller). To resize an image, first click on it to display solid sizing handles. Then click one of the corner handles and drag it toward the center of the image to make it smaller or away from the center of the image to make it larger.

❹ To move the image, click and drag it to the beginning of the first paragraph of the document; drop it there by releasing the mouse button.

❺ Format the image by double-clicking on it, which displays the **Format Picture** dialog box. Click **Layout, Tight** for the **Wrapping style,** and **Left** for **Horizontal alignment** so that the first paragraph of the document is wrapped around the image. Click **OK.**

❻ To insert a scanned or digital image using one of the file formats previously described, follow the same procedure for inserting clip art except begin by clicking **Insert | Picture | From File.**

Creating Headers and Footers in a Document

For a multi-page document you may want a title at the top (called a header) and/or a title or page number at the bottom of the page (called a footer).

❶ To insert a header, click **View | Header and Footer** and click in the Header box at the top of the page (the box with a dashed border). Click **Align Right,** select **10** for the **Font Size,** and then type **World Wide Web Report.**

❷ Click the down arrow of the **Outside Border** icon to draw a bottom border on the header. Select **Bottom Border** from the pop-up menu, and the tool will draw a bottom border on the line on which the cursor currently rests in the header.

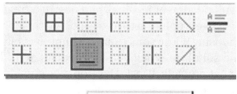

Bottom Border

③ Now enter a centered page number for a Footer. In the Header and Footer Toolbar, click **Switch Between Header and Footer.** Click in the Footer box at the bottom of the page (the box with a dashed border).

④ Click **Center** on the **Formatting Toolbar.** Now click **Insert Page Number** on the **Header and Footer Toolbar.** The page number will appear on all pages.

Insert Page Number

⑤ You may want to bold the page number or change its size. To do so, first highlight the number and then change these attributes.

⑥ Save and close the document and exit *Word.* An example of the completed **Ch3Report.doc** may be found in a document file named **Ch3ReportFinal.doc** in the **WP folder** on the **T3 Practice CD.** You can use it to compare with your solution.

FOLLOW-UP PRACTICE PROJECTS

For more practice on layout and graphics skills in *Word*, perform the following practice exercises.

① Start *Word* and open the *Word* document **Ch3EarthquakeReport.doc** from the **T3 Practice CD.** Perform each of the following practice exercises using this document. If you make a mistake on any of these operations, Undo the change and then perform the operation again. When you have completed the practice exercise, save the document and exit *Word.*

   a. Select all text in the document and double-space it. (If you have extra blank lines in some places, delete the blank lines.)

   b. Center and bold the report title, increase its font size, and bold or underline the section headings.

   c. Insert a report title that is right-aligned in the header and a page number that is centered in the footer.

   d. Near the middle of the report is a list or table of Earthquake Magnitudes. Place this information (cut and paste) in a text box with a 2¼ pt border, and locate it along the right margin of the report.

   e. Insert two or three more clip art images into the report (for example, one for each section of the report).

   f. Preview the document and then print it.

   g. Develop a lesson idea or plan for the entire activity you just completed that is targeted for the grade level you teach or plan to teach. Add it to the **Lesson Plans ePortfolio.**

Lesson Plans

2 Open a new blank document in *Word*, and design a treasure hunt lesson that describes using a geography, history, or ecology theme (or subject or theme of your own choosing). For your treasure hunt, use clip art and text to create clues for the solution. When you have completed the practice exercise, save the document and exit *Word*. Develop a lesson idea or plan for this activity that is targeted for the grade level you teach or plan to teach. Add it to the **Lesson Plans ePortfolio.**

3 Open a new blank document in *Word*, and in it create a math lesson about place value using hieroglyphics to represent different place values.

     a. Create your own set of hieroglyphs using clip art to represent numbers with place values up to the thousands place. This would require four clip art images—one for the ones place, tens place, hundreds place, and thousands place. If you used a basket to represent the tens place and a ball to represent the ones place, then 2 [basket image] + 5 [ball image] would be 25.

     b. Create a place value worksheet for students to work with items made up of groups of the hieroglyphs to learn what numbers are represented. When you have completed the practice exercise, save the document and exit *Word*.

     c. Develop a lesson idea or plan for this entire activity that is targeted for the grade level you teach or plan to teach. Add it to the **Lesson Plans ePortfolio.**

LESSON 3.2: LAYING OUT TEXT IN COLUMNS AND USING DRAWING TOOLS IN *WORD*

Lesson 3.2: Learning Activities

Laying out text in columns
Inserting WordArt in a document
Inserting horizontal lines in a document
Inserting graphics from a file
Using shading to highlight headings

The principal has asked Julia if her creative writing class would publish a quarterly newsletter for the high school. The principal will submit to Julia and her class most of the content for the newsletter, but they will need to rewrite or edit some articles and format the newsletter.

     Julia knows that there are several desktop publishing features in *Word* in addition to those functions she has already learned. So Julia decides that *Word* would be a good software tool for creating and publishing the school newsletter. In this lesson Julia will use two desktop publishing features of *Word* that are useful for publishing a newsletter: column layout and drawing tools. She will learn how to format a newsletter in columns and how to use the drawing tools of *Word* to enhance the appearance of the document and emphasize or reinforce text information.

LESSON 3.2: TUTORIAL

Laying Out Text in Columns

When students or teachers are producing a document such as a newsletter or brochure, additional ways to structure text are to format text into columns and change the line spacing.

❶ Open *Word* and then the file **Ch3Newsletter.doc** that you loaded previously from the **T3 Practice CD** onto your own disk.

❷ Move the cursor in front of the text "CURRENT EVENTS AND UPCOMING ACTIVITIES." Select **Format I Columns** and click **Two** below **Presets**. Select **This point forward** from the drop-down list on the **Apply to** box. Click **OK.**

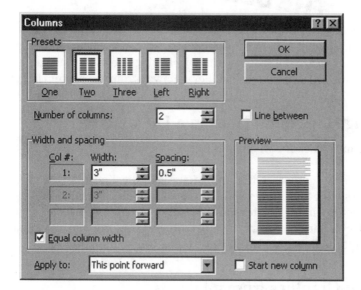

❸ The titles of the newsletter should be listed at the top while the remaining content is divided into two columns.

Inserting WordArt in a Document

You can apply **WordArt** to a title to improve the appearance and emphasize certain text elements.

❶ Select the title of the newsletter, "The Del Rio Reporter", and select **Insert I Picture I WordArt.** When the **WordArt Gallery** dialog box appears, select the diagonal **WordArt style** that is the second from the left in the top row. Click **OK** to close the **WordArt Gallery** dialog box and again to close the **Edit WordArt Text** dialog box.

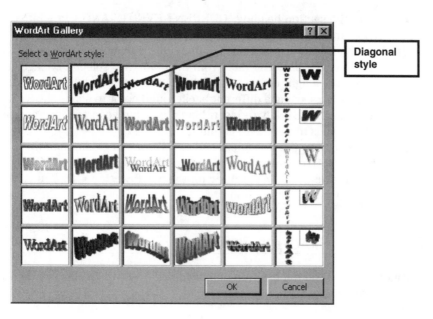

❷ The heading on the newsletter should be similar to the following example:

THE DEL RIO REPORTER

❸ You may need to delete the original title after the WordArt text appears.

❹ You can resize the WordArt title by clicking one of the end handles and dragging towards the center (smaller) or away from the center (larger).

Inserting Horizontal Lines in a Document

This line can be used for Web pages or text documents.

Macintosh®: Select **Insert | Picture** and select **Horizontal Line.** Select a line style from the list and click **Insert.**

❶ Place the cursor at the end of the subtitle line that reads "A Quarterly Newsletter for Parents and Patrons of Del Rio High School."

❷ Select **Format | Borders and Shading | Horizontal Line.**

❸ Select a line style from the **Horizontal Line** drop-down list and click **OK.** Insert the line directly following the newsletter subtitle.

Inserting Graphics from a File

You can insert original art or images into a document.

❶ Be sure the **T3 Practice CD** is inserted in the CD drive on your computer. Click beside the heading "From the Principal," and click **Insert | Picture | From File.**

❷ Use the arrow beside Look in: to select the **T3 Practice CD,** select the file **Notebutton.gif** from the **WP Folder** and click **OK.**

Using Shading to Highlight Headings

You can add a background color around each of the section headings of the newsletter to highlight the text.

❶ Select the section heading "CURRENT EVENTS AND UPCOMING ACTIVITIES," and click **Bold.**

❷ While the heading text is highlighted, select **Format | Borders and Shading** and select the **Shading** tab. From the color grid select a background color (preferably a light color) and click **OK.** Repeat 1 and 2 for each of the section headings, using a different background color to shade the text.

❸ Press the **ENTER** key to insert blank lines between sections and push section headings to the top of columns.

❹ Save and close the document and exit *Word.* An example of the completed **Ch3Newsletter.doc** may be found in a document file named **Ch3NewsletterFinal.doc** in the **WP folder** on the **T3 Practice CD.** You can use it to compare with your solution.

FOLLOW-UP PRACTICE PROJECTS

For more practice on the desktop publishing skills in *Word,* perform the following practice exercises.

1 Start *Word* and open the *Word* document **Ch3Newsletter.doc** you used in the preceding lesson. Perform each of the following practice exercises using this document. If you make a mistake on any of these operations, Undo the change and then perform the operation again. When you have completed the practice exercise, save the document and exit *Word.*

   a. Create the following graphic for the newsletter in the space at the end of the newsletter using **AutoShapes.** Click **AutoShapes** on the **Drawing Toolbar,** and click **Basic Shapes** from the pop-up menu. Click on a triangle-shaped object to select it, and then click in the document to insert it into the document.

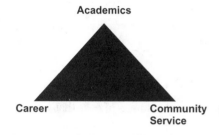

   b. Add fill to the shape by clicking the **Fill Color** arrow and selecting a color from the grid.

   c. Use the **Text Box** tool to create the text at each point of the triangle. In the **Format Text Box** dialog box (double-click the box border) remove the lines around the boxes, and add a colorfill to each box.

   d. Adjust the position as necessary of each object either by clicking and dragging it or by selecting it, clicking **Draw I Nudge,** and then using the pop-up menu that appears.

   e. Group the four objects together so that they will remain together in their relative positions even if text is added above or around them. Select each of the four objects by pressing the **SHIFT** while clicking each of the objects. Then when all four objects are selected, click **Draw I Group** on the **Drawing Toolbar.** Hollow sizing handles appear around the new group of objects.

   f. Insert a WordArt heading over the group image, similar to the one shown in the example.

   g. Develop a lesson idea or plan for the entire activity you just completed that is targeted for the grade level you teach or plan to teach. Add it to the **Lesson Plans ePortfolio.**

2 Open a new blank document in *Word,* and in it create a document that is similar to a section of a page from a local newspaper. Include columns, separate filled text boxes for the headlines, bulleted items when appropriate, and a border for the page (click **Format I Borders** and **Shading I Page Border** and choose settings). When you have completed the practice exercise, save the document and exit *Word.* Develop a lesson idea or plan for this activity that is targeted for the grade level you teach or plan to teach. Add it to the **Lesson Plans ePortfolio.**

3 Open a new blank document in *Word,* and in it use *Word* drawing tools to illustrate a math word problem or one of your own choosing. When you have completed the practice exercise, save the document and exit *Word.* Develop a lesson idea or plan for this activity that is targeted for the grade level you teach or plan to teach. Add it to the **Lesson Plans ePortfolio.**

LESSON 3.3: USING TABLES IN *WORD* DOCUMENTS

Lesson 3.3: Learning Activities

Inserting a table in a document
Entering text in a table
Sizing text in a table
Inserting a large table in a document

In this lesson Julia learns how to use tables in *Word* documents. Tables can be used to control the layout of text and graphics in a document; in this lesson tables are used to organize and report information.

LESSON 3.3: TUTORIAL

Open *Word* and the file Ch3Newsletter.doc you loaded previously from the T3 Practice CD onto your own disk.

Inserting a Table in a Document

A table is composed of rows and columns of cells that you can fill with text and graphics.

❶ Move the cursor to the section of the newsletter called "TEACHER AND STUDENT SURVEYS" and click after the first paragraph of text (first inserting a blank line after it).

❷ Create a table by selecting **Table | Insert | Table.** In the **Insert Table** dialog box, enter **3** for **Number of columns** and **5** for **Number of rows.** Click **OK.** You will see a blank table that looks similar to this:

❸ Adjust the column width of this table. Pass your mouse without clicking over the line between two columns until you see a "wedge" tool that looks like the one shown here. Click and drag the tool to make the left column larger and the middle and right columns smaller.

Entering Text in a Table

Create titles for each column to show the names of the parts of speech and add text to the table.

❶ Click in the first column, first row and type **Students Who Reported That They:.** Click in the second column, first row and type **YES.** Click in the last column, first row and type **NO.**

2 Now enter the following data in the table starting from the left column of each row. **TAB** to move the cursor from one cell to the next. **NOTE:** Do not press **TAB** from the last cell of a table, because doing so will add a blank row at the end.

Look forward to going to school.	175	30
Study hard for tests.	100	105
Feel safe at school.	180	25
Talk with parents about school/homework.	95	110

3 Adjust column widths if necessary so text does not wrap to a second line.

Sizing Text in a Table

Make the titles larger by highlighting them and selecting a larger font size. Normal type size is 10- to 12-point, so 14- or 16-point type would make the titles stand out. Make them bold, if you like.

1 Again adjust column widths to correct text wrapping.

2 Add a title and subtitle above the table so that your completed table looks similar to the following example:

Student Attitude Survey
Number of Students Reporting = 205

Students Who Reported That They:	**YES**	**NO**
Look forward to going to school.	175	30
Study hard for tests.	100	105
Feel safe at school.	180	25
Talk with parents about school/homework.	95	110

3 Center the text in columns 2 and 3 so that it appears neater. Pass the mouse above column 2 until the cursor changes to a thick down arrow, and then click and drag it over column 3. Release the mouse button and both columns should be highlighted. Click **Center.**

Inserting a Large Table in a Document

Create a table on your own. This table should be located above the table you just inserted. Insert one or two blank lines above the table you already created so that the two tables will not be joined.

1 Create a table by selecting **Table | Insert | Table.** In the dialog box, enter **3** for **Number of columns** and **9** for **Number of rows.** Click **OK.**

2 Insert a title above the table and text in the table cells so that it looks similar to the following example:

Teacher Survey
Number of Teachers Reporting = 66

Number of teachers who report improvements among students in the following behaviors:	YES	NO
Improved in turning in his/her homework on time	40	26
Improved in completing classroom homework on time and correctly	42	24
Improved in participating in class	44	22
Improved in attending class regularly	38	28
Improved in being attentive in class	37	29
Improved in behaving well in class	43	23
Had classroom academic performance that was satisfactory or better	47	19
Improved in coming to school ready/prepared to learn	41	25

❸ Adjust column width as necessary to prevent wrapping, if possible.
❹ Center all of columns 2 and 3.
❺ Save and close the document and exit *Word*.

FOLLOW-UP PRACTICE PROJECTS

For more practice on using tables in *Word* documents, perform the following practice exercises.

❶ Start *Word* and open the document **Ch2PartsofSpeech.doc.** Perform each of the following practice exercises using this document. If you make a mistake on any of these operations, Undo the change and then perform it again.

     a. Insert a table in the document that is 3 columns and 10 rows. Students can practice identifying the parts of speech they identified previously by copying the words from the paragraph of text and pasting them into the appropriate columns of the table (use Copy, not Cut).

     The final table should look something like the following example:

Adjectives	Nouns	Verbs
<u>a</u> (4)	*hole* (3)	**lived**
<u>the</u> (2)	*ground*	**filled**
<u>nasty</u>	*hobbit*	**sit**
<u>dirty</u>	*ends*	**eat**
<u>wet</u>	*worms*	**was**
<u>oozy</u>	*smell*	**means**
<u>dry</u>	*nothing*	
<u>bare</u>	*hobbit-hole*	
<u>sandy</u>	*comfort*	

b. When you have completed the practice exercise, save the document as **Ch3PartsofSpeechTable.doc** and exit *Word*.

c. Develop a lesson idea or plan for the activity you just completed that is targeted for the grade level you teach or plan to teach. Add it to the **Lesson Plans ePortfolio.**

❷ Perform the following practice exercise, a table in which students fill in a number sequence. (*Word* is used instead of a spreadsheet program like *Excel* so that students will need to use mental analysis, not a formula, to calculate the results.) In *Word* open a new blank document.

a. Create a document that looks similar to the following example by entering the text and experimenting using the **Table** menu, **Format** menu, and **Formatting Toolbar.**

b. Develop a lesson idea or plan for this activity that is targeted for the grade level you teach or plan to teach. Add it to the **Lesson Plans ePortfolio.**

Type Your Name Here:

_____

**Do the following exercises to prepare for the ITBS next week.
When you finish, e-mail me the file to the usual e-mail address.**

DESCRIBE THE PATTERN FOR EACH ONE,
AND TYPE THE NEXT FOUR NUMBERS IN THE SERIES:

Describe the Pattern:

	3	9	15	21			
	5	8	6	9			
	7	14	13	26			

TYPE THE ANSWERS BELOW:

$2^2 =$		$2^3 =$		$2^4 =$	
$3^2 =$		$3^3 =$		$3^4 =$	
$4^2 =$		$4^3 =$		$4^4 =$	

EXERCISES TO REVIEW AND EXPAND YOUR SKILLS

Set 1: Reviewing Terms and Concepts—For each question below, provide a term on the blank that matches the description.

_____ **1.** This *Word* feature lets you add titles with special effects such as curved or slanted text.

_____ **2.** An option on the Drawing Toolbar that lets you merge two or more images into one.

_____ **3.** Select this feature on the View menu to insert automatic page numbers.

_____ **4.** Prepared images and photos that come with *Word* or that you can buy from other sources.

_____ **5.** An object consisting of rows and columns of cells that you can fill with text and graphics.

Set 2: **Expanding Your Skills**—Expand on the skills you learned in this chapter with these activities. Open a new blank document and perform each activity.

1. **Change a Table by Inserting or Deleting Rows and/or Columns.** Insert a table into the document. Delete a row or column, by clicking inside the row or column. Then, click **Table | Select | Row Table | Select | Column.** Then select **Table | Delete | Rows** or **Table | Delete | Columns.** To insert a row, click the row adjacent to where you want to insert, then select **Table | Insert | Rows. Above** or **Table | Insert | Rows Below.** To insert a column, click a column adjacent to where you want to insert, then select **Table | Insert | Columns to the Left** or **Table | Insert | Columns to the Right.**

2. **Different Headers/Footers for Different Pages.** Books often have a header on the right pages different from a header on the left pages. If you want a document to have a different header for odd and even pages, select **View | Header and Footer.** In the **Header and Footer Toolbar,** click **Layout,** then click the check box beside **Different odd and even.**

3. **Change Line Width.** To draw a line in the document, click the **Line** icon on the **Drawing Toolbar.** In the document click and drag the cross that the cursor changes into until the line is drawn. To change the width of the line, click on the line and then either **Line Style** or **Dash Style** on the **Drawing Toolbar.** From the pop-up list select a different width or type of line.

Set 3: **Use Microsoft® Help**—In the Microsoft® *Office* Help Menu look up the following features to get further information and tips, and then try out each of these features with one or more of the documents you used in this chapter.

- Look up **Header** and **Footer** to learn how to put different headers and footers in different parts of a document (e.g., a header in all pages except the title page).
- Look up **Draw** to learn how to draw curve and freeform objects using the Curve, Freeform, and Scribble tools under the Autoshapes and Lines icons.
- Look up **Drawing Object** to learn how to arrange images behind or in front of text or other images.
- Look up **Watermark** to learn how to use an image as a watermark.

Set 4: **Create Your Own Lesson**— After reviewing the lessons in this chapter, develop and describe a lesson targeted for the grade level you teach or plan to teach that makes effective use of each of the following *Word* features. Describe the document you or the students would need to create to carry out the lesson. Enter your lesson idea or plan into the **Lesson Plans ePortfolio.**

- Students create their own letterhead and note paper for a fictional business.
- Students create a class newsletter.
- Students use tables filled with WordArt, text, and images to create a cartoon strip or to tell a story.
- Students use drawing tools and AutoShapes to illustrate a math concept visually (e.g., tessellations).

CONSTRUCTING INTERACTIVE FORMS AND WEB DOCUMENTS WITH *WORD*

NEW TERMS

form	hyperlink	template
find and replace	HTML format	thesaurus
FTP	spelling checker	

OVERVIEW

The lessons in this chapter expand your skills with Microsoft® *Word* by adding three capabilities: 1) creating forms and templates; 2) checking and changing the spelling and grammar of a document, and 3) preparing documents that can be published on the World Wide Web.

Each lesson consists of guided practice that demonstrates how teachers and students can use Microsoft® *Word* features in classroom learning activities. Practice files for the tutorials are located in the **WP folder** on the **T3 Practice CD.** Following each lesson are several exercises that include activities from the **Lesson Plans ePortfolio.** Complete these exercises to reinforce the learning activities demonstrated in the tutorial and to build your collection of technology-based lesson plans and ideas.

Lesson 4.1: Creating *Word* Forms and Templates

Lesson 4.2: Using *Word* Language Tools

Lesson 4.3: Publishing *Word* Documents on the Web

LESSON 4.1: CREATING *WORD* FORMS AND TEMPLATES

Lesson 4.1: Learning Activities

Creating a form
Creating a document template
Using a form
Using a template

Julia often creates worksheets and tests that her students must complete and return. Now that she has learned to use word processing for several classroom instructional activities, she wants to use *Word* to help automate this process. *Word* forms are one possible solution. With *Word* forms her students can complete assignments and return a document file containing the completed assignment.

A form is a document with blank areas for users to fill in information. A teacher can use *Word* form options to make fill-in exercises for vocabulary or other practice. The teacher can then save the document as a template to use for other exercises in the future. Practice these options with the following exercise on science vocabulary. It is based on an exercise called "Building Science Vocabulary with Electronic Encyclopedias" designed by Harriss (1992).

LESSON 4.1: TUTORIAL

Creating a Form

A form can be designed as a *Word* document structured with spaces for entering information. The form is designed so that users can fill it in on paper or in *Word*.

❶ Open *Word* and the file **Ch4Vocabex.doc** that you loaded previously from the **T3 Practice CD** onto your own disk.

❷ Activate the **Forms Toolbar** by selecting **View I Toolbars Forms**. Review the illustration below to become familiar with the various icons. Each kind of field—text, check box, and drop-down—can be helpful in creating various kinds of learning activities. For example, a text field could be used for a fill-in-the-blank response, a check box field for a multiple-choice response, and a drop-down field for a yes/no or true/false response.

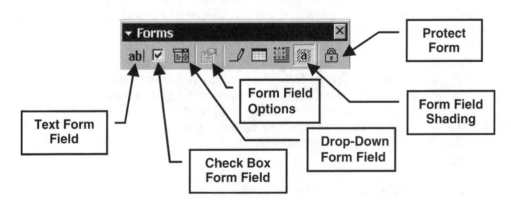

❸ The document uses a table to format the information for the learning activity. In the "FILL IN CLOUD" column, highlight the underline in the table cell beside the first appearance of "thunderheads" and press **DELETE** to delete it.

❹ Click **Text Form Field** on the **Forms Toolbar** to insert a form field.

❺ Click **Form Field Options** on the **Forms Toolbar.** The **Text Form Field Options** dialog box, similar to the following illustration, will display.

❻ To make this field the length of the longest word, enter **13** for **Maximum length** (or click the up-arrow to reach 13).

❼ Be sure the **Fill-in enabled** option is checked, then click **OK**.

❽ The field will be shaded automatically. If you do not want it to be shaded, click **Form Field Shading** to erase it. (Although, you cannot see it if it is not shaded.)

❾ Repeat steps 3–8 for each underline field. Or copy and paste the text form field you just created to each underline field, by selecting the text form field, copy, and then select all the other underline fields and paste. **OPTIONAL:** Add a form field at the top of the form to allow the student to enter a name.

❿ When you have created all the necessary fields, click **Protect Form** on the **Forms Toolbar.** This feature protects the document so students can change or enter text *only* in the areas you have designated. Protection is necessary for the document to function as a form rather than a regular word processing document.

⓫ Save the document as a form for use as a learning activity by selecting **File | Save** as and save the form document as **Ch4CloudsVocab.doc.** You may close the **Forms Toolbar** by clicking the **X** at the top right of it.

Creating a Document Template

Microsoft® *Word* has several templates, or ready-made document types, to use as a start for creating forms. Most templates are for items such as letters and faxes, but you can create your own instructional templates. Follow these steps to create an exercise template based on the form document from the previous exercise. (If you closed the **Forms Toolbar,** you will need to activate it again.)

❶ To use the form as a template, you need to unprotect the form so you can make changes to it and allow it to be adapted for other learning activities. Select **Tools | Unprotect Document** or click **Protect Form** on the **Forms Toolbar.**

❷ Select **File | Save As**. In the **Save As** dialog box, select **Document Template** from the drop-down list in the **Save as type** box.

3 *Word* may default to the **Templates** folder to save the document, but you can select another disk or hard drive location.

4 In the **File Name** box, type template name, **Ch4VocabFillinTemplate.doc,** and click **Save**. Later, you can open this template and make changes to it to create similar exercises and exercise templates.

5 Close the template document.

Using a Form

You should try out a form before distributing to students to determine that it functions properly and is easy to understand and use.

1 Load the form named **Ch4VocabClouds.doc** just created.

2 When you open the form, the cursor is set at the first input field. Enter **Cumulonimbus** in the first text form field.

3 Press **TAB** and enter **Cirrostratus** in the second text form field.

4 Continue pressing **TAB** to advance to each of the following fields. In the remaining text fields enter, **Cirrus, Cirrocumulus, Altostratus, Altocumulus, Stratocumulus.**

5 When you complete the last field and press **TAB,** the cursor returns to the first field.

6 Save the file as **CloudsAnswerSheet.doc** (a *Word* document file). When your students complete a learning activity using a form, they should save the form using their name and the name of the activity, for example, SmillsCloudsWorksheet.doc.

7 Close the form document.

Using a Template

You can create templates for different types of learning or assessment strategies. Julia has given a copy of her template for fill-in-the-blank exercises to a science teacher in her school. The science teacher is going to use the template to create a fill-in-the-blank exercise on the planets of the solar system based on matching the planet name by classification and relative position from the sun. The first column will have the text form field. The second column will contain the planet classifications, and the third column will contain the planet's relative position to the sun. The fourth, or right-most, column will contain a list of the planets to be used to fill in the appropriate text form field. The title and instructions for the exercise will need to be changed on the new form to correspond with the solar system exercise.

1 Load the template file named **Ch4VocabFillinTemplate.doc.**

2 When you open the form, change the title of the exercise. Select or highlight the existing title and enter **Planets of the Solar System**.

3 Select or highlight the instructions and enter **Fill in the name of the planet according to the relative size and position of its orbit around the sun using the list of planets at the right**.

4 Change the column headings: FILL IN CLOUD to **FILL IN PLANET;** APPEARANCE to **CLASSIFICATION;** CLOUD HEIGHT to **POSITION FROM SUN;** CLOUD TYPES to **PLANETS.**

5 Delete the list of Cloud Types and replace with a list of Planets in the solar system. Select the cells with the list of clouds and select **Edit | Clear** and then select **Contents.** Enter the list of planets in alphabetical order down the column: **Earth, Jupiter, Mars, Mercury, Neptune, Pluto, Saturn, Uranus, Venus.**

6 Delete the list of Cloud Heights and replace with the Position from Sun. Select the cells with the list of Cloud Heights and select **Edit | Clear** and then select **Contents.** Enter the list of planet positions in ascending numerical order down the column: 1st, 2nd, 3rd, 4th, 5th, 6th, 7th, 8th, 9th.

7 Delete the list of cloud Appearances and replace with Classifications of each planet. Select the cells with the list of cloud heights and select **Edit | Clear.** Then select **Contents** and enter the classifications for each planet down the column:

Inner, Terrestrial, Small, Inferior, Classical
Inner, Terrestrial, Small, Inferior, Classical
Inner, Terrestrial, Small
Inner, Terrestrial, Small, Superior, Classical
Outer, Jovian, Giant, Superior, Classical
Outer, Jovian, Giant, Superior, Classical
Outer, Jovian, Giant, Superior, Modern
Outer, Jovian, Giant, Superior, Modern
Outer, Small, Superior, Modern

8 With the **Forms Toolbar** replace each of the underline fields in the first column with a text form field. (You could create one text form field and then copy and paste to all the other underline fields.)

9 When you have created all the necessary fields, click **Protect** on the **Forms Toolbar.**

10 Save the template file as a form file named **Ch4PlanetsFillin.doc** and close the file.

11 Load the form just created named **Ch4PlanetsFillin.doc** and test it to make sure it works correctly. Enter the answers in text fields: **Mercury, Venus, Earth, Mars, Jupiter, Saturn, Uranus, Neptune, Pluto.**

12 Save the file as **PlanetsAnswerSheet.doc.** When your students complete a learning activity using a form, they should save the form using their name and the name of the activity.

13 Close the form document.

FOLLOW-UP PRACTICE PROJECTS

For more practice on the forms and templates skills you just learned in this lesson, perform the following projects.

1 Open *Word* and then load the document **Ch2PartsofSpeech.doc.** Perform the following steps using this document. When you have completed the practice exercise, save the document and exit *Word*.

  a. Copy the paragraph and paste it to a new blank document.
  b. In the new document, list key words from the first document from the paragraph. In the new document insert a drop-down form field in front of each key word. From the **Forms Toolbar,** click **Drop-Down Form Field.** Point to a field, and double-click it to open the **Drop-Down Form Field Options** dialog box. Type each item in the **Drop-down item:** box clicking **Add** after each one, and then click OK.
  c. The items in the drop-down list should be **Adjective, Noun,** and **Verb.**
  d. Protect the document from changes, and save it as a template.
  e. Develop a lesson idea or plan for this activity that is targeted for the grade level you teach or plan to teach. Add it to the **Lesson Plans ePortfolio.**

❷ Open a new blank document in *Word*, and design a survey lesson that describes using a health/nutrition, social studies, or mathematics theme (or a subject or theme of your own choosing). In a form, create a simple survey that students can answer on the computer. You could use the questions from the student survey in Chapter 3, Lesson 3. Use the check box form option so survey takers can check a response to each question. When you have created the form, save the document and exit *Word*.

❸ Develop a lesson idea or plan for the activity you just completed that is targeted for the grade level you teach or plan to teach. Add it to the **Lesson Plans ePortfolio**.

Lesson 4.2: Using *Word* Language Tools

Lesson 4.2: Learning Activities

Finding and replacing text in a document
Checking the spelling of words in a document
Using the thesaurus to find a synonym

Since Julia is an English teacher, she is particularly interested in the language features of *Word*. With these powerful tools her students can better prepare written assignments that are free from spelling and grammar errors.

    This lesson demonstrates how students can improve their writing skills and products using find and replace, spelling checker, and thesaurus.

Lesson 4.2: Tutorial

Finding and Replacing Text in a Document

Word can find and replace text, formatting, paragraph marks, page breaks, and other items in documents.

❶ Open *Word* and the file **Ch3Report.doc.** In the report an acronym WWW, was used for the World Wide Web, when W3C, for World Wide Web Consortium, should have been used. Using Find and Replace this problem is easy to correct.

❷ Select **Edit | Replace.** Enter **WWW** in the **Find what** box and **W3C** in the **Replace with** box.

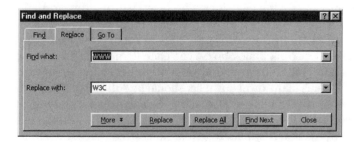

❸ Click **Replace**. *Word* advances to the next occurrence of the Find criteria ("WWW"). Click **Replace** to replace it and advance to the next occurrence.

❹ Click **Replace All** to replace all remaining occurrences. When the Replace is complete, a message displays telling you how many times the term was replaced. Click **OK** to close the message. Then, click **Close** to close the dialog box.

❺ Save and close the document.

Checking the Spelling of Words in a Document

By default, *Word* checks spelling and grammar automatically as you type text in a document. *Word* uses wavy red underlines to indicate possible spelling problems and wavy green underlines to indicate possible grammatical errors. You can also check spelling and grammar all at once.

The spelling checker should be used in addition to manual proofreading, when used alone, the spelling checker cannot detect the difference between *pair* and *pear* or determine whether *the*, not *a*, should be used, for example.

❶ Locate the file **Ch4Spelling.doc** that you loaded previously from the **T3 Practice CD** onto your own disk and open the document.

❷ Click in front of the first word of the document and select **Tools | Spelling and Grammar**. The misspelled words will be displayed in red in the **Spelling and Grammar** dialog box as they are located. See the example below.

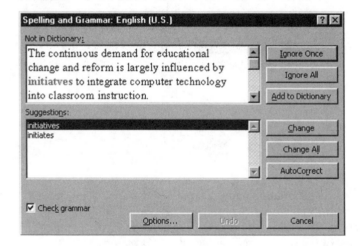

❸ For each word, the spelling checker suggests some possible correct spellings. Click on the correct suggestion for each misspelled word, and then click **Change** to complete the substitution. If no suggestion is correct, click in the **Not in Dictionary** box, type the correct substitution, and then click **Change.**

❹ Click **Close** to close the dialog box.

Using the Thesaurus to Find a Synonym

The thesaurus provides a list of synonyms for the text you look up. The thesaurus is useful for helping students focus on definitions and synonyms of words.

❶ Using the same document, highlight "integrate" in the first sentence of the document and select **Tools | Language | Thesaurus** (on Macintosh® select **Tools | Language**).

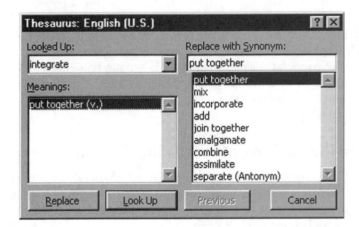

2 Select a synonym, such as "incorporate," by highlighting it and then clicking **Replace**.

3 Now select the word "entails" in the last sentence of the document by highlighting it or clicking on the word. Select **Tools | Language | Thesaurus** (on Macintosh® select **Tools | Language**).

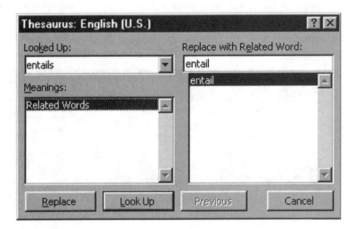

4 When the **Thesaurus** dialog box displays, click the **Look Up** button to look up additional words. Select a synonym and click **Replace.**

5 Use the Thesaurus to find a synonym for the word "enhance" in the last sentence of the document. Replace it with a synonym.

6 Save and close the document and exit *Word*.

Follow-up Practice Projects

Students can use *Word* language tools to improve the quality and readability of reports. For more practice using *Word* language tools you just learned, perform the following practice exercise.

1 Open *Word* and the document **Ch3EarthquakeReport.doc** from the **T3 Practice CD** (or from the location you saved it to when you used it in Chapter 3). Perform each of the following steps using this document. When you have completed the practice exercise, save the document and exit *Word*.

    a. Replace all occurrences of the word "properties" with the word "characteristics."

b. Replace all occurrences of the word "earthquakes" with an italicized and bold form of the same word. Formatting attributes can be entered into either the Find or Replace criteria. Click in the **Replace** box and then click **More I Format I Font I Bold Italic.** Then run the Find and Replace.

c. Find an occurrence of the word "amplify" and use the thesaurus to find a replacement synonym.

d. Using **Tools I Word Count,** count the number of words in the report

e. Check the document for grammar errors by selecting **Tools I Spelling and Grammar**. *Word* will perform a spelling and grammar check. For each spelling error (if any) either ignore or accept the recommended change. (Sometimes words are not misspelled; they are just unrecognized by the spelling checker dictionary.) For each grammar error (if any) either ignore or change it.

❷ Develop a lesson idea or plan for the activity you just completed that is targeted for the grade level you teach or plan to teach. Add it to the **Lesson Plans ePortfolio.**

LESSON 4.3: PUBLISHING *WORD* DOCUMENTS ON THE WEB

Lesson 4.3: Learning Activities

Inserting hyperlinks in a document
Creating hyperlinks in a document with text
Saving a document as a Web page
Browsing Web pages using *Word*

Julia realized that she could use *Word* to create Web-based exercises for her students to use. With *Word* she can prepare documents that can be used as Web pages and posted on the School Web server, or let her students create Web pages. *Word* includes features that allow you to construct documents for publishing on the Web. This lesson lets you practice classroom uses of some of these capabilities.

LESSON 4.3: TUTORIAL

Inserting Hyperlinks in a Document

Word automatically creates a hyperlink to a Web site when you type the address of an existing Web site, such as www.microsoft.com. A hyperlink provides a clickable link to a Web site or to a file or another location. **NOTE:** You can turn off the automatic formatting of hyperlinks by selecting **Tools I AutoCorrect I AutoFormat As You Type** and clearing the Internet and network paths with hyperlinks check box.

❶ To prepare a handout of Web sites for students to browse in preparation for a report or to prepare their own Web site, open a new *Word* document and insert a centered heading, such as **Great Resources for Your Web Sites.**

❷ Minimize *Word* and at the desktop connect to the Internet with the browser program on your computer. Surf a site you might want your students to see. For example, surf to the Smithsonian Institution Web site at http://www.si.edu.

❸ Copy the Web address for the site from the address line of the brower by highlighting it and selecting **Edit I Copy.**

❹ Click in the new *Word* document, and paste the Web address by selecting **Edit I Paste** and then press **ENTER.** *Word* automatically formats the Web address as a hyperlink.

Creating Hyperlinks in a Document with Text

Another way to insert a hyperlink in a *Word* document is to create one with text. Again, these are clickable links if your computer is connected to the Internet. Insert another hyperlink in your Web resources document.

❶ Enter the following text into your document: **Click here for the NASA Space Center Site.**

❷ Highlight the words you just typed by dragging the mouse over them.

❸ Click **Insert | Hyperlink** or click on **Insert Hyperlink.** In the **Type the file or Web page name** box, enter **www.nasa.gov.** Click **OK.** The text becomes a hyperlink (text color is changed to blue and the text is underlined) that you can click in order to link to the NASA Web site.

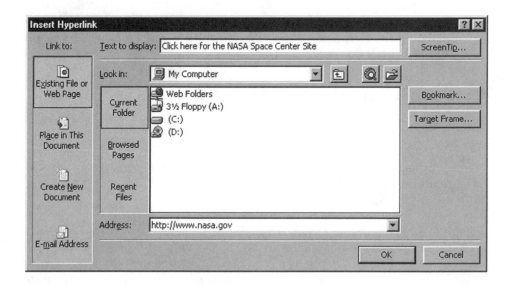

❹ Save the document as **Ch4Links.doc** and close it.

Saving a Document as a Web Page

Word lets you prepare documents for publishing as Web pages by saving them as HTML documents. The following exercises will let you prepare a Web page that can be viewed with a Web browser like *Internet Explorer*.

❶ Open the file **Ch4HomePage.doc** that you loaded previously from the **T3 Practice CD** onto your own disk. The document contains a list of English and language arts Web resources (hyperlinks) and descriptions. The document uses a table to layout the hyperlinks and descriptions.

❷ To save the file as a Web page, select **File | Save as Web Page.** Name the file and save it to a desired location on a disk or hard drive (you can use the same file name). The **Save as Web Page** option saves a document file as a Web page (HTML document).

❸ The resulting file may look different from the original one, since HTML formatting is different from word processing formatting. HTML pages can be edited with *Word* and then posted to a Web server using a FTP (File Transfer Protocol) program or by copying the file to the Web server through your local area network.

Browsing Web Pages Using *Word*

By using the **Web Toolbar,** which is available in *Word* and in other Microsoft® *Office* programs, you can browse Web pages and other documents that have hyperlinks with or without a browser program open if your computer is connected to the Internet.

① To practice using the Web browsing features of *Word*, open the **Web Tool-bar** by selecting **View | Toolbars | Web.**

② Click **Go | Open**. Enter **www.nasa.gov** and click **OK.** Close the Web page.

③ To open the Web page you created in the previous step, click the **Go** button and then select **Open Hyperlink** and click the **Browse** button. Find the file, **Ch4HomePage.htm,** or the file name you gave it. Select some of the links on the Web page.

④ Select **Favorites** on the **Web Toolbar.** Click on the Web sites you entered as a hyperlink in Step 1 to go to the page in your browser. Then go back to the *Word* document and select **Favorites** from the **Web Toolbar.** Select **Add to Favorites.** This Web page will be added to the list automatically.

⑤ To check the list of Favorites, select **Open Favorites** under **Favorites** on the **Web Toolbar.**

⑥ Exit *Word*.

FOLLOW-UP PRACTICE PROJECTS

For more practice on publishing *Word* documents with Web features, complete the following exercises. Create Web resources that encourage students to research, analyze, and think critically about information.

① Open a new blank document in *Word*, and design an online news resources lesson that describes language arts or social studies sites (or sites of a subject or theme of your own choosing) and provides links to each.

② Using *Word*, design a current events resource Web page document using a layout table similar to the one used in Lesson 3. Locate Web sites for several large newspapers, such as *USA Today* and the *Washington Post*. Make a handout of these sites for students by going to each Web site, copying the Web address, and pasting it in the *Word* document in one column of the table. In the next column of the layout table, identify the Web site by name and description.

Save the document and print it as a *Word* document, and save it also in HTML format for posting to a Web site. View the HTML document using *Word* as your Web browser. Exit *Word*.

③ Develop a lesson idea or plan for the above activity that is targeted for the grade level you teach or plan to teach. Add it to the **Lesson Plans ePortfolio.**

④ Open a new blank document in *Word*, and design a creative writing lesson that describes using a language arts or writing theme (or subject or theme of your own choosing).

⑤ Design a Web page document that reports on a recent class or school activity by preparing such a composition as a *Word* document and inserting clip art images or pictures. Save the document in HTML format for posting to a Web site, so students can use it as a model for their own compositions or reports.

View the HTML document using *Word* as your Web browser. When you have completed the practice exercise, save the document and exit *Word*.

⑥ Develop a lesson idea or plan for the activity you just completed that is targeted for the grade level you teach or plan to teach. Add it to the **Lesson Plans ePortfolio.**

EXERCISES TO REVIEW AND EXPAND YOUR SKILLS

Set 1: Reviewing Terms and Concepts—For each question below, provide a term on the blank that matches description.

_____ 1. Create this so that users can click on it and go to a Web site.

_____ 2. Select this menu to find Spelling and Thesaurus options.

    _____ **3.** Save a *Word* document in this format to make it ready for posting on the Web.

    _____ **4.** Use this type of form field to let people click a yes/no option.

    _____ **5.** Find *Word*'s Web page options on this toolbar.

Set 2: Expanding Your Skills—Expand on the skills you learned in this chapter with these activities.

1. Find and Replace can be refined to look *only* for words that begin with upper- or lowercase letters. Begin a Find and Replace, and click on **More** then **Match case** to search for and replace only words that are in the same case as the Find word. For example, if you typed "Micro" in the **Find what** box, *Word* would find and replace all instances of "Micro" but not "micro."

2. Templates, documents with prepared formats, are available for you to use to create memos, letters, fax forms, resumes, and other documents. Select **File | New** and choose one from within one of the tabs listed. (Then click **OK.**) Follow the directions embedded within the document to enter your own text.

3. Hyperlinks can be used to "jump" to locations *within* documents as well as to link a *Word* document to an Internet Web page. Create a Table of Contents page for a document you have created. Use the same procedure you practiced in this chapter for linking each of the items in the table of contents to the page that contains the item.

   Use **Insert | Bookmark** at each section to be linked, and type a bookmark name, then click **Add.** Then, in the table of contents, select an item and insert a hyperlink. At the **Insert Hyperlink** dialog box, click **Bookmark,** double-click **Bookmarks** to see a list of bookmarks, select one from the list, then click **OK.**

Set 3: Use Microsoft® Help—Look up the following features to get further information and tips and then practice each of these features with one or more of the documents you used in this lesson.

- Look up **Wildcard** to fine-tune a search using Find and Replace.
- Look up **Letter Wizard** to learn to quickly create a letter.
- Look up **Track** to let reviewers change a document by inserting comments and changes.

Set 4: Create Your Own Lesson—After reviewing the lessons in this chapter, develop a lesson targeted for the grade level you teach or plan to teach that makes effective use of each of the following *Word* features. Describe the document you or the students would need to create to carry out the lesson. Enter your lesson idea or plan into the **Lesson Plans ePortfolio.**

- Students use a *Word* form with fields to collect data from observations or measurements.
- Students use **Find and Replace** for a vocabulary exercise.
- Students create a list of items for their classmates to find and a list of clickable Web site links where the items can be found (e.g., a scavenger hunt).

PART

2

INTEGRATING TECHNOLOGY IN THE CLASSROOM WITH MICROSOFT® *EXCEL*

OVERVIEW

Shelly Edwards is a middle school science teacher. Her school recently installed five new computers in her classroom. Each of the computers is equipped with Microsoft® *Office*, with network capabilities, and access to the Internet. Shelly is excited about the possibility of using the new computers for classroom instructional activities that integrate the technology standards now incorporated in the science curriculum.

Shelly has a computer at home and uses word processing to prepare lesson plans and handouts for science projects and experiments. After reviewing the technology standards in the science curriculum, Shelly found that spreadsheets were recommended for instructional use in performing simulations and to support decision making and problem solving. As Shelly began to research the uses of spreadsheets for teaching and learning, she discovered that there are more classroom uses reported for spreadsheets than for any other productivity tool. Roblyer (2003) notes that, while its teaching role is primarily in mathematics, spreadsheets can also be integrated into science, social studies, and even language arts curricula.

- **Demonstrations.** Spreadsheet demonstrations can help clarify abstract concepts by presenting them as numerical "pictures." Frequently used to present math concepts such as multiplication and percentages, spreadsheets also may be used to demonstrate numerical concepts such as the difference between electoral and popular votes.
- **Student products.** Students can use spreadsheets to create their own charts, graphs, and timelines to illustrate a project or presentation.

- **Support for problem solving.** Spreadsheets do mathematical calculations so students can focus on the higher level numerical concepts involved in problem solving.
- **Storing and analyzing data.** When students have to keep track of data during a project or experiment, spreadsheets help them organize the data and do statistical analyses.
- **Projecting grades.** Spreadsheets can help students be more responsible for their own progress by allowing them to do "what if?" projections of future grades.

Shelly is beginning a unit on nutrition in her sixth grade science class. One goal for the study of nutrition is for students to select appropriate foods and food amounts to build a nutritious menu based on calorie counts and nutrition values for certain ages or weights. Shelly thought that her students could build tables of foods with their associated nutrient values, including counts of calories, fats, proteins, carbohydrates, vitamins, and minerals. They could then create nutritious menus for persons of varying ages and weights.

Before Shelly attempted this ambitious application of technology to science instruction, she first needed to learn how to use a spreadsheet program. Since all her new classroom computers were installed with Microsoft® *Office*, she began to use Microsoft® *Excel* and then develop instructional units and projects for her students that integrate *Excel* into classroom learning activities.

In Part 2 you will learn how to use the Microsoft® *Office* spreadsheet application, *Excel*, to create documents called worksheets. Spreadsheet programs organize and manipulate numerical data (Roblyer, 2003). Spreadsheets themselves are computerized, numerical record-keeping systems that were originally designed to automate paper-based ledger systems (Jonassen, 2000). Spreadsheets, or worksheets, are organized into a grid or table of rows and columns. The intersection of each row-column position in the worksheet is called a cell. Each cell may contain text, numbers, mathematical formulas, or logical operations that manipulate the contents of other cells.

Spreadsheets have three primary functions: storing data, performing calculations, and presenting information (Jonassen, 2000). Roblyer (2003) provide several examples of how electronic spreadsheets can be used to perform classroom management tasks and instructional activities:

- Recording and maintaining student grades and preparing grade charts
- Student clubs or classroom budgets
- Attendance charts
- Performance assessment checklists
- Problem-solving and decision-making learning activities
- Collecting and storing data from experiments or other classroom research
- Demonstrating numerical, statistical, and logical concepts and computations
- Creating charts and graphs

Technology Standards and Educational Best Practices for Technology

The lessons in this section assist learners in developing skills for the following International Society for Technology in Education (ISTE) National Educational Technology Standards for Students (NETS·S):

1. Basic operations and concepts

   - Students demonstrate a sound understanding of the nature and operation of technology systems.
   - Students are proficient in the use of technology.

2. Social, ethical, and human issues

    *   Students practice responsible use of technology systems, information, and software.
    *   Students develop positive attitudes toward technology uses that support lifelong learning, collaboration, personal pursuits, and productivity.

3. Technology productivity tools

    *   Students use technology tools to enhance learning, increase productivity, and promote creativity.

4. Technology research tools

    *   Students use technology tools to process data and report results.

5. Technology problem-solving and decision-making tools

    *   Students use technology resources for solving problems and making informed decisions.
    *   Students employ technology in the development of strategies for solving problems in the real world.

The chapters in Part 2: Integrating Technology in the Classroom with Microsoft® Excel address indicators in five of the NETS·S standards. The tutorials and activities in Part 2 require you to open files from a CD, floppy disk, and/or a hard disk, use a keyboard and mouse, and manage files you create, save, or copy. Excel is a productivity tool for storing numbers and computations and a research tool for analyzing, processing, and reporting data. It is useful for problem-solving and decision-making learning activities, especially in performing "what if" analyses. The tutorials and learning activities in Part 2 provide learning experiences in which students create work products such as reports and graphs that analyze scientific data and on-line spreadsheets that facilitate collaboration at a distance.

The chapters in Part 2 demonstrate how Microsoft® Excel is a powerful technology integration resource in constructing and conducting curriculum-related learning activities and classroom management tasks. All learning activities in Part 2 are designed to promote responsible use of computer technology and help students develop positive attitudes about the use of technology to accommodate lifelong learning.

Chapters in Part 2

The step-by-step lessons in each chapter demonstrate the text, numbers, and graphics processing features of Microsoft® Excel. Each tutorial consists of guided practice that demonstrates how teachers and students can use Excel features in classroom learning activities. For each chapter, use the practice files in the **SP folder** of the **T3 Practice CD** to complete the step-by-step lessons.

Several exercises follow each lesson, which may also include activities using files from the **T3 Practice CD** and the **Lesson Plans ePortfolio.** Complete these exercises to reinforce the learning activities demonstrated in the tutorial and expand your skills.

The tutorials in the following lessons do not include every feature of Microsoft® Excel but are designed to address those features that will allow you to perform text and graphics processing tasks that support classroom instruction and student learning. The tutorials also provide activities that encourage you to investigate other features of Excel not specifically included in these lessons.

Chapter 5:   Navigating, Updating, and Formatting Worksheets in Excel

Chapter 6:   Excel Formulas, Functions, and Forms

Chapter 7:   Printing and Publishing Excel Data

NAVIGATING, UPDATING, AND FORMATTING WORKSHEETS IN *EXCEL*

NEW TERMS

active cell	formula bar	template
cell	row	workbook
column	scroll bar	worksheet
default folder		

OVERVIEW

This chapter contains three tutorial lessons of step-by-step exercises to build skills in basic Microsoft® *Excel* file operations, navigation of the *Excel* window, and entering and formatting data in *Excel* worksheets.

Each tutorial consists of guided practice that demonstrates how teachers and students can use Microsoft® *Excel* features in classroom learning activities. Practice files for the tutorials are located in the **SP folder** on the **T3 Practice CD.** Several exercises follow each lesson, including activities from the **Lesson Plans ePortfolio.** Complete these exercises to reinforce the learning activities demonstrated in the tutorials and to build your collection of technology-based lesson plans and ideas.

Lesson 5.1: Opening and Saving *Excel* Worksheet Files
Lesson 5.2: Managing and Navigating Workbooks
Lesson 5.3: Entering and Formatting Data in *Excel* Worksheets

LESSON 5.1: OPENING AND SAVING *EXCEL* WORKSHEET FILES

Lesson 5.1: Learning Activities

Opening a worksheet document
Saving a worksheet document
Saving a worksheet for use in another program
Changing the default working folder for *Excel*
Closing the worksheet document
Exiting *Excel*

A worksheet is a grid or table of empty cells. Columns of the worksheet are identified by letters in alphabetical order (A, B, C, etc.) from left to right, and rows are identified by numbers in numerical order (1, 2, 3, etc.) from top to bottom. A cell is located at the intersection of each column and row, and a cell address is defined by its column and row location (A1, B2, C3, etc.). In the following *Excel* window each of the cells has been labeled with its corresponding cell address:

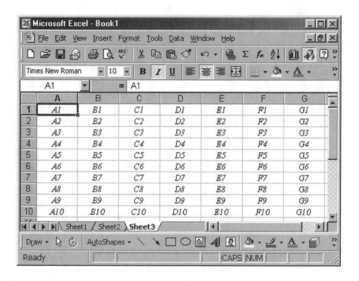

Shelly is beginning to construct her unit on nutrition. She first had to obtain a data table with food and nutrition information from an Internet download site of the U.S. Department of Agriculture. The table she downloaded was provided in *Excel* format. (An abridged version of this table, **Ch5NutritionTable.xls,** is used in this tutorial.) Shelly opened the table and reviewed its contents. The following procedure demonstrates how to use *Excel* to open an existing worksheet document file.

LESSON 5.1: TUTORIAL

Opening a Worksheet Document

The **T3 Practice CD** contains a file called **Ch5NutritionTable.xls.** Place the CD in the CD drive, and open the file as follows.

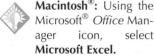

Macintosh®: Using the Microsoft® *Office* Manager icon, select **Microsoft Excel.**

❶ Open *Excel* by double-clicking on the *Excel* icon or by selecting **Microsoft® Excel** from the **Start | Programs** menu on the Windows® screen. Your screen should look very similar to that shown in Figure 5–1.

❷ From the *Excel* program window select **File | Open.** The Open dialog box displays the default working folder. The default folder for *Excel* files is the folder that is automatically selected by *Excel*. For computers using the Win-

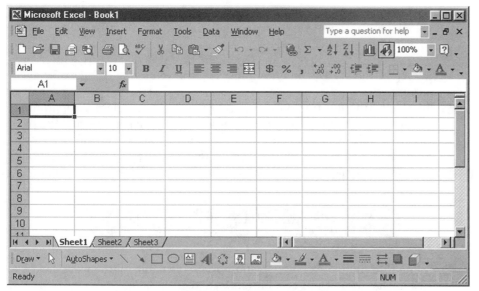

FIGURE 5–1
The Microsoft® *Excel*
Window with Standard,
Formatting, and Drawing
Toolbars
Source: Screen captures of
Microsoft® *Excel* used in the
chapters in Part 2 are reprinted by
permission from Microsoft®
Corporation.

dows® operating system, the default working folder is **My Documents.** To select the CD drive, click the down arrow on the **Look in** box and then select the appropriate location from the list.

❸ Select the **SP Folder** on the **T3 Practice CD** and open it by double-clicking on it or by pointing at the name with the mouse, clicking on it to highlight it, and then clicking **Open.**

❹ Select the file named **Ch5NutritionTable.xls** from the file list. (The .xls file name extension may not appear on the file name based on the hardware platform and system settings of your computer.) Your screen should look similar to the following example:

Macintosh®: To select the CD drive, make sure the **T3 Practice CD** is in the CD drive. In the **File | Open** dialog box, select the CD drive from the **Desktop** folder. Select the CD drive and then double-click on **SP folder.**

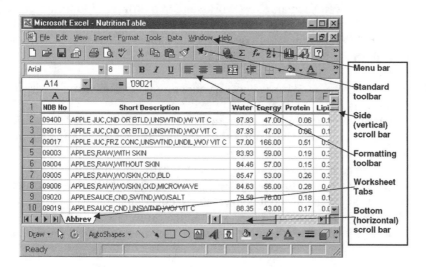

Saving a Worksheet Document

You will need to save the *Excel* worksheet that you loaded from the CD to your computer in order to perform the procedures and exercises in this tutorial.

Macintosh®: Macintosh® may remember the last folder you selected especially with **Open** or **Save As.** You should verify the folder in which you are opening or saving your file each time you perform these operations.

1 To save a copy of the worksheet on your computer, select **File | Save As**. (Similar to *Word*, use **Save** only when you are saving your file to the same location with the same file name.)

Ⅰ The first time you open the **Open** and **Save As** dialog boxes after starting *Excel*, the **My Documents** folder is displayed as the default working or active folder.

2 To change the location, in the **Save As** dialog box select an appropriate folder to store the worksheet file. Be sure a disk is inserted in the floppy or CD drive unless you are saving to the hard drive. Click the down arrow by the **Save in** box, and select the appropriate location. (Remember the location of the workbook file, as you will use it in several of the following lessons.)

Macintosh®: In the Macintosh® **File | Save** dialog box, select an appropriate folder and click the **Save** button. You can also close the document by clicking on the □ in the upper left-hand corner of the document window.

3 In the **File name** box enter an appropriate file name for the worksheet file. Use the file name **Ch5FoodTable.xls,** and click **Save**.

4 When the file is saved, the **Save As** dialog box closes and the program returns to the worksheet window.

Saving a Worksheet for Use in Another Program

You can save a worksheet for use by another program, such as a word processing or database program. By default worksheets are saved in *Excel* format for the version you are using. If you work with other people who use earlier versions of *Excel* or other spreadsheet programs, you can use another format as the default for saving worksheets. If you save an *Excel* worksheet in a different file format, features unique to the version of *Excel* you are using may be lost. Therefore, you should use a file name that is different from your worksheet name when you save the worksheet in an alternate format for use with another program.

1 To save a copy of the worksheet on your computer as text for use with a word processing program, select **File | Save As.**

2 In the **Save As** dialog box enter an appropriate file name for the worksheet file (The file name **Ch5FoodTable.xls** already appears as the file name.) such as **Ch5FoodTableText.xls.**

3 At the **Save as type** box, click the down arrow and drop down a list of file types. Click **Text (Tab delimited)** and then **Save** button. If you receive a message about the file containing features not compatible with the format you chose, click **Yes.** (In the Follow-up Practice Projects at the end of this lesson you will see what this file looks like when you open it in word processing.)

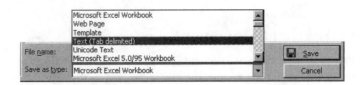

Changing the Default Working Folder for *Excel*

You can specify the default working folder (the folder that *Excel* automatically selects to save files in) for *Excel*. (You can also change the default working folder for all of your *Office* programs and for the **Open Office Document** button and command by renaming the **My Documents** folder or by moving the folder to a new location, or both.)

1 To change the default working folder, select **Tools | Options | General.**

2 In the Default file location: window, type the path for the folder you want to display as the default working folder. For example, you could type **C:\My Worksheets,** and then click **OK.** (Before you change the default working folder, you must first create the folder.) **NOTE:** For purposes of this tutorial, DO NOT change the default file location at this time.

> **Macintosh®:** Macintosh® may remember the last folder you selected, especially with **Open** or **Save as.** You should verify the folder in which you are opening or saving your file each time you perform these operations.

Closing the Worksheet Document

Although the worksheet file has been saved, the worksheet document still resides in computer memory allocated to the *Excel* program.

1 To close the worksheet document (release the computer memory allocated to the worksheet document), select **File | Close.** If you have not already saved your worksheet document in a file or saved your document since you made modifications to it, you will be prompted to save the worksheet in a file before closing it.

2 You may also close the worksheet by clicking the **X** on the upper right-hand corner of the worksheet window (just below the **X** on the top right of the *Excel* program window).

> **Macintosh®:** You can also close the document by clicking on the □ in the upper left-hand corner of the worksheet window.

Exiting *Excel*

Closing a Worksheet does not exit the *Excel* Program. When you close the worksheet document, the *Excel* program remains in computer memory and you may open another worksheet document or quit the program.

1 To exit the *Excel* program, select **File | Exit.** If you have not already closed your document and you made modifications to it, you will be prompted to save the file before exiting the program.

2 You can also exit *Excel* by clicking the **X** on the top right corner of the *Excel* program window (not the **X** at the extreme right of the menu bar).

> **Mactintosh®:** To exit the *Excel* program, select **File | Quit.** If you have not already closed your document and have made modifications to it, you will be prompted to save the document in a file before exiting the program.

FOLLOW-UP PRACTICE PROJECTS

In the following lessons in this chapter and the following chapters of Part 2, you will use several practice files from the **T3 Practice CD.** The following projects allow you to practice the skills you learned in this lesson.

Insert the **T3 Practice CD,** open *Excel*, and complete the projects below.

1 From the **SP folder** of the **T3 Practice CD,** open the document named **Ch5FastFood1.xls.** Save it to the hard drive of your computer or a personal disk then close it. Repeat the entire procedure with **Ch5FastFood2.xls**

2 Expand your skills. Use the Open and Save procedures of *Excel* to save each of the following document files on the hard drive of your computer or a personal disk, or use the Windows® or Macintosh® operating system to copy or drag each of the files to the hard drive of your computer or a personal disk: **Ch5GrdBook.xls, Ch6NutritionSurvey.xls, Ch7CalorieCalc.xls**

❸ Open the **Ch5FoodTableText.txt** file in *Word*. Notice how the spacing of a spreadsheet occurs in word processing. Some data elements in the text file are contained within quotation marks while others are not? Why?

LESSON 5.2: MANAGING AND NAVIGATING WORKBOOKS

Lesson 5.2: Learning Activities

Switching to another sheet in a workbook
Selecting worksheets in a workbook
Inserting a new worksheet in a workbook
Moving or copying worksheets
Renaming a worksheet
Deleting worksheets from a workbook
Moving and scrolling through a worksheet
Viewing two parts of a worksheet at the same time
Keeping row and column labels visible during scrolling

So far in this tutorial we have been using the term "worksheet" to describe the *Excel* work area. *Excel* uses the term "workbook" to describe the file that contains one or more worksheets. A workbook is like a book with multiple pages of worksheets. Each workbook in *Excel* can contain many sheets, and you can organize various kinds of related information in a single file.

The capability of having several worksheets in a workbook allows you to enter and edit data on several worksheets simultaneously and perform calculations based on data from multiple worksheets. When you create a chart, you can place the chart on the worksheet with its related data or in a separate worksheet. The names of the worksheets appear on tabs at the bottom of the workbook window.

Before Shelly can start entering or modifying data in a worksheet, she must know how to navigate in the worksheet window and to manage worksheets in a workbook. For this lesson, follow the steps you learned in the last lesson to start *Excel* and then open the **Ch5FoodTable.xls** workbook you used in the previous lesson.

LESSON 5.2: TUTORIAL

Switching to Another Sheet in a Workbook

You can switch among the worksheets in a workbook by pointing at the sheet tabs and clicking the mouse.

❶ Once you have opened the **Ch5FoodTable.xls** workbook, click the sheet tab for **Sheet2** to access the second worksheet in the workbook.

Selecting Worksheets in a Workbook

You might want to use the contents of a worksheet as a template for a similar worksheet or move a worksheet from one position in a workbook to another position. To manipulate a whole worksheet, you must first select it. You can select adjacent or nonadjacent worksheets.

❶ To select multiple adjacent worksheets in your workbook (sheets 2 and 3), click the **Sheet2** tab and then at the same time press **SHIFT** and click the **Sheet3** tab. Notice that both **Sheet2** and **Sheet3** are selected.

❷ To select multiple nonadjacent worksheets in your workbook (sheets 1 and 3), click the **Sheet1** tab and then at the same time press and hold **CTRL** and click the **Sheet3** tab. Notice that both **Sheet1** and **Sheet 3** are selected.

❸ To select all worksheets in your workbook, right-click on any sheet tab and then click **Select All Sheets.** Notice that all worksheets are selected.

Macintosh®: Click the sheet tabs while pressing **COMMAND (APPLE).**

Macintosh®: Click on any sheet tab while pressing **CONTROL** and from the pop-up menu select **Select all Sheets.**

Inserting a New Worksheet in a Workbook

Sometimes it is necessary to add a new worksheet to a workbook. Worksheets are 65,536 rows by 256 columns. The number of worksheets you can have in a workbook is limited only by the memory that is available for the *Excel* program on your computer. The default number of worksheets in a new workbook is three.

❶ To add a single worksheet to the **Ch5FoodTable.xls** workbook, click the **Sheet1** tab and then select **Insert | Worksheet.** A new worksheet, **Sheet4,** is inserted into the workbook in front of Sheet1.

❷ To add multiple worksheets, press and hold **SHIFT** and click the **Sheet4** and **Sheet1** worksheet tabs, and then select **Insert | Worksheet.** Two new worksheets, **Sheet5** and **Sheet6,** are inserted into the workbook in front of **Sheet4.**

Moving or Copying Worksheets

You can change the order of worksheets in a workbook or duplicate the contents of a worksheet.

❶ To move a worksheet within the current workbook, drag the selected sheet along the row of sheet tabs to another position in the order of worksheets. Select the **Sheet4** tab and drag it to the right until the positioning arrow that appears above the tab is located on the right side of the **Sheet3** tab and release the mouse button. **Sheet4** is now located after **Sheet 3.** Repeat this procedure for **Sheet5** and **Sheet6** to order the sheets from 1 to 6.

❷ To copy a worksheet within the current workbook, press and hold **CTRL** while dragging the selected sheet along the row of sheet tabs. Select the **Sheet4** tab. Next, press and hold **CTRL,** and drag the tab until the positioning arrow that appears above the tab is located on the right side of the **Sheet6** tab, and then release the mouse button and the **CTRL** key. A copy of **Sheet4** named **Sheet4(2)** is now located after **Sheet6.**

Macintosh®: Hold down **OPTION (ALT)** while dragging the selected sheet along the row of sheet tabs.

Renaming a Worksheet

You can name a sheet using any label you want. Do not use spaces or special characters in a sheet name.

❶ Double-click the **Sheet4(2)** tab, type **Sheet7,** and press **ENTER.**

Deleting Worksheets from a Workbook

You can delete a worksheet from a workbook.

❶ To delete Sheet7 from the workbook, select the **Sheet7** tab and then select **Edit | Delete Sheet.** Select **OK** in the warning message box to delete the sheet.

Moving and Scrolling Through a Worksheet

To move between cells on a worksheet, click any cell or use the arrow keys. When you move to a cell, it becomes the active cell. To see different areas of the worksheet, use the scroll bars. Using the vertical scroll bar and the horizontal scroll bar, you can view parts of the worksheet not shown on the screen.

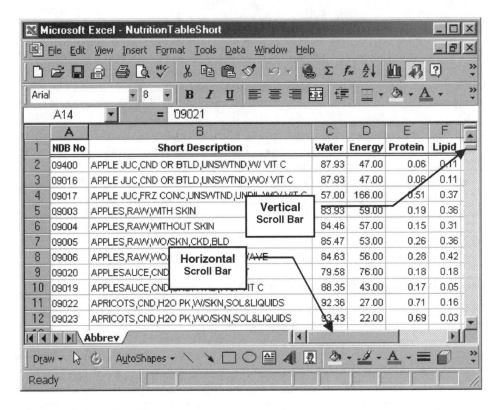

❶ Use the right arrow key (→) to move to the right, the down arrow key (↓) to move down, the left arrow key (←) to move to the left, and the up arrow key (↑) to move up in the worksheet. Practice moving in the worksheet using each arrow.

❷ To scroll towards the right side of the worksheet, drag the scroll box on the horizontal scroll bar to the right or click the right arrow on the horizontal scroll bar. Practice moving to the right using both methods.

❸ To scroll down the worksheet, drag the scroll box on the vertical scroll bar down or click the down arrow on the vertical scroll bar. Practice moving down using both methods.

❹ To scroll one window to the left or right, click to the left or right of the scroll box in the horizontal scroll bar. Practice moving left and right one window with the horizontal scroll bar.

❺ To scroll one window up or down, click above or below the scroll box in the vertical scroll bar. Practice moving up and down one window using the vertical scroll bar.
NOTE: Notice two features of the scroll box: (1) The size of a scroll box indicates the proportional amount of the used area of the sheet that is visible in the window. (2) The position of the scroll box indicates the relative location of the visible area within the worksheet.

Viewing Two Parts of a Worksheet at the Same Time

For large worksheets that extend off the right or bottom of the screen, you may need to be able to align column or row headings with rows or columns that extend off the viewable worksheet area. To view and scroll independently in different parts of a worksheet, you can split a worksheet horizontally and vertically into separate panes. Splitting a worksheet into panes allows you to view different parts of the same worksheet side by side and is useful for viewing, entering, or pasting data between different areas of a large worksheet.

1 At the top of the vertical scroll bar, point to (do not click) the split box.

2 When the pointer changes to a split pointer, drag the split box line down and position between rows 4 and 5.

3 Scroll the worksheet down in each pane. Notice that the text and data in the other pane remain in place while you scroll through the data in the worksheet.

Keeping Row and Column Labels Visible During Scrolling

An extension of the split window feature is to freeze a pane as you scroll the other side. This feature is useful for freezing column or row headings on large worksheets that extend off the bottom or right of the screen.

1 Point at the right end of the horizontal scroll bar. When the pointer changes to a split pointer, drag the split box line to the left and position between Columns B and C.

2 Two horizontal scroll bars now appear on the worksheet window, one for each pane. To freeze the left vertical pane, click in any cell in the first pane and click **Window | Freeze Panes.** The horizontal scroll bar on the left vertical pane disappears. Use the horizontal scroll bar on the right vertical pane to scroll the data. The description stays in place while you scroll through the nutrient data for each food item in the table.

3 To unfreeze the panes and restore the worksheet window to a single pane, select **Window | Unfreeze Panes** and then **Window | Remove Split.**

4 A simple technique to keep labels and data visible in both columns and rows is to freeze both the upper and left panes at the same time. To keep the top heading row and the food description column visible in the nutrition table while you scroll through the nutrient data for each food item, you need to freeze Row **1** and Columns **A** and **B.** Click in Cell **C2** to make **C2** the active cell. Columns **A** and **B** are to the left of **C2** and Row **1** is above **C2.** Select **Window | Freeze Panes.**

The worksheet is divided into four panes. Try scrolling both vertically and horizontally in the worksheet and notice how easy and accurate it would be to enter or modify table data with column headings and food item descriptions visible from any cell.

Remember, you cannot both split a worksheet and freeze parts of a worksheet at the same time.

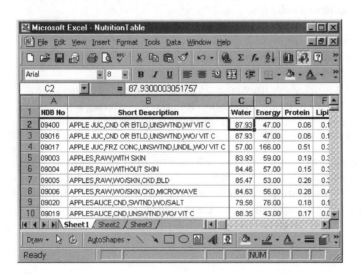

❺ Close the workbook and exit *Excel.* If prompted, do not save any changes you made to the workbook file.

FOLLOW-UP PRACTICE PROJECTS

For more practice on the basic workbook operations and navigation skills you learned in this lesson, perform each of the following projects. Start the *Excel* program and open the workbook **Ch5FoodTable.xls** that you used in this lesson. Perform each of the following practice exercises using this workbook. When you have completed the practice exercises, exit *Excel.*

❶ Move to the right on **Sheet1** until you find the last column with data. What is the alphabetic column label? What does *Excel* do when it has used all the letters of the alphabet for column labels? Scroll to the extreme right of the worksheet. What is the alphabetic column label of the last column of a worksheet? Press **HOME.** What happens to the active cell?

❷ Move down on **Sheet1** until you find the last row with data. What is the numeric row label? Scroll to the extreme bottom of the worksheet. What is the numeric row label of the last row of a worksheet?

❸ Move to the top of the worksheet. Split the screen on the right side of the Short Description column. Move the active cell to the right until the Cholesterol column is lined up beside the Description column. Move down the worksheet and find how many grams of cholesterol are in a hard-boiled egg.

LESSON 5.3: ENTERING AND FORMATTING DATA IN *EXCEL* WORKSHEETS

Lesson 5.3: Learning Activities

Creating a new blank workbook
Entering numbers, text, and dates in a worksheet cell
Undoing data entry mistakes
Editing cell contents
Formatting numbers in cells
Formatting dates in cells
Selecting cells, rows, and columns
Changing the font or font size
Adjusting column width or row height
Applying borders to cells
Inserting columns and rows
Deleting rows or columns
Clearing contents and formats from cells

Each cell of a worksheet may contain either data or formulas that perform operations on data in other cells. This lesson focuses on entering and formatting different types of data in a worksheet. Remember the following guidelines when entering different types of data in an *Excel* worksheet:

- **Characters as numbers.** In *Excel* a number can contain only the following characters: 0 1 2 3 4 5 6 7 8 9 + − ( ) , / $ % . E e. *Excel* ignores leading plus signs (+) and treats a single period as a decimal. All other combinations of numbers and nonnumeric characters are treated as text.
- **Fractions.** To avoid entering a fraction as a date, precede fractions with a "0" (zero); for example, type "0 1/2".

- **Negative numbers.** Precede negative numbers with a minus sign ($-$), or enclose the numbers in parentheses ( ).
- **Fifteen-digit limit.** Regardless of the number of digits displayed, *Excel* stores numbers with up to 15 digits of precision. If a number contains more than 15 significant digits, *Excel* converts the extra digits to zeros (0).
- **Dates and times are actually numbers.** *Excel* treats dates and times as numbers. The way a time or date is displayed on a worksheet depends on the format applied to the cell. When you type a date or time that *Excel* recognizes, the format of the active cell changes to a built-in date or time format. By default, dates and times are right-aligned in a cell. If *Excel* cannot recognize the date or time format, the date or time is entered as text, which is left-aligned in the cell.

Before Shelly can start creating her own instructional activities using *Excel* for the nutrition unit, she needs to know how to properly enter and format data in a worksheet. She is going to use a lesson by Justice (1996), *Teaching Math and Nutrition with Spreadsheets*, to practice entering and formatting spreadsheet data. This activity is designed for students to develop their own daily balanced eating plan with the right number of servings from each food group and the correct calories and fat requirements.

LESSON 5.3: TUTORIAL

Creating a New Blank Workbook

You need to create a blank worksheet for this lesson. *Excel* furnishes you with a number of worksheet templates, which can be used as a basis for creating similar workbooks. For example, *Excel* supplies you with templates for invoices, purchase orders, income statements, balance sheets, vehicle mileage logs, and others.

❶ Open *Excel*. Then open a new workbook by clicking **New** on the Menu Bar.

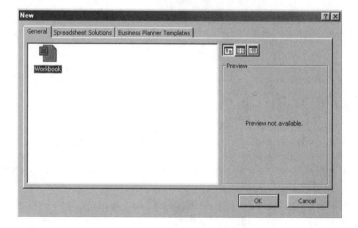

❷ A new blank workbook is created and displayed on the screen with Cell **A1** of **Sheet1** outlined (or highlighted) as the active cell.

Entering Numbers, Text, and Dates in a Worksheet Cell

You can enter several different types of data in a worksheet cell. Generally, worksheet cells contain numbers, but cells can also contain text, dates, times, special characters, and even formulas that perform operations on other cells in the worksheet.

❶ Enter a number in a cell. Click in Cell **B3** to make it the active cell, type **31.02** and then press **ENTER**. Notice when you press **ENTER** that the new active cell becomes the next cell down in the same column, Cell **B4**.

❷ Enter **1.88** in Cell **B4** and press **ENTER**. Enter **2.98** in **B5** and press **ENTER**. Enter **8.80** in **B6** and press **ENTER**.

❸ Enter a date in Cell **A1**. Type the date **4/01/2002** (use slashes or hyphens) and then press **ENTER**. Notice the date value in Cell **B1** is reformatted to a two-digit year date when you press **ENTER**.

❹ Your worksheet should be similar to the following example. Notice that the unformatted cell contents are displayed in the **Formula Bar** while the worksheet cell displays the cell contents using the *Excel* default format based on the data type. In later steps in this lesson you will learn the very important process of formatting your worksheet data.

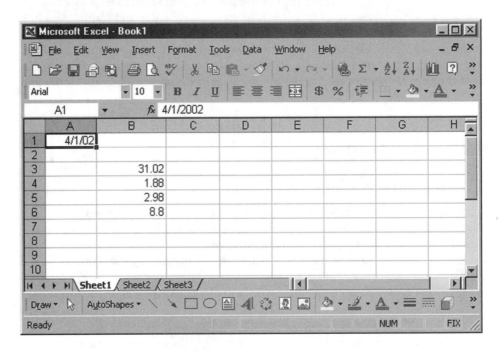

Undoing Data Entry Mistakes

In *Excel* it is quite simple to fix or undo data entry errors. You may cancel and erase an entry in a cell before you press **ENTER** by pressing **ESC**.

❶ In cell **A2** type **999** and press **ENTER**. To undo this entry, select **Edit | Undo** typing **999** in **A2**.

❷ Type **999** in Cell **A2** and press **ENTER** and type **222** in Cell **A3** and press **ENTER**. This time click the **Undo** icon twice and undo these two actions. If at any time you change your mind about an **Undo** action, select **Edit | Redo** or click the **Redo** icon.

Editing Cell Contents

Editing cell contents is different from undoing data entry mistakes. When you edit cell contents, you make modifications to the existing data in the cell. You may edit cell contents either directly in the cell or on the **Formula Bar.**

❶ Enable the option to edit directly in cells. Select **Tools | Options,** click the **Edit** tab, and be certain the **Edit directly in a cell** checkbox is checked. Click on it if it is not checked. Click **OK.**

❷ In Cell **A2** type **Menu** and press **ENTER.**

❸ Change the contents of Cell **A2** to **Healthy Menu.** Double-click on Cell **A2,** move the cursor in front of "Menu" and type, **Healthy,** and press **ENTER.**

❹ Change the contents of Cell **A2** to "Healthy Meal Menu" by clicking the cell, then editing the cell contents in the **Formula Bar,** and then pressing **ENTER.** (If the **Formula Bar** is not displayed, select **View | Formula Bar.**)

Macintosh®: Select **Edit | Preferences** and then click the **Edit** tab. Be certain the **Edit directly in a cell** checkbox is checked (click on it if it is not checked). Click **OK.**

Formatting Numbers in Cells

You can change the appearance of numbers in cells without changing the value of the numbers in the cells.

❶ To display the contents of a cell as currency, set the active cell to **B3,** select **Format | Cells,** and select the **Number** tab. Then select **Currency** in the **Category** list. In the **Decimal places** box choose **2,** set the Symbol to **$,** set the **Negative numbers** box to **−$1234.10,** and click **OK.** The cell now displays as **$31.02.**

❷ To display the contents of a cell as a percentage, set the active cell to **B3,** select **Format | Cells,** and select the **Number** tab. Then select **Percentage** in the **Category** list. In the **Decimal places** box choose **0,** and click **OK.** The cell now displays as **3102%.** When you format cells as a percentage, numbers above 1 are automatically entered as percentages. Numbers below 1 are converted to percentages by multiplying by 100. For example, **.5** displays as **50 %** when the cell format is set to Percentage.

❸ Format Cell **B3** to a plain number with 2 decimal places. Select **Format | Cells,** select the **Number** tab, and select **Number** in the **Category** list. In the **Decimal places** box choose **2,** and click **OK.** The cell now displays as **31.02.** There are many other cell formats you can select for numbers in cells including special formats such as **Social Security Number, Zip Code,** or **Phone Number.**

Formatting Dates in Cells

You can change the appearance of dates and times in cells without changing the value of the dates or times in the cells.

❶ Change the date of Cell **A1.** Select the cell, then select **Format | Cells,** and select the **Number** tab. Select **Date** in the **Category** list. In the **Type** box choose the format **March 14, 2001** and click OK. The cell now displays as "April 01, 2002." By default, as you enter dates in a worksheet, the dates are formatted to display two-digit years. When you change the date format to a different format using this procedure, all previously entered dates in your workbook will change to the new format.

❷ Change the date of Cell **A1** to **14-March.** The cell now displays as "1-Apr."

Selecting Cells, Columns, and Rows

You may want to format several cells, columns, or rows at once. To do so, select a group of cells, a column, or a row in *Excel.*

❶ To select a group of cells, place the mouse pointer in Cell **B3,** hold the mouse button, and drag the mouse pointer down **Column B** to Cell **B6,** and release the mouse button. Cells **B3** to **B6** are highlighted with color and a box with a heavy border. Now formatting can be applied to all of these cells at once.

② To select **Column B,** point at the column heading for the column and click the mouse. **Column B** is highlighted with color and a box with a heavy border noting the selected column. Now formatting can be applied to all cells in the entire column at once.

③ To select **Row 2,** point at the row heading for the row and click the mouse. **Row 2** is highlighted with color and a box with a heavy border as the selected row. Now formatting can be applied to all cells in the entire row at once.

Changing the Font or Font Size

You can set the font and font size for single cells or a group of cells.

① Select cells **B3** to **B6.**

② To change the font size, select the down arrow on the **Font Size** box on the **Formatting Toolbar** and click **16.** (If the **Formatting Toolbar** is not displayed on your screen, select it by clicking **View | Toolbars | Formatting.**)

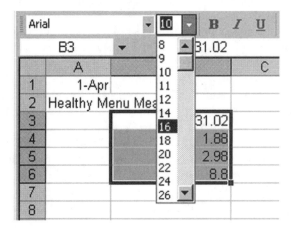

③ Some of the cells may now be displayed with pound signs (#), because the format of the cell contents is too big for the width of the cell. The next step will show you how to alleviate this problem.

Adjusting Column Width or Row Height

You may need to adjust column width or row height to fit the contents of a cell or cells.

① To make the width of Column **A** fit the contents, double-click the vertical boundary on the right side of the column heading when the mouse pointer becomes a thin, black cross with horizontal arrows (**+**). The column expands to display the full contents of the widest cell.

② You can also change the column width by dragging it. Point at the right vertical boundary Column **B.** When the mouse pointer changes, click and drag the boundary until the column width is about **14,** as displayed in the pop-up Screen Tip.

③ You can also manually change a column width using menu commands. Select Column **B** by clicking its column heading. Select **Format | Column | Width.** Type **8** and press **OK.** The column width will be decreased to **8.**

❹ You can reset row heights by clicking and dragging the horizontal bottom border of a row or by selecting **Format | Row | Height** and typing a number in the **Row Height** box. Generally, it is not necessary to change the height since it changes automatically based on the font size.

Applying Borders to Cells

You can insert additional rows or columns between existing rows and columns on a worksheet.

❶ Add a border to Cells **A1** to **A5.** First, select the cells.
❷ Click the click the **Borders** icon on the **Formatting Toolbar,** and click **Outside borders.**

Inserting Columns and Rows

You can insert additional rows or columns between existing rows and columns on a worksheet.

❶ To insert a new column between columns A and B, click on a cell in column **B.** Click **Insert | Columns,** and a new column is inserted to the left of Column B. The new column is the same width as the column to the left of it (in this case, Column A).
❷ To insert a new row between row 1 and 2, click Row **2.** Click **Insert | Rows** and a new row is inserted above Row 2.

Deleting Rows or Columns

You can delete rows or columns in *Excel.* Generally, you should delete rows or columns and not individual or groups of cells. The next exercise describes how to clear the contents of individual or groups of cells.

❶ Select Column B and click **Edit | Delete** to delete the column.
❷ Select Row 2 and click **Edit | Delete** to delete the row.

Clearing Contents and Formats from Cells

You may need to remove the contents or format of a cell or group of cells.

❶ To remove the formats of the cells in Columns A and B, select both columns. Point at the Column **A** heading and drag the mouse pointer to the right to select Column **B** also and release the mouse. Select **Edit | Clear | Formats.**
❷ To remove the contents of the cells in Columns **A** and **B,** select both columns and then click **Edit | Clear | Contents.**
❸ To delete the contents of a single cell, you can click the cell and then press **DELETE** or **BACKSPACE.** *Excel* removes the cell contents but does not remove cell formats or comments. If you clear a cell, *Excel* removes both the contents and formats from the cell. (The value of a cleared cell is 0.)
❹ Click **Undo** twice to recover the cell formats.
❺ Save the workbook as **Ch5HealthyMeal.xls** and exit *Excel.*

FOLLOW-UP PRACTICE PROJECTS

For more practice on the data entry and formatting skills you learned in this lesson, perform each of the following practice exercises. Open *Excel* and open the workbook, **Ch5HealthyMeal.xls,** to complete each of the following practice exercises. When you have completed the practice exercises, save the workbook and exit *Excel.*

Enter and format the following data in the workbook:

Healthy Meal Menu					
NDB No	Short Description	Protein	Fat	Carbohydrate	Calories
05064	CHICKEN BREAST,MEAT ONLY,CKD,RSTD	31.02	3.57	0.00	
11371	POTATOES,MSHD,HOME-PREPARED,WHL MILK& MARGARINE	1.88	4.23	16.71	
11742	BROCCOLI,CKD,BLD,DRND,W/SALT	2.98	0.35	5.06	
18066	BREAD,WHEAT BRAN	8.80	3.40	47.80	
09098	FRUIT COCKTAIL,CND,EX LT SYRUP,SOL&LIQUIDS	0.40	0.07	11.63	
14355	TEA,BREWED,PREP W/TAP H$_2$O	0.00	0.00	0.30	
	TOTAL				

❶ Set the font to **Arial** and the font size to **8** for all data on the worksheet.

❷ Set the column widths appropriate for the content of each column. (If any cell displays its contents # # # # # #, increase the column width.)

❸ Insert a row for the column headings. Bold the column headings and place top and bottom borders on the column heading's row.

❹ Set the font size for the title, "Healthy Menu Meal", to **16.** Bold the title and center it across columns by selecting **Columns A–F** in the title row. Click the **Merge and Center** icon on the **Formatting Toolbar.**

❺ Select all numbers and format with two decimal places.

❻ Bold and align right the TOTAL cell.

❼ Change the date to the current date and format as **3/14/01.**

EXERCISES TO REVIEW AND EXPAND YOUR SKILLS

Set 1: Reviewing Terms and Concepts—For each question below, provide a term on the blank that matches the description.

_____ **1.** A bar at the top of the worksheet window used to enter or edit values or formulas in cells or charts.

_____ **2.** The shaded bars along the right side and bottom of a worksheet used to navigate around the worksheet.

_____ **3.** The selected cell in which data is entered when you begin typing.

_____ **4.** The folder that is automatically selected by *Excel.*

_____ **5.** A workbook you can create and use as a basis for similar workbooks.

Set 2: **Expanding Your Skills**—Expand on the skills you learned in this chapter with this activity. Use **Ch5FoodTable.xls** and save the workbook when you are finished.

    You can use worksheet formatting features to effectively display worksheet data. For example, the data in a column is sometimes narrow while the heading or title for the column is wider. Instead of creating wide columns or abbreviated column headings, you can rotate text and apply borders that are rotated to the same degree as the text.

- Rotate text in a cell. Select the heading Cells **A1** to **AB1.** Click **Format | Cells | Alignment.** In the **Degrees** box, click **60** (or drag the indicator to the 60-degree angle) and click **OK.**
- Apply borders to cells. Select heading Cells **A1** to **AB1.** Click **Format | Cells | Border.** Click **Inside** and then **OK.**
- Change column width. Select Columns **C** to **AB.** Click **Format | Column | Width.** Type **5** and click **OK.** Notice how much more of the worksheet is now displayed in the window.

Set 3: **Use Microsoft® Help**—The Microsoft® *Office* Help Menu can give additional information on any topic and help with troubleshooting procedures when you encounter problems. Look up the following features to get further information and tips, and then try out each of these features with one or more of the workbooks you used in this chapter.

- Look up **Check** spelling to check the spelling of text data in a worksheet.
- Look up **Template** to customize the default settings for a workbook or worksheet.
- Look up **AutoFormat** to format cells and lists quickly.

Set 4: **Create Your Own Lesson**—After reviewing the lessons in this chapter, develop and describe a lesson targeted for the grade level you teach or plan to teach that makes effective use of each of the following *Excel* features. Describe the workbook you or the students would need to create to carry out the lesson. Enter your lesson idea or plan into the **Lesson Plans ePortfolio.**

- Students create a worksheet to collect data for a science experiment and format the data in the worksheet appropriately.
- Students create a worksheet to collect data and then transfer the data to a table in a *Word* file and create a report to explain the data.

EXCEL FORMULAS, FUNCTIONS, AND FORMS

NEW TERMS

absolute reference	formula	reference
autofill	function	reference style
comments	list	relative reference
dependent cell	precedents	sort order
drag and drop	R1C1	syntax
form		

OVERVIEW

The use of spreadsheets for decision making and problem solving is largely based on their capability to perform mathematical and logical calculations with groups or ranges of numbers. Each of the tutorial lessons in this chapter consists of guided practice that demonstrates how to construct worksheets that perform powerful calculations easily and accurately.

The guided practice in each tutorial demonstrates how teachers and students can use Microsoft® *Excel* features in classroom learning activities. Practice files for the tutorials are located in the **SP folder** on the **T3 Practice CD.** The exercises following each lesson include activities from the **Lesson Plans ePortfolio.** Complete these exercises to reinforce the learning activities demonstrated in the tutorials and to build your collection of technology-based lesson plans and ideas.

Lesson 6.1: Using Formulas to Perform Calculations in *Excel*

Lesson 6.2: Using Functions to Perform Calculations in *Excel*

Lesson 6.3: Using Forms to Enter Data in *Excel*

Lesson 6.1: Using Formulas to Perform Calculations in *Excel*

Lesson 6.1: Learning Activities

Referencing ranges of cells
Changing the reference style
Copying or moving whole cells
Entering a formula
Copying or moving a formula
Ordering operations in formulas
Controlling the recalculation of formulas

A formula is an equation that performs operations on worksheet data. Formulas can perform mathematical operations, such as addition and multiplication, or logical operations, such as comparisons, contrasts, and combinations. Formulas can refer to cells on the same worksheet, cells on other sheets in the same workbook, or cells on sheets in other workbooks.

  Shelly wants to begin setting up an *Excel* worksheet to begin her nutrition unit. Shelly wants her students to learn about the nutritional content of various foods by using *Excel* to construct their own personal eating plan. She decides to build student interest in the science of nutrition by creating a worksheet to demonstrate the nutritional value of food items most commonly eaten by her students: fast foods. For this spreadsheet to be effective, it must calculate and summarize the number of calories and fat grams contained in typical fast-food items. Shelly wants her students to use the mathematical power of *Excel* to solve problems and perform repetitive calculations with large amounts of data, so she sets out to learn how to perform calculations using *Excel*.

Lesson 6.1: Tutorial

Referencing Ranges of Cells

A reference identifies a cell or a range of cells on a worksheet and tells *Excel* where to look for the values or data you want to use in a formula. With references, you can use data contained in different parts of a worksheet in one formula or use the value from one cell in several formulas. You can also refer to cells on other sheets in the same workbook, other workbooks, and data in other programs.

  By default, *Excel* uses what is called the A1 reference style. The A1 reference style refers to columns with letters (A through IV for a total of 256 columns) and refers to rows with numbers (1 through 65536). As you learned in Chapter 5, these letters and numbers are called row and column headings.

❶ Open *Excel* and the workbook **Ch6FastFood1.xls** that you loaded previously from the **T3 Practice CD** onto your hard disk or own disk.

❷ Refer to cells first by column letter followed by row number. For example, C2 refers to the cell at the intersection of Column C and Row 2. Notice that the **Name** box just above the column labels on the left side of the worksheet shows the active cell reference. Click in the **Name** box and type **C2** over the highlighted active cell reference. Press **ENTER,** and the cursor moves to the cell you entered.

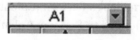

3 To refer to a range of cells, enter the reference for the cell in the upper-left corner of the range, a colon (:), and then the reference to the cell in the lower-right corner of the range. For example, A1:E6 refers to the range of cells beginning at (and including) Cell A1 and ending at (and including) Cell E6. Enter **A1:E6** in the **Name** box, and press **ENTER.** Notice that the cell range is highlighted on the worksheet.

4 To refer to a range of cells that includes all cells in a column or row, enter the reference to the beginning column or row, a colon (:), and the reference to the ending column or row. For example, A:A refers to all cells in Column A, and 5:5 refers to all cells in Row 5.

Enter **A:A** in the **Name** box and press **ENTER** to refer to Column A. Enter **5:5** in the **Name** box and press **ENTER** to refer to Row 5. Enter **A:C** in the **Name** box and press **ENTER** to refer to Columns A, B, and C. Enter **2:8** in the **Name** box and press **ENTER** to refer to Rows 2 through 8. Notice that the cells in the columns or rows you indicated become highlighted on the worksheet.

5 A more common way to reference a range of cells is to click the first cell of the range and then drag to the last cell. To reference the range of cells from **A2** to **E6**, click Cell **A2.** While holding down the mouse button, drag to Cell **E6** and release the mouse button. The area from **A2** to **E6** should be highlighted. Click the mouse button again to deselect the cell range.

6 Close the workbook without saving it.

Changing the Reference Style

You can also use a reference style in which both the rows and the columns on the worksheet are numbered, called the R1C1 reference style. In the R1C1 style, *Excel* indicates the location of a cell with an "R" followed by a row number and a "C" followed by a column number.

1 To change the reference style, select **Tools | Options | General.** Click in the **R1C1 reference style** check box, then click **OK.** Now deselect the **R1C1 Reference style** to return to the standard reference style.

Macintosh®: To change the default working folder, select **Tools | Preference** and then click the **General** tab. Click in the **R1C1 Reference style** check box then click **OK.** Now deselect the **R1C1 Reference style** to return to the standard reference style.

Copying or Moving Whole Cells

When you copy a cell by dragging or by using Cut or Copy and Paste, *Excel* copies the entire cell contents, including formulas and their resulting values and cell formats, to its new location.

1 Open the *Excel* workbook **Ch6FastFood2.xls.** In Cell **B7** type **TOTAL** in bold and right-aligned. Click Cell **B7** then click **Copy** or select **Edit | Copy.** Click Cell **B13** then click **Paste** or **Edit | Paste.**

2 You can copy the contents of a cell using drag and drop. Click Cell **B13,** point the mouse pointer at the cell (so it remains a pointer, not a four-sided arrow), press and hold **CTRL,** and click and drag the box to Cell **B19,** and release the mouse button and **CTRL.** The contents of Cell **B13** are copied to Cell **B19. NOTE:** If you do not press **CTRL** as you drag the mouse, the contents of the cell will be moved instead of copied.

3 Save the worksheet as **Ch6FastFood2Upd.xls.** The worksheet should look similar to the following example:

NDB No.	Description	Calories	Fat	Cholesterol
	BREAKFAST			
21007	FAST FOODS,BISCUIT,W/EGG,CHS,&BACON	331.00	21.80	181.00
14209	COFFEE,BREWED,PREP W/TAP H2O	2.00	0.00	0.00
09209	ORANGE JUC,CHILLED,INCL FROM CONC	44.00	0.27	0.00
21026	FAST FOODS,POTATOES,HASHED BROWN	210.00	12.80	13.00
	TOTAL			
	LUNCH			
21100	FAST FOODS,CHEESEBURGER,LRG,DOUBLE PATTY, W/CONDMNT&VEG	273.00	16.92	55.00
21138	FAST FOODS,POTATO,FRENCH FR IN VEG OIL	342.00	18.43	0.00
14346	SHAKE,FAST FOOD,CHOCOLATE	127.00	3.70	13.00
	TOTAL			
	DINNER			
22902	SAUSAGE&PEPPERONI PIZZA,FRZ	264.00	13.49	21.00
14400	CARBONATED BEV,COLA,CONTAINS CAFFEINE	41.00	0.00	0.00
19271	FROZEN DSSRT,ICE CRM,STRAWBERRY	192.00	8.40	29.00
	TOTAL			

Entering a Formula

A formula in *Excel* always begins with an equal sign (=). The equal sign tells *Excel* that the subsequent characters constitute a formula. The equal sign is followed by the elements to be calculated or operands, which are separated by calculation operators.

Formulas calculate values in a specific order. *Excel* calculates the formula from left to right, according to a specific order for each operator in the formula. You can change the order of operations by using parentheses.

A formula can refer to both constant values and to other cells. The cell that contains the formula is known as a dependent cell when its value depends on the values in other cells. The cells that provide data to a specific cell to the dependent cell are called precedents.

The following procedure sums the Calories, Fat, and Cholesterol columns for each of the fast-food meals.

❶ To sum the Calories for a fast-food breakfast meal, click Cell **C7**, type = (an equal sign), type **C3+C4+C5+C6,** and press **ENTER.** The formula calculates the total Calories for a breakfast meal.

❷ Whenever a precedent cell changes, the dependent cell also changes. For example, change the value in Cell **C3** from **331** to **300,** and the result of the formula in Cell **C7** changes accordingly. Now change Cell C3 back to **331.**

Copying or Moving a Formula

When you create a formula, references to cells or ranges are based on their position relative to the cell that contains the formula. For example, the formula =C3+C4+C5+C6 in Cell C7 sums the values for Cell C3, which is four cells above Cell C7; plus Cell C4, which is three cells above Cell C7; plus Cell C5, which is two cells above Cell C7; plus Cell C6, which is one cell above Cell C7. This is known as a relative reference.

When you copy a formula that uses relative references, *Excel* automatically adjusts the references in the pasted formula to refer to different cells relative to the position of the formula. When you move a formula, the cell references within the formula do not change.

Absolute references refer to cells in a specific location. In a formula the absolute reference is the exact address of a cell, regardless of the position of the cell that contains the formula. An absolute cell reference takes the form $A$1. If you used this absolute cell reference in a formula, the dollar sign in front of A would mean you do not want the column reference to change and the dollar sign in front of 1 would mean you do not want the row reference to change. Relative references automatically adjust relative to the row and column when a formula is copied from one cell to another. Absolute references do not adjust.

Depending on the task you want to perform in *Excel*, you can use either relative cell references or absolute references. You will usually use relative cell references when copying formulas in a worksheet.

Although absolute cell references is a concept that seems complex, in application it is quite simple to use and a powerful feature of a spreadsheet program. If you entered a formula into a cell to sum or total numbers in Column C and you had an equal number of items to total in Columns D and E, you would not have to enter the formula three times. The formula entered in Column C could be copied to Columns D and E, and those formulas would automatically be adjusted to sum the numbers in those columns.

❶ Copy the formula from Cell **C7** to Cells **D7** and **E7,** since it uses relative references. First, Click Cell **C7** and format it in bold. Then, click **Copy,** click Cell **D7,** and click **Paste.** The formula is copied and calculated relative to the values under the Fat column for a Breakfast meal.

❷ To copy the formula from Cell **C7** using point and drag, click Cell **C7,** point at the cell (so the pointer remains a pointer), press and hold **CTRL,** click and drag the box to Cell **E7,** and release the mouse button and **CTRL.** The contents of Cell **C7** are copied to Cell **E7.** The formula is copied and calculated relative to the values under the Cholesterol column for a Breakfast meal.

❸ You can also copy formulas into adjacent cells with **AutoFill.** Select Cell **C13,** point at the **Fill Handle** (solid black square) in the lower right corner of the cell, click and drag the **Fill Handle** over Cells **D13** and **E13,** and release the mouse button. The value in Cell **C13** is copied to Cells **D13** and **E13.**

❹ Copy the formula in Cell **C19** to Cells **D19** and **E19.**

❺ Save the file with the new updates and close it. Your solution should look similar to the following example.

NDB No.	Description	Calories	Fat	Cholesterol
	BREAKFAST			
21007	FAST FOODS,BISCUIT,W/EGG,CHS,&BACON	331.00	21.80	181.00
14209	COFFEE,BREWED,PREP W/TAP H2O	2.00	0.00	0.00
09209	ORANGE JUC,CHILLED,INCL FROM CONC	44.00	0.27	0.00
21026	FAST FOODS,POTATOES,HASHED BROWN	210.00	12.80	13.00
	TOTAL	587.00	34.87	194.00
	LUNCH			
21100	FAST FOODS,CHEESEBURGER,LRG, DOUBLE PATTY, W/CONDMNT&VEG	273.00	16.92	55.00
21138	FAST FOODS,POTATO,FRENCH FR IN VEG OIL	342.00	18.43	0.00
14346	SHAKE,FAST FOOD,CHOCOLATE	127.00	3.70	13.00
	TOTAL	742.00	39.05	68.00
	DINNER			
22902	SAUSAGE&PEPPERONI PIZZA,FRZ	264.00	13.49	21.00
14400	CARBONATED BEV,COLA,CONTAINS CAFFEINE	41.00	0.00	0.00
19271	FROZEN DSSRT,ICE CRM,STRAWBERRY	192.00	8.40	29.00
	TOTAL	497.00	21.89	50.00

Ordering of Operations in Formulas

The order in which formula elements are calculated determines the final result of the calculation. Starting with the equal sign (=), *Excel* performs formula operations from left to right according to the order of operator precedence based on the algebraic hierarchy. You can control the order of calculation by using parentheses to group operations that should be performed first. For example, the formula =3+2*4 produces 11 because *Excel* first multiplies 2 by 4 and then adds 3 to the result. If you use parentheses to change the order of operations, the formula =(3+2)*4 adds 3 and 2 together and then multiplies the result by 4 to produce 20.

For Shelly's students to learn to calculate their own healthy menu, they need to understand some math related to the calculation of calories in food items. The main sources of calories in food are protein, carbohydrates, and fat. In food, 1 gram of protein equals 4 calories, 1 gram of carbohydrates equals 4 calories, and 1 gram of fat equals 9 calories. You can construct a formula to calculate the number of calories in food items if you know the number of grams of protein, carbohydrates, and fat.

❶ Open *Excel* and the workbook **Ch5HealthyMeal.xls** that you created in the previous chapter. The workbook contains a menu for a healthy meal and provides the number of grams of protein, carbohydrates, and fat for each food item in the menu, but you need to calculate the calories for each food item; sum the total grams of protein, carbohydrates, fat, and calories; and determine what percent of calories are based on fat.

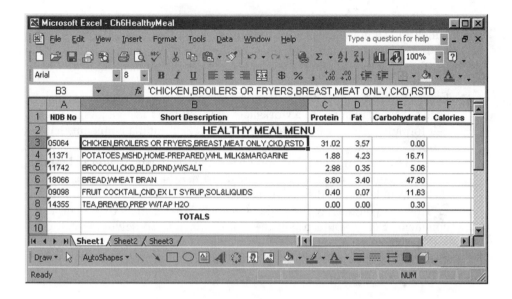

❷ Construct a formula that calculates the number of Calories. The formula would use an algorithm like this: *Protein times 4 plus Carbohydrates times 4 plus Fat times 9.* Using cell references, this algorithm expressed as an *Excel* formula would be **=C3*4+D3*4+E3*9** (* represents ×). Would parentheses be necessary to ensure the proper order of operations?

❸ Once you have the formula constructed, type it into Cell **F3** and then copy it down the column to calculate the approximate number of calories for each of the food items on the worksheet.

Controlling the Recalculation of Formulas

Excel automatically recalculates dependent cells when the values in the precedent cells have changed. This type of calculation helps to avoid unnecessary calculations. *Excel* also calculates workbooks each time they are opened or saved.

❶ The default value on calculation/recalculation is automatic. In a large spreadsheet with many formulas, you might want to manually control when the worksheet recalculates, because it will slow down considerably if it recalculates each time a precedent or dependent cell is changed. Select **Tools | Options | Calculation,** then click **Manual** and **OK.** To recalculate the worksheet, press **F9.**

❷ Set **Calculation** back to **Automatic.**

❸ Save the worksheet with the new updates and close it. Exit *Excel.*

FOLLOW-UP PRACTICE PROJECTS

For more practice on skills using and copying formulas, perform each of the following practice exercises. Open *Excel* and the workbook **Ch6FastFood2.xls.** Perform each of the following practice exercises using this workbook. When you have completed the practice exercises, save and close the workbook and exit *Excel.*

❶ You can enter the same formula into a range of cells by selecting the range first, typing the formula, and then pressing **CTRL+ENTER.** Enter and copy formulas to calculate the totals for Calories, Fat, and Cholesterol for the Lunch and Dinner Meals and save your work. Can you use the same formula for Lunch that calculates the totals for Breakfast? Why or why not? Can you use the same formula for Dinner that calculates the totals for Lunch? Why or why not?

2 In *Excel* you can add a note to a cell by using comments. Comments may be used to record changes to a worksheet or to explain the contents of a cell, a cell formula, or other information about a cell. To add a comment that describes the purpose of this worksheet, click in Cell A1, select **Insert | Comment,** and in the pop-up box type **This worksheet calculates the nutritional value of three fast-food meals.** When you finish typing the text, click outside the comment box.

How do you display the cell comments? What signals that a cell has a comment? See if you can edit the cell comments. To delete the cell comments, select Cell **A1,** and click **Edit | Clear | Comments.** Remember, if you clear the contents of a cell, *Excel* removes the cell contents but does not remove any comments or cell formats.

Lesson 6.2: Using Functions to Perform Calculations in *Excel*

Lesson 6.2: Learning Activities

Using math functions
Using date and time functions
Using statistical functions
Using logical functions
Using reference and lookup functions

Functions are predefined formulas that perform calculations by using specific values, called arguments, in a particular order, or structure. With functions you can have students easily perform complex calculations with large amounts of data. For example, the SUM function adds values or ranges of cells, and the PMT function calculates the loan payments based on an interest rate, the length of the loan, and the principal amount of the loan. Functions perform a series of calculations with one command.

- **Arguments.** Arguments for functions can be numbers, text, logical values such as TRUE or FALSE, arrays, error values such as #, N/A, or cell references. The argument you designate must produce a valid value for that argument. Arguments can also be constants, formulas, or other functions.
- **Structure.** The structure of a function begins with the function name, followed by an opening parenthesis, the arguments for the function separated by commas, and a closing parenthesis. If the function starts a formula, include an equal sign before the function name. As you create a formula that contains a function, the **Formula Palette** will assist you.

Lesson 6.2: Tutorial

Using Math Functions

With math functions, you can perform simple calculations, such as rounding a number, calculating the total value for a range of cells, or complex calculus calculations. The most frequently used math function is the SUM function, which is used to add the numbers in a range of cells. The syntax for the sum function is: =SUM(number1,number2,. . .) where number1, number2, . . . are 1 to 30 arguments for which you want the total value or sum. A common example for the SUM function would be to sum a range of numbers: =SUM (C5:C9), which would equal 150 if Cells C5:C9 contain 10, 20, 30, 40, and 50.

❶ Open *Excel* and the workbook **Ch6FastFood2.xls.** In Lesson 2 you used formulas to calculate totals for Calories, Fat, and Cholesterol. This lesson will show you a simpler way to perform this calculation using *Excel* functions.

❷ Use the SUM function in a formula to sum the Calories for a fast-food breakfast meal. Click in Cell **C7,** (the formula from the previous lesson will be deleted when you start typing), enter the formula **=SUM(C3:C6),** and press **ENTER.** The formula calculates the total Calories for a breakfast meal.

❸ You can also use point and click to enter the range for a SUM function. Click in Cell **D7** and type the beginning of the formula and the left side of the parentheses: **=SUM(.** Then, with the mouse pointer select the range **D3:D6** and press **ENTER.**

❹ You can also use **Paste Function** (**Insert Function** in *Office® XP*) to enter and edit formulas. Click Cell **E7** and click **Paste Function.** When the **Paste Function** dialog box is displayed, select **Math Trig** in the **Function category** box and then **SUM** in the **Function Name** box and click **OK.** When the **SUM** dialog box is displayed, type **E3:E6.** Or, when the **SUM** dialog box (**Function Arguments** dialog box in Office XP) appears, click the **Collapse Dialog** icon to the right of the **Number 1** box (the dialog box is collapsed), select the range of cells to sum, click the **Expand Dialog** icon to the right of the data entry box on the "collapsed" dialog box, and then click **OK.** You can also use the mouse pointer to select the range **E3:E6** and click **OK.**

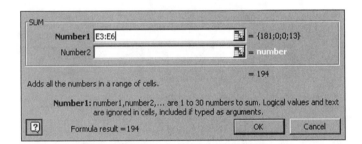

❺ *Excel* has a useful feature called AutoSum that automatically tries to distinguish a column or row range you want to SUM and then selects it for you. If it is not the range you want, you can adjust it. Click Cell **C13** and click **AutoSum.** If the range **C10:C12** is selected, press **ENTER.** (If it is not, enter the correct range in the highlighted part of the cell, then press **ENTER.**)

❻ Copy the formula to the Fat and Cholesterol columns for Lunch and then for Dinner. Save the worksheet.

Using Date and Time Functions

With date and time functions, you can analyze and work with date and time values in formulas. For example, if you need to use the current date in a formula, use the TODAY function, which returns the current date based on your computer's system clock.

❶ To include the current date on your worksheet, click Cell **A22.** Click **Paste Function,** select the **Date & Time** category, select the **TODAY** function name, and click **OK.** When the **TODAY** dialog box is displayed, click **OK** again and the current date in mM/dD/YY format is displayed.

❷ Save but do not close the worksheet.

Using Statistical Functions

Statistical worksheet functions perform statistical analysis on ranges of data. Statistical functions can perform sophisticated data analyses such as standard deviations, correlations, and confidence.

A frequently used statistical function is finding the mean or average of a range of numbers. The syntax for the AVERAGE function is: =AVERAGE(number1, number2,. . .) where number1, number2, . . . are 1 to 30 arguments for which you want the mean or average. A common example for the AVERAGE function would be to find the average of a range of cells: =AVERAGE (C5:C9), which would equal 30 if Cells C5:C9 contain 10, 20, 30, 40, 50.

❶ With the **Ch6FastFood2.xls** workbook still open, open the workbook **Ch6FastFood1.xls.** (You can switch between the workbook windows by pressing **ALT+TAB** or **CMD+TAB** on Macintosh®). You can use statistical functions to analyze the fast-food nutrition data in this workbook. In the following steps you will use the statistical functions AVERAGE, MIN, and MAX to display the average smallest and largest nutritional values for the fast-food items in the table. Additionally, you will use COUNT and COUNTIF to display the number of fast food items in the table as well as the number of food items that meet certain conditions.

❷ In Cell **B122** of **Ch6FastFood1.xls** type **Average=,** then bold and right-align it. In Cell B123 type **Lowest=,** then bold and right-align it. In Cell B124 type **Highest=,** then bold and right-align it. In Cell **B125** type **No. of Fast-Food Items=,** then bold and right-align it. In Cell **B126** type **No. of Fast-Food Items > 250 Calories=,** then bold and right-align it. These cells should look similar to the following example:

Average=
Lowest=
Highest=
No. of Fast-Food Items=
No. of Fast-Food Items > 250 Calories=

❸ Find the Calorie average by entering the formula **=AVERAGE(C2:C121)** in Cell **C122.** Use one of the three methods you learned with the SUM function to enter the formula: 1) type the complete formula; 2) type the function name and use point and click to enter the range; or 3) use **Paste Function** (select **Statistical** for **Function category** and **AVERAGE** for **Function name**).

❹ Find the lowest Calorie value in the list by entering the formula **=MIN(C2:C121)** in Cell **C123** using one of the three methods listed in step 3.

❺ Find the highest Calorie value in the list by entering the formula **=MAX(C2:C121)** in Cell **C124** using one of the three methods listed in step 3.

❻ Copy the formulas in Cells **C122:C124** and paste them in Cells **D122:E124.**

❼ Find the number of fast-food items on the list by entering the following formula **=COUNT(C2:C121)** in Cell **C125.** Format the cell to **Number** with **0** decimal places. (There is no need to copy the formula as it will return the same result in each column.)

❽ Find the number of fast-food items on the list with more than 300 Calories by entering the following formula **=COUNTIF(C2:C121,">250")** in Cell **C126.** Format the cell to **Number** with **0** decimal places. (There is no need to copy the formula as it relates only to Calories.)

Your solution should look similar to the following example:

Average=	241.07	12.43	51.25
Lowest=	16.00	0.07	0.00
Highest=	543.00	33.01	426.00
No. of Fast-Food Items=	120		
No. of Fast-Food Items > 250 Calories=	27		

9 Save the workbook but do not close it.

10 Switch the *Excel* window to the **Ch6FastFood2.xls** workbook. Select all the active cells in the worksheet (**A1:E22**), and select **Edit | Copy** or click **Copy.** Switch back to the **Ch6FastFood1.xls** workbook, and click on the **Sheet2** tab. Click in Cell **A1,** and select **Edit | Paste** or click **Paste** to place a copy of the worksheet in **Sheet2** of the **Ch6FastFood1.xls** workbook.

11 Switch to **Ch6FastFood2.xls** and close the document.

Using Logical Functions

You can use logical functions either to test whether a condition is true or false or to test for multiple conditions. For example, you can use the IF function to determine whether a condition is true or false. One value is returned if the condition is true, and a different value is returned if the condition is false.

Shelly discovered in her preparation for the nutrition unit that the USDA recommends that people should consume about 2,500 calories per day, of which only 30 percent of the calories should be from fat. Additionally, she found that health experts recommend a diet that consists of less than 300 milligrams of cholesterol a day. Now Shelly wants to create a formula in the worksheet that tests the total calories and total cholesterol and displays a warning if either exceeds the recommended maximum allowance.

1 In order to construct these logical formulas, it is necessary to total the Calories, Fat, and Cholesterol for all meals. The SUM function will not work for this formula because the total is not a contiguous set of numbers. In Cell **B21** of **Sheet2** of **Ch6FastFood1.xls,** enter the heading **TOTAL FOR ALL MEALS.** Bold and right-justify the cell contents.

2 In Cell **C21** enter the formula **=C7+C13+C19** to total the Calories for all meals. Copy this formula to the Fat and Cholesterol columns.

3 In Cell **B22** enter the heading **TOTAL DAILY ALLOWANCE IS.** Bold and right-justify the cell contents.

4 Construct a formula that determines if the number of Calories exceeds 2,500. The formula would use an algorithm such as: IF Total Calories is greater than 2,500, then display the word HIGH; otherwise, display the word OK.

Using the logical function IF, this algorithm expressed as an *Excel* formula would be **=IF(C21>2500,"HIGH","OK").** Enter this formula in Cell **C22.** The syntax for the IF function is to state a logical condition and then evaluate the condition to determine if the condition stated in the logical function is true or false based on the values in the precedent cells. If the condition is true, the formula fills the cell with the information provided after the first comma. If the condition is false, the formula fills the cell with the information provided after the second comma.

5 Repeat this logical formula in Cell **E22** for Total Cholesterol > 300. Your solution should be similar to the following example:

TOTAL FOR ALL MEALS	1826.00	95.81	312.00
TOTAL DAILY ALLOWANCE	OK		HIGH

6 Save the workbook as Ch6FastFood3. Close it and exit *Excel.* An example of the completed workbook may be found in a workbook file named **Ch6FastFood3.xls** in the **SP folder** on the **T3 Practice CD.** Use it to compare with your solution.

Using Reference and Lookup Functions

So far Shelly has been creating learning activities to use *Excel* as an instructional tool for teaching a science unit on nutrition. She determines that *Excel* will also be a great way to maintain her grade records and decides to construct an electronic gradebook using it.

One of the most time-consuming grading tasks for Shelly is to convert a numerical grade to a letter grade for the student report cards. *Excel* can automatically find cells in a table based on a specified value. You will create a grading scale table to look up a letter grade that corresponds with the numerical grade average.

1 Open *Excel* and the workbook **Ch6GrdBook.xls** that you loaded from the **T3 Practice CD** onto your own disk or hard disk.

2 In Cell **L4** enter the formula **=AVERAGE(B4:K4)** for averaging the grades for the first student on the list.

3 The result of the calculation is a number with decimal places. Select **Format I Cells I Number,** and set the decimal places to **0.** Notice that formatting the cells properly rounds the grade average.

4 Copy the formula down the column for all students in the gradebook and save the worksheet. Notice that the AVERAGE function calculates only for nonempty cells, and a numerical grade of 0 should be entered as 0, not left blank. Your worksheet should look similar to the following example:

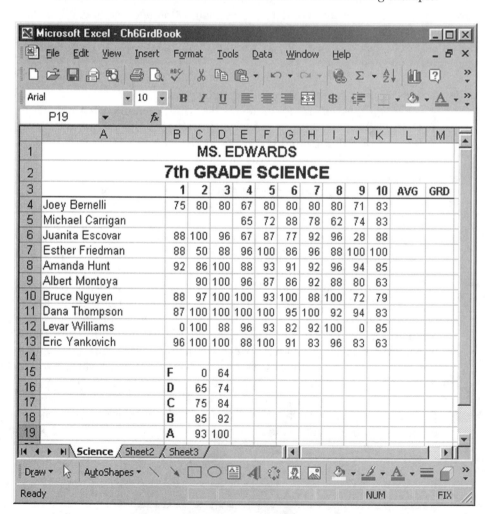

5 *Excel* will automatically find cells in a table based on a specified value. To create a grading scale table to look up a letter grade that corresponds with the numerical grade average, use LOOKUP to find values in a single column table, VLOOKUP (vertical lookup) to find values in tables arranged in multiple columns, and HLOOKUP (horizontal lookup) to find values in tables arranged in multiple rows.

To use a lookup function, you must have a table with appropriate values arranged in the proper order. Construct a grade table in the **Ch6GrdBook.xls** worksheet as shown above (starting with **F** in Cell **B15**).

Although the grading scale table you have created actually has multiple columns to show the beginning and ending range of values for each letter grade, you will only need the value in the middle column to perform the lookup. The rightmost column is only for your benefit to show the end of each range of values for the corresponding letter grade.

6 After you have entered the grading scale table, click in Cell **M4** to enter the lookup formula. Since a table lookup is a complex function, it is best to use **Paste Function** to enter the formula. Select **Paste Function,** then select **Lookup & Reference** for the function category and **LOOKUP** as the function name and click **OK.**

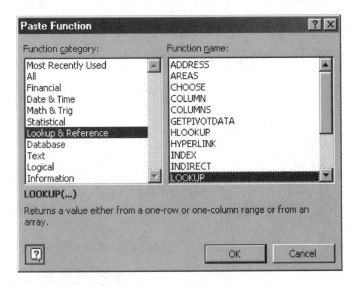

7 The syntax is: =LOOKUP(lookup_value,lookup_vector,result_vector). Lookup_value is the grade average cell. Lookup_vector (vector is one column of a table) is the one column of values designed to correspond with or be referenced by the lookup_value (must be in ascending order). Result_vector is the column with the corresponding letter grade to be returned from the LOOKUP. Select the appropriate argument in the **Select Arguments** dialog box as shown below and click **OK.**

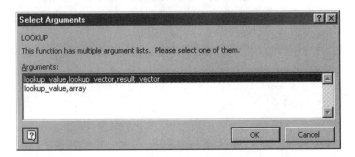

8 In the **LOOKUP** dialog box, click the icon on the right side of the **Lookup_value** data entry box to select a value to look up in the grading scale table. When the full worksheet displays on the screen, click Cell **L4** and then press **ENTER.**

⑨ When the **LOOKUP** dialog box reappears, click the icon on the right side of the **Lookup_vector** box and select Cells **C15:C19** to select a vector (single table column) for looking up the Lookup_value. Press **F4** to make the cell range absolute and press **ENTER**. When you copy the formula to other cells, you do not want the position of the grading scale table to adjust relative to the cell being copied.

Notice that the lookup_vector is arranged in ascending order. *Excel* will search the lookup_vector for the lookup_value. If an exact match is not found, the LOOKUP function will return the value that matches the largest value in lookup_vector that is less than or equal to lookup_value.

⑩ When the LOOKUP dialog box reappears, click the icon on the right side of the **Result_vector** box, then select Cells **B15:B19**. Press **F4** to make the cell range absolute then press **ENTER**. When you copy the formula to other cells, you do not want the position of the grading scale table to change relative to the cells being copied.

⑪ Click **OK** in the **LOOKUP** dialog box to complete data entry of the formula. The letter grade "C" is displayed in Cell **M4**.

⑫ The formula in cell M4 should read: **=LOOKUP(L4,$C$15:$C$19, $B$15:$B$19)**. Now copy this formula in cell down Column **M** for every student in the gradebook.

Your gradebook worksheet solution should look similar to the following example.

Ms. Edwards 7th GRADE SCIENCE												
	1	**2**	**3**	**4**	**5**	**6**	**7**	**8**	**9**	**10**	**AVG**	**GRD**
Joey Bernelli	75	80	80	67	80	80	80	80	71	83	**78**	C
Michael Carrigan				65	72	88	78	62	74	83	**75**	D
Juanita Escovar	88	100	96	67	87	77	92	96	28	88	**82**	C
Esther Friedman	88	50	88	96	100	86	96	88	100	100	**89**	B
Amanda Hunt	92	86	100	88	93	91	92	96	94	85	**92**	B
Albert Montoya		90	100	96	87	86	92	88	80	63	**87**	B
Bruce Nguyen	88	97	100	100	93	100	88	100	72	79	**92**	B
Dana Thompson	87	100	100	100	100	95	100	92	94	83	**95**	A
Levar Williams	0	100	88	96	93	82	92	100	0	85	**74**	D
Eric Yankovich	96	100	100	88	100	91	83	96	83	63	**90**	B
	F	0	64									
	D	65	74									
	C	75	84									
	B	85	92									
	A	93	100									

⑬ Save and close the workbook. Exit *Excel*.

FOLLOW-UP PRACTICE PROJECTS

To expand your skills and allow you more practice on skills using logical functions, open *Excel* and the workbook **Ch6FastFood3.xls** used in this lesson. When you have completed the practice exercise, save and close the workbook and exit *Excel*.

1 After reviewing maximum recommended daily levels for Calories, Fat, and Cholesterol, you want students to use *Excel* to analyze the fast foods on the list and determine which ones are acceptable. You have calculated that no more than one-third of the recommended daily levels of Calories (300), Fat (20 g), and Cholesterol (100 mg) should be in any food item.

   a. Place a new column on the right side of the worksheet that contains the results of the analysis. You could label the column "**GOOD/BAD**," or some label of your choosing.

   b. The formula would use an algorithm like this: *IF Calories is less than or equal to 300 AND Fat is less than or equal to 20 AND Cholesterol is less than or equal to 100, THEN display the word GOOD; otherwise display the word BAD.* Using the logical functions IF and AND, this algorithm expressed as an *Excel* formula is:

   ```
   =IF(AND(C2<=300,D2<=20,E2<=100),"GOOD","BAD")
   ```

   The AND function is embedded in the IF function using parentheses. The AND function allows you to provide a list of conditions such as C2<=300, D2<=20, E2<=100.

   c. Copy the formula down the column. Add a comment on either the column heading or the first occurrence of the formula with the algorithm that explains how the formula works.

   d. Publish a list of GOOD fast food items. Copy and paste the GOOD items into a *Word* document, and write a short report explaining how the list was derived.

   e. Develop a lesson idea or plan related to the activity you just completed. It should describe using a science or math theme (or subject or theme of your own choosing) for organizing and analyzing data and target the grade level you teach or plan to teach. Add it to the **Lesson Plans ePortfolio.**

2 To expand your skills and allow you more practice on skills using statistical and math functions, open *Excel* and the workbook **Ch6GrdBook.xls** used in this lesson. When you have completed the practice exercise, close and save the workbook and exit *Excel*.

   a. You can name a range of cells and then use that range name in a formula. Select Cells **C15:C19** in the grade scale table. Click **Insert | Name | Define.** In the **Define Name** dialog box enter **GradeScale** and click **OK.** Repeat the process for Cells **B15:B19,** naming the range of cells **LetterGrade.**

   Click Cell **M4** and select **Paste Function** to enter the lookup formula. In the **Lookup_vector** box enter **GradeScale** and in the **Result_vector** box enter **LetterGrade** and click **OK.** Copy the cell formula down the column. Notice it is not necessary to specify absolute values in the formula for a named range since the absolute value is built into the range name.

   b. Insert four new rows between the last student name on the list and the grading scale table. Use the AVERAGE function to find the average grade for each of the ten grades recorded in the grade book. Use Column A to label the row. Use the statistical functions MIN, MAX, and MEDIAN to display the smallest, largest, and middle grade for each of the ten grades recorded in the grade book. Use Column A to label the calculation for each row. Your solution might look like the following example:

Ms. Edwards 7th GRADE SCIENCE												
	1	2	3	4	5	6	7	8	9	10	AVG	GRD
Joey Bernelli	75	80	80	67	80	80	80	80	71	83	**78**	C
Michael Carrigan				65	72	88	78	62	74	83	**75**	D
Juanita Escovar	88	100	96	67	87	77	92	96	28	88	**82**	C
Esther Friedman	88	50	88	96	100	86	96	88	100	100	**89**	B
Amanda Hunt	92	86	100	88	93	91	92	96	94	85	**92**	B
Albert Montoya		90	100	96	87	86	92	88	80	63	**87**	B
Bruce Nguyen	88	97	100	100	93	100	88	100	72	79	**92**	B
Dana Thompson	87	100	100	100	100	95	100	92	94	83	**95**	A
Levar Williams	0	100	88	96	93	82	92	100	0	85	**74**	D
Eric Yankovich	96	100	100	88	100	91	83	96	83	63	**90**	B
Average	77	89	95	86	91	88	89	90	70	81	**85**	
High	96	100	100	100	100	100	100	100	100	100	**95**	
Low	0	50	80	65	72	77	78	62	0	63	**74**	
Median	88	97	100	92	93	87	92	94	77	83	**88**	
	F	0	64									
	D	65	74									
	C	75	84									
	B	85	92									
	A	93	100									

c. An example of the completed workbook may be found in a workbook file named **Ch6GrdBookFinal.xls** in the **SP folder** on the **T3 Practice CD.** You can use it to compare with your solution.

d. Although the electronic grade book was intended as a classroom management tool for teachers, allowing students to develop a grade book (and providing them with fictitious grade data) or having them create a grade book of all their own subject grades is an excellent exercise for demonstrating basic statistical operations and the analysis of data. Develop a lesson idea or plan for the electronic grade book activity you just completed that is targeted for the grade level you teach or plan to teach. Add it to the **Lesson Plans ePortfolio.**

LESSON 6.3: USING FORMS TO ENTER DATA IN *EXCEL*

Lesson 6.3: Learning Activities

Using data forms to input data
Adding a record to a list by using a data form
Scrolling through records in a list
Finding records in a list
Editing a record in a list by using a data form
Deleting a record in a list by using a data form
Sorting a list

A data form is a dialog box that gives you a convenient way to enter or display information one record or one complete row at a time. Data forms are especially useful in worksheets with numerous rows and columns that extend off the screen. You can also use data forms to locate and delete records. To use data forms to add records to a worksheet, the worksheet must have labels at the top of each column in the worksheet. *Excel* uses these labels to create field names on the form. Data forms can display a maximum of 32 fields at one time.

In designing her instructional activities for the nutrition unit, Shelly wants her students to conduct research and use *Excel* worksheets to analyze and interpret the results. Through discussions with her students about the unit on nutrition, Shelly realized that many students did not have healthy eating habits. Shelly decided to conduct a nutrition survey among the students at her school and enter the responses to the nutrition survey into a workbook for analysis. The survey gave a list of food types and asked students to check off any foods they had eaten on the previous day. Shelly created a workbook with the survey responses that grouped the student responses by the Food Pyramid with an additional category for Fast Foods.

LESSON 6.3: TUTORIAL

Using Data Forms to Input Data

Excel will automatically create a data entry form for you to use to enter and update your worksheet data. In a form each column of the worksheet is a field and each row of the worksheet is a record. All the data in a worksheet is called a list or database. Forms manipulate data for a complete record.

1 Open *Excel* and the workbook **Ch6NutritionSurvey.xls** that you loaded previously from the **T3 Practice CD** onto your hard drive or own disk.

2 To create a worksheet to use for data analysis, Shelly grouped the responses by food category. For each survey she entered a 1 under the food categories corresponding to each food type marked on the student survey. Using a 1 to indicate a survey response instead of an X or * or + makes it easier to analyze the data, because you can perform mathematical operations such as SUM.

3 To create a data form automatically, click on any data cell within the worksheet and select **Data | Form.** You should have a data entry form that looks like the following:

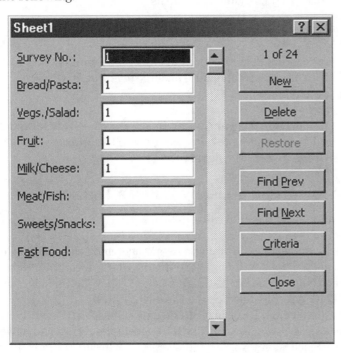

❹ Notice that the form displays the label over the column as the field name and shows all the columns in the row. You can add (New), edit, or delete rows (or records) using the form.

Adding a Record to a List by Using a Data Form

You can easily add records (or rows) of data to a list (or worksheet) using the data form automatically generated by *Excel*. A list is an *Excel* worksheet that contains rows with related data. A list has the characteristics of a database in which rows are records and columns are fields.

❶ To enter the following data into the form, click **New.** To move to the next field in a form, press **TAB.** To move to the previous field in a form, press **SHIFT+TAB.** Survey No.: **25** Bread/Pasta: **1** Milk/Cheese: **1** Sweets/Snacks: **1** Fast Food: **1** When you finish, press **ENTER** to add the record. *Excel* adds the record when you move to another record or close the data form.

❷ When you finish adding the data, click **Close** to add the new record and close the data form.

❸ When using forms, fields that contain formulas also display the results of the formula. You cannot enter data into a formula field, but the formula is copied into the new record relative to the fields in the new record. The formula is not calculated until you press **ENTER** or click **Close** to add the record.

❹ While you are adding a record, you can undo changes by clicking **Restore** before pressing **ENTER** or clicking **Close.**

Scrolling Through Records in a List

On a form you can scroll through all the records in a list using the scroll bar arrows in the dialog box.

❶ To create a data form automatically, click on any data cell within the worksheet and click **Data | Form.**

❷ To scroll through the list one record at a time, click the down arrow on the scroll bar in the middle of the form. To scroll ten records at a time, click the scroll bar anywhere beneath the scroll box.

❸ Scroll back to the beginning of the list.

Finding Records in a List

On a form you can set search conditions or comparison criteria to find specific records of data. This is a useful feature on large lists where all the records (or rows) are not displayed on the screen.

❶ Click **Criteria.** In the **Survey No.** field, type **25** and click **Find Next.** Clicking **Find Prev** finds a previous record with the criteria you specified.

❷ Click **Close** to close the data form.

Editing a Record in a List by Using a Data Form

Forms also allow you to edit existing data in a list.

❶ Click on any data cell within the worksheet and select **Data | Form.**

❷ You can use the scroll bar in the middle of the form to find the record you want to edit, or you can use a Find action. Click **Criteria** and in the **Survey No.** field, type **25** and click the **Find Next** button.

❸ When Survey No. 25 is displayed, enter a **1** in the **Meat/Fish** field. When you finish editing the data, press **ENTER** to update the record and move to the next record. Since Survey No. 25 is the last record in the list, the form displays no data.

④ When you finish editing the records, click **Close** to update the displayed record and close the data form.

Deleting a Record in a List by Using a Data Form

Forms allow you to delete rows of data from a list. When you delete a record by using a data form, you cannot undo the deletion and all the data in the row is permanently deleted.

① Click any data cell within the worksheet and select **Data | Form.**
② You can use the scroll bar in the middle of the form to find the record you want to change or you can use a Find action. Click **Criteria** and in the **Survey No.** field, type **25** and click **Find Next.**
③ When Survey No. 25 is displayed, click **Delete.** When the confirmation box appears on the screen, click **OK.**
④ When you finish deleting records, click **Close** to update the displayed record and close the data form.
⑤ Close the workbook without saving it.

Sorting a List

Excel uses specific sort orders to arrange data according to the value of specified cells (or fields). In ascending (small to large) sort order, *Excel* sorts numbers from the smallest negative number to the largest positive number. *Excel* sorts text left to right, character by character. The sort order for text and text that includes numbers is numbers, then special characters, then alphabetic characters. For example, 1A would be sorted in front of A1. Blanks are always last in the sorting order. Descending sort order would be the reverse of ascending for both numeric and text data.

① Open *Excel* and the workbook **Ch5FoodTable.xls.**
② To sort the worksheet in descending order by calories (food items with the most calories down to food items with the least calories), click a cell in the Calories column and select **Data | Sort.** A **Sort** dialog box that looks like the following is displayed:

③ Notice that the Sort command automatically chooses the Calories column to perform the sort. Click on the **Descending** radio button for the **Sort by** box.

④ The radio button for **Header row** should be selected because there is a heading row at the beginning of the list and you want it to remain in place and not sort with the data in the list.

⑤ Click **OK** and the list is sorted with the food items with the most calories at the top of the list (see the following example).

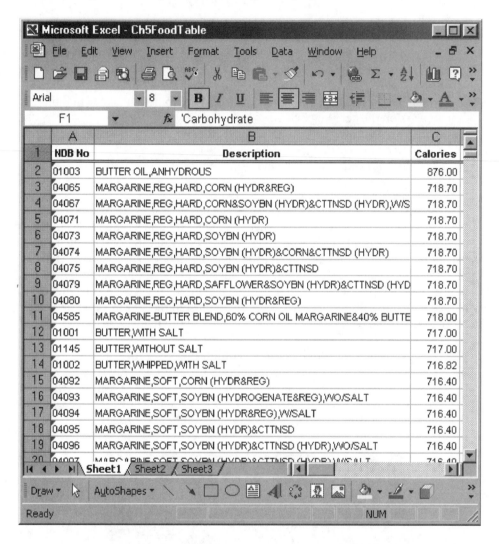

⑥ Close the workbook and exit *Excel.* If prompted, do not save any changes you made to the workbook file.

FOLLOW-UP PRACTICE PROJECTS

For more practice on sorting and filtering data in *Excel* worksheets, perform each of the following practice exercises. Open *Excel* and the workbook **Ch5FoodTable.xls.** Perform each of the following practice exercises using this workbook. When you have completed the practice exercises, close and save the workbook and exit *Excel.*

❶ The Sort command will allow you to arrange data according to multiple criteria. What food items have the least amount of calories and protein? When you select the Sort command, the last sort criteria used is the default sort criteria and is displayed in the **Sort** dialog box. Sort the food table by **Calories** and **Protein,** both in descending order.

② The Data command has a filter operation that makes it easy to filter out worksheet data and display items according to certain selection criteria. To filter out the fast-food items in the food table, select **Data | Filter | AutoFilter.** Any field (column) or combination of fields may be used to filter worksheet data. Click the down arrow on the Description Column and Select Custom. Change the dialog box to **contains** and enter **fast foods.**

③ A macro is a stored series of commands and functions that can be run whenever you need to perform the task. Macros are especially useful to automate tasks that are run repeatedly. When you record a macro, *Excel* stores information about each step you take as you perform a series of commands. You then run the macro to repeat, or play back, the commands.

    a. Before you record a macro, plan the steps and commands you want the macro to perform. If you make a mistake when you record the macro, corrections you make are also recorded. When you record macros, *Visual Basic* stores each macro in a new module attached to a workbook.

    b. As an example, if you often sort and re-sort your worksheet, you can record a macro to perform a specific sort. The steps for this macro would be as follows:

MACRO STEP	*EXCEL* COMMANDS
1. Name the macro	**Tools	Macro, Record New Macro,** *SortbyDescriptionAscending*, **CTRL+D**
2. Start the sort	**Data	Sort**
3. Select the sort criteria	**Description, Ascending**
4. Save the macro	**Tools	Macro, Stop Recording**
5. Test the macro	**CTRL+D**

    c. Create a macro named **CaloriesDescending** with a Shortcut key of **CTRL+C** that sorts the worksheet by Calories in Descending order and then test the macro.

    d. Save the worksheet so that the macros are saved with the workbook.

④ Develop a lesson idea or plan or add to one you developed previously) related to the activity you just completed. It should describe using a science or math theme (or subject or theme of your own choosing) for organizing and analyzing data and target the grade level you teach or plan to teach. Add it to the **Lesson Plans ePortfolio.**

EXERCISES TO REVIEW AND EXPAND YOUR SKILLS

Set 1: Reviewing Terms and Concepts—For each question below, provide a term on the blank that matches the description.

    _____ **1.** A cell that contains a formula, and its value is based on the values in other cells.

    _____ **2.** Cell references that always refer to cells in a specific location—denoted by a $.

_____   **3.** A cell or a range of cells on a worksheet.

_____   **4.** Predefined formulas that perform calculations by using specific values.

_____   **5.** Criteria for arranging data according to the value of a specified cell.

Set 2:   Expanding Your Skills—Expand on the skills you learned in this chapter with these activities. Use **Ch6FastFoods2.xls** to perform the following activities.

1. *Excel* provides tools to find problems on your worksheets. For example, the value you see in a cell may be the result of a formula, or it may be used by a formula that produces an incorrect result. The auditing commands graphically display, or trace, the relationships between cells and formulas with tracer arrows. When you audit a worksheet, you can trace the precedents (the cells that provide data to a specific cell) or you can trace the dependents (the cells that depend on the value in a specific cell). Select **Tools | Auditing** and select **Show Auditing Toolbar.**

   a. Click in Cell **C22** and then select **Trace Precedents** from the toolbar (the leftmost icon). Blue tracer arrows show cells on the active worksheet that provide data to the formula. Click **Trace Precedents** again and *Excel* goes one level deeper and traces any cells on the active worksheet referenced by the precedent cells. If the selected cell contains a reference to another worksheet or workbook, a black tracer arrow points from the worksheet icon

   b. Click Cell **D21** and then select **Trace Dependents** from the **Auditing Toolbar** (the third icon from the left). Notice that no tracer arrows are displayed because the formula in that cell has no dependents. Now click in Cell **D7** and click **Trace Dependents.** Blue tracer arrows show which formulas on the active worksheet depend on that cell. If a cell on another worksheet refers to the selected cell, a black tracer arrow points to a worksheet icon.

   c. Click on each cell in the worksheet with a formula and trace precedents and dependents. When you have viewed all the relationships among the formulas, click **Remove All Arrows** to clear all tracer arrows from the worksheet.

Set 3:   Use Microsoft® Help—Look up the following features to get further information and tips and then practice each of these features with one or more of the workbooks you used in this lesson.

- Look up **Formula** to find information about correcting formulas and the Formula Auditing toolbar for tracing the relationship between formulas and cells.
- Look up **Troubleshoot Formula** to find information to describe error values in a cell when an improper formula is used.
- Look up **CHOOSE, COUNTA,** and **COUNTBLANK** functions.
- Look up **Form** for additional practice in creating a customized on-screen or printed form.
- Look up **Macro** for additional practice in automating tasks in a workbook.

Set 4: **Create Your Own Lesson**—After reviewing the lessons in this chapter, develop and describe a lesson targeted for the grade level you teach or plan to teach that makes effective use of each of the following *Excel* features. Describe the workbook you or the students would need to create to carry out the lesson. Enter your lesson idea or plan into the **Lesson Plans ePortfolio.**

- Students create a worksheet and forms to collect and input data for a science experiment and use formulas and functions to perform statistical calculations with the data.
- Students conduct a survey of the eating habits of other students to determine the nutritional value of what they eat. Create a worksheet and use forms to input the survey data. Use formulas and functions to analyze the calories, fat, carbohydrates, protein, vitamins, minerals, and cholesterol content of the students' responses.
- Students create a worksheet of each food item they consume and how many calories and grams of fat each contains. They use these data to design their own daily balanced eating plan: the right number of servings from each food group in the Food Pyramid, the correct calories and fat requirements for their age, and correct calories and fat requirements for their activity levels.

PRINTING AND PUBLISHING *EXCEL* DATA

NEW TERMS

chart sheet	interactive data	Web browser
Chart Wizard	landscape	X axis
embedded chart	noninteractive data	Y axis
hyperlink	portrait	

OVERVIEW

Microsoft® *Excel* provides a variety of ways to display or print and then publish the results of a data analysis. Each of the tutorial lessons in this chapter demonstrates the various features of *Excel* that provide ways to report and communicate the results of data analyses and calculations performed with *Excel* worksheets, using printed reports, graphs, and the World Wide Web.

Each tutorial consists of guided practice that demonstrates how teachers and students can use Microsoft® *Excel* features in classroom learning activities. Practice files for the tutorials are located in the **SP folder** on the **T3 Practice CD.** Following each lesson are several exercises. Some exercises include activities from the **Lesson Plans ePortfolio.** Complete these exercises to reinforce the learning activities demonstrated in the tutorials and to build your collection of technology-based lesson plans and ideas.

Lesson 7.1: Creating Reports Using *Excel*
Lesson 7.2: Creating Charts Using *Excel*
Lesson 7.3: Publishing a Worksheet on the Web Using *Excel*

LESSON 7.1: CREATING REPORTS USING *EXCEL*

Lesson 7.1: Learning Activities

Previewing how your worksheet will print
Printing the active sheets, a selected range, or an entire workbook
Printing a worksheet with row numbers and column letters
Printing a worksheet with cell gridlines
Setting page, header, and footer margins
Inserting a page break
Making a printed worksheet fit the paper width

Microsoft® *Excel* provides a number of optional settings that let you adjust the final appearance of your printed worksheets. *Excel* can produce professional looking reports in which teachers and students can take pride. The tutorial in this lesson will demonstrate how to make sure you have checked everything likely to affect your printout. For this lesson be certain that your computer is connected to a printer. (Check with your instructor before performing any print operations.)

LESSON 7.1: TUTORIAL

Previewing How Your Worksheet Will Print

Microsoft® *Excel* provides three ways to preview the appearance of a worksheet. Open *Excel* and the workbook **Ch6FastFoods2.xls** that you used in the previous chapter.

❶ **Normal View:** This view is the default and probably the way you are currently viewing your worksheet. It is best for on-screen viewing and working. Select **View | Normal.**

❷ **Print Preview:** This view shows you the printed page and lets you easily adjust columns and margins. Click **Print Preview.** Click **Close** to close Print Preview mode and return to Normal view mode.

❸ **Page Break Preview:** This view shows the layout of each page and lets you quickly adjust the print area and page breaks. Select **View | Page Break Preview** (read then close the message box by clicking **OK**). Select **View | Normal** to return to **Normal** view mode.

   As you make settings that affect how your worksheet will print, you can switch between the different views to see the effects before you send the data to the printer.

❹ Close the worksheet without saving it.

Printing the Active Sheets, a Selected Range, or an Entire Workbook

When you print a worksheet, Microsoft® *Excel* prints all of the active worksheet. You can define and print only a certain area. If you select a range of cells to print and then issue the command to print the selection, *Excel* prints the selection and ignores any print area you previously defined for the worksheet. Open the *Excel* workbook **Ch6GrdBook.xls** that you used in the previous chapter.

❶ To print all the active sheet, select **File | Print** and click **OK.** The worksheet is printed on the printer.

❷ Select the cell range **B15:D19** containing the grading table. To print only the selected range of cells, select **File | Print.** In the **Print** dialog box under

Print what click **Selection** then **OK.** The grading scale table is printed on the printer.

❸ To print all the worksheets in your workbook, select **Entire workbook** under **Print what.** To print multiple sheets, select the worksheets to print, then click **Selection** and **OK.**

Printing a Worksheet with Row Numbers and Column Letters

You can print a worksheet with row and column headings to make it easier to identify the contents of cells.

❶ To set a worksheet to print row and column headings on the active sheet, select **File | Page Setup | Sheet.** Then select the **Row and column headings** and **OK.**

❷ Select **File | Page Setup | Sheet.** Clear the **Row and column headings** check box and click **OK.**

Printing a Worksheet with Cell Gridlines

You can print a worksheet with cell gridlines to make it easier to read across columns and down rows. Large worksheets print faster if you do not select the gridlines option.

❶ To set a worksheet to print cell gridlines on the active sheet, select **File | Page Setup | Sheet.** Then select **Gridlines.**

❷ To print the sheet, from the **Page Setup** dialog box click **Print** and click **OK.** The worksheet is printed on the printer.

❸ Select **File | Page Setup | Sheet,** clear the **Gridlines** check box, and click **OK.**

Setting Page, Header, and Footer Margins

You can adjust various margins in a worksheet.

❶ To print the worksheet in the middle of the page starting from the top, you should center the worksheet on the page vertically. Select **File | Page Setup | Margins.** In the **Center on** box click **Vertically.**

❷ You can also reset the margins by entering the margin size you want in the **Top, Bottom, Left,** and **Right** boxes or the header and footer margins in the **Header** and **Footer** boxes.

❸ To add a header, select the **Header/Footer** tab and then click **Custom Header.** In the **Header** dialog box in the **Center section** box, enter **Calorie and Fat Counter for a Day of Fast Foods,** and click **OK.**

❹ To see how the header will appear on the printed document, click **Print Preview** from the **Page Setup** dialog box before clicking **OK** to print.

     If necessary, change the height of the header margin in print preview by first clicking **Margins** and then dragging one of the handles above or below the header to decrease or increase the height of the header area.

     Place a header or footer on each page. You can add page headers or footers to the report in the **Page Setup** dialog box.

❶ Click on the **Header/Footer** tab.

❷ Click the down arrow on the **Footer** box and select a built-in footer from the list for the report and click **OK.**

Inserting a Page Break

Regular page breaks are based on the paper size, margin settings, and scaling options you set. You can change which rows print on a page by inserting horizontal page breaks, or you can change which columns print on a page by inserting vertical page breaks.

❶ To insert horizontal page breaks so that the menu for each meal is printed on a different page, click in the row below the row where you want to insert the page break. To insert a page break above the Lunch row, click in Row **9** and then select **Insert | Page Break.** Repeat this step to insert a page break above the Dinner menu.

❷ Use **Print Preview** to see how the pages break and the header is printed on each page. Close **Print Preview** without printing the document.

❸ Click in Row **9** and select **Insert | Remove Page Break** to remove the page break above the Lunch menu. Remove the page break above the Dinner menu also.

❹ Close the worksheet without saving it.

Making a Printed Worksheet Fit the Paper Width

You can set a worksheet to automatically shrink or expand to make the worksheet fit the paper width. Open the *Excel* workbook **Ch5FoodTable.xls.**

❶ Select **File | Page Setup** and then click **Page.** Since the worksheet is extremely wide, it would fit best in a landscape orientation (sideways) rather than portrait orientation. Click **Landscape.**

❷ In the **Page Setup** dialog box click **Fit to** and in the first box beside **Fit to** enter **1** (for 1 page wide).

❸ In the second box beside **Fit to** delete the value so that the number of pages tall is unspecified.

❹ *Excel* ignores manual page breaks when you use the **Fit to** option. When you change the values for **Fit to**, *Excel* shrinks the printed image or expands it up to 100 percent, as necessary.

❺ Click **Print Preview** to view the worksheet without printing it. Click **Zoom** to enlarge the display of the report, then click **Close** to exit **Print Preview** mode.

❻ Close the workbook and exit *Excel.* If prompted, do not save any changes you made to the workbook file.

FOLLOW-UP PRACTICE PROJECTS

To expand your skills and allow you more practice on printing *Excel* worksheets, perform each of the following practice exercises. Start *Excel* and open the workbook **Ch5FoodTable.xls.** Use this workbook for each of the following practice exercises. When you have completed the practice exercises, close and save the workbook and exit *Excel.*

❶ In addition to setting headers and footers in a worksheet, you can print the column heading rows of your worksheet at the top of each page for worksheet reports with multiple pages.

    a. Fit the worksheet to paper width. Then, preview the report and scroll through the report, noticing the top of each page. It is hard to understand the content of each column because the column heading is printed on the first page only.

b. To repeat the column heading row at the top of each printed page, close **Print Preview** mode and select **File | Page Setup | Sheet.** In the **Rows to repeat at top** box, click the worksheet icon on the right side; the dialog box "hides." In the worksheet select Row 1 and then click the worksheet icon in the "hidden" dialog box. Click **Print Preview** and notice that the column headings are now printed at the top of each page.

② Print filtered data from a worksheet.

a. Select all of the fast-food items in the worksheet by using **Data | Filter** and selecting **AutoFilter.** Click the down arrow on the Description column and select Custom and click **OK.** Change the dialog box to **contains** and enter **fast foods.**

b. Once all fast-food items are displayed, select Columns **A–F** of the table for printing.

c. Click **File | Page Setup | Page** and click **Landscape.** On the Header/Footer tab select **Custom Header,** and enter **Fast-Foods Nutrition Table** into the **Center** section box and click **OK.** Click the down arrow in the **Footer** box, and select one of the choices from the drop-down menu. On the **Sheet** tab select Row 1 to repeat at the top of the page.

d. Once you have made your Page Setup selections, click **OK.** Select **File | Print | Selection.** You may preview the page first by clicking **Preview.** If the report appears to be correct, click **Print** to print the worksheet to the printer. It should print about four pages.

③ Macros are useful for automating print tasks. Create a macro that automates the AutoFilter and print task in the preceding activity. The steps for this macro would be as follows:

MACRO STEP	*EXCEL* COMMANDS
1. Name the macro	**Tools	Macro, Record New Macro, AutoFilterFastFoodsPrint, Ctrl+f**
2. Filter the worksheet data	**Data	Filter, AutoFilter, Description, Custom, contains, fast foods**
3. Page setup and printing the worksheet	**File	Page Setup, Page, Landscape, Header/Footer, Custom Header, Center Section, Fast Foods Nutrition Table, OK, Footer (down arrow), select footer, Sheet, Row 1**
4. Print the worksheet	**File	Print, Selection, OK**
5. Save the macro	**Tools	Macro, Stop Recording**
6. Test the macro	**CTRL+f**
Save the workbook with the new macro.	

LESSON 7.2: CREATING CHARTS USING *EXCEL*

Lesson 7.2: Learning Activities

Creating a chart in one step
Creating a chart using the Chart Wizard
Selecting chart components using point and click

Editing chart or axis titles
Linking a chart title or text box to a worksheet cell
Editing category axis labels
Sizing and setting up a chart for printing
Selecting the chart type

Charts provide a visually appealing way to portray worksheet data that is summarized in printed reports. With charts it is easy for students to see comparisons, patterns, and trends in data. In *Excel* you can create a chart on its own sheet or as an embedded object in a worksheet. *Excel* also allows you to publish a chart on a Web page.

To create a chart, you must first enter the data for the chart on the worksheet. You can also create a chart in one step by using the Chart Wizard. Since charts are linked to data in a worksheet, they are updated automatically when you change the worksheet data.

An embedded chart is considered a graphic object and is saved as part of the worksheet on which it is created. Use embedded charts to display or print one or more charts with your worksheet data. A chart sheet is a separate sheet within your workbook that has its own sheet name. Use a chart sheet to view or edit large or complex charts separately from the worksheet data or to preserve screen space as you work on the worksheet.

In Chapter 6 Shelly created a learning activity in which students conducted research using surveys and used an *Excel* worksheet to organize, analyze, and display survey results. Shelly wants to expand the lesson to use *Excel* charts to analyze data and interpret the worksheet survey data. The survey workbook grouped student responses by the Food Pyramid with an additional category for Fast Foods.

LESSON 7.2: TUTORIAL

Creating a Chart in One Step

When you create a chart using this quick procedure, the default chart type for *Excel* is used. The default chart type is a column chart.

❶ Open *Excel* and **Ch6NutritionSurvey.xls.** In the chart, Shelly grouped the responses by food category. For each survey she entered a number one (1) under the food categories corresponding to each food type marked on the student survey. To create a chart, you must total each food category column. Use the SUM function to total each food category column, then save the workbook as **Ch7NutritionSurveyGr.xls.**

❷ To create a chart sheet that uses the default chart type, select the cells that contain the totals for each food category type (**B27:H27**) and then press **F11.** A chart sheet named **Chart1** is created with only minimal formatting. Examine the chart sheet.

❸ When you create a chart in *Excel*, you can determine which part of your data you want to emphasize. Unless you specify differently, *Excel* plots whatever you have fewer of: rows or columns. In this example, the Chart Wizard plotted columns for Food Categories rather than Surveys because there were fewer Food Category columns than Survey rows.

Creating a Chart Using the Chart Wizard

The Chart Wizard simplifies the procedure for creating a chart by prompting you to enter the proper information to construct a chart.

1 In **Sheet1** select Cells **B27:H27.** Click **Insert | Chart.**

2 Select **Clustered Column** in the **Chart sub-type** box, then click **Next >.**

3 In the **Chart Wizard - Step 2 of 4 - Chart Source Data** dialog box, click the **Series** tab. In the **Name** box type **Food Category.** Click the icon of the **Category (X) axis labels** box, select Cells **B2:H2,** and press **ENTER.** Click **Next >.**

4 In the **Chart Wizard - Step 3 of 4 - Chart Options** dialog box, type **Number of Students** in the **Value (Y) axis** box. Click **Next >.**

5 In the **Chart Wizard - Step 4 of 4 - Chart Location** dialog box, click the radio button **As new sheet** and type **Chart2** in the window if it does not appear. Click **Finish** and examine the chart sheet that was created by the Chart Wizard.

6 Save the worksheet again.

Selecting Chart Components Using Point and Click

You can select and edit various components of a chart. Data series, data labels, and the legend have individual elements that can be selected after you select the group.

1 Select **Chart2.** Point at the gray background with the mouse, and *Excel* displays the name of the chart component (Plot Area). When the name is displayed, double-click the component. In the **Format Plot Area** dialog box, click the **None** radio button under **Area** and click **OK.**

2 Point at one of the columns in the data series with the mouse. When the name of the series is displayed, double-click the component. In the **Format Data Series** dialog box, select **Options,** click the **Vary colors by point** check box, and click **OK.** Notice that the Legend changes to accommodate the different colors in the data series.

Editing Chart or Axis Titles

If chart or axis titles are not linked to worksheet data, you can edit them by selecting the title box and reentering the title.

1 Click the chart title. When a box surrounds the title, type the new title **Daily Consumption by Food Category** (appears in Formula Box) and press **ENTER.** Then Click outside of the title area.

2 Point at the **Value axis title (Y axis).** Follow the procedure in step 1 to replace the title with **Number of Student Responses.** Click outside of this title area.

Linking a Chart Title or Text Box to a Worksheet Cell

You can link an existing chart title to a worksheet cell or create a new text box that is linked to a worksheet cell.

1 To link the Chart Title to a cell on the worksheet, click the chart title and in the formula bar type **=.** Select **Sheet1,** click Cell **A1,** and press **ENTER.** The text in Cell A1 becomes the chart title.

2 Point at the chart title to select it and set the font size to **14** and the text to **Bold.** Click outside of the title area.

Editing Category Axis Labels

Excel uses column or row headings in the worksheet data for category axis names. You can change category axis labels by changing the data in the linked cell in the worksheet.

❶   To change category axis labels, on **Sheet1** click Cell **G2,** enter **Junk Food,** and press **ENTER.** On the chart notice that the category axis label and the legend are changed from Snacks/Sweets to Junk Food. Your completed chart should look similar to the following example:

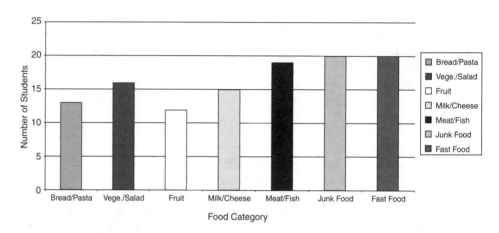

MS. EDWARDS NUTRITION SURVEY

❷   Save the worksheet again.

Sizing and Setting Up a Chart for Printing

If the chart is embedded in a worksheet, you can adjust it where it will print on the page by sizing and moving the chart with the mouse in **Page Break Preview.** If you are working with a chart sheet, you can use **Page Setup** to size and scale the chart area, specify how it should be placed on the printed page, and then view it in the preview window.

❶   Click **Chart2.** To set printing options for the chart sheet, click **File | Page Setup | Chart.**

❷   To move and size the chart area of a chart sheet by using the mouse, click **Custom** and then click **OK** to return to the chart sheet. Try re-sizing the chart by clicking and dragging the handles, and then click **File | Page Setup | Chart,** and select the **Scale to fit page** radio button. Preview the chart and then print to the printer.

❸   You can print an embedded chart without its associated worksheet data. First, click the embedded chart to select it, and then click **File | Print | Selected Chart.** You can move and size the chart area of an embedded chart without using the Custom option on the Chart tab.

Selecting the Chart Type

For most 2-D charts, you can change the chart type of either a data series or the entire chart. For bubble charts, you can change only the type of the entire chart. For most 3-D charts, changing the chart type affects the entire chart. For 3-D bar and column charts, you can change a data series to the cone, cylinder, or pyramid chart type.

❶ Select the **Chart2** sheet and click on any plot in the data series. Right-Click the mouse (without moving the pointer) and select **Chart Type.** In the **Chart Type** dialog box on the **Standard Types** tab select **Pie** and click **OK.**

❷ Repeat step 2 selecting **Cylinder, Cone,** and **Pyramid** chart types.

❸ Close the workbook and exit *Excel.* If prompted, do not save any changes you made to the workbook file.

FOLLOW-UP PRACTICE PROJECTS

To expand your skills and allow you more practice on charts, perform each of the following practice exercises. Open *Excel* and the workbook **Ch6GrdBook.xls.** Perform each of the following practice exercises using this workbook. When you have completed the practice exercises, close and save the workbook and exit *Excel.*

❶ Create a chart showing the count of students in a class who received an A, B, C, D, or F. To create the chart, you must first create data indicating the number of each kind of grade.

   a. In the last column of the grading table at the bottom of the worksheet, create a formula that counts the quantity of each letter grade using the COUNTIF function. For example, in the F row of the grading table enter a formula that counts the number of F's in Column M.

   b. The formula might look like this **=COUNTIF(M4:M13, "F").** This formula performs a cumulative count for the number of F's in the range M4:M13. Your count column should look something like the following:

F	0	64	0
D	65	74	2
C	75	84	2
B	85	92	5
A	93	100	1

   c. Can you use the results of a formula or function to plot data on a graph?

❷ Use the grading table data of the count for each letter grade to create an embedded column chart, embedded pie chart, embedded doughnut chart, and an embedded line chart.

   a. Properly label the chart title, axis titles, and legends. Use different colors for each plot on the graph.

   b. Size the embedded graphs to a size where all four graphs will fit on one page of paper. Statistically, you would want the distribution of grades in your class to resemble a normal (or bell) curve.

   c. Examine the line chart and see if you have a normal distribution of grades. If not, is the distribution skewed toward F or toward A?

❸ To the **Lesson Plans ePortfolio** add procedures for communicating results through charting to the procedures for the lesson plan you developed previously for the electronic grade book.

Lesson Plans

LESSON 7.3: PUBLISHING A WORKSHEET ON THE WEB USING *EXCEL*

Lesson 7.3: Learning Activities

Inserting hyperlinks in a worksheet
Publishing an interactive worksheet on a Web page
Publishing a noninteractive chart on a Web page
Browsing Web pages

By using the publishing and saving features in *Excel*, you can save a workbook or part of a workbook as a Web page that others can access by using their Web browsers. Web browsers are programs that allow you to view and interact with files that store information as Web pages.

You can save your data in either interactive or noninteractive form. If you save your data in interactive form, Microsoft® *Office* users can work with the worksheet data and make changes to it by using Microsoft® *Internet Explorer 4.01* or later in a way that is similar to the way they would use *Excel* to work with the data. If you save your data in noninteractive form, others can view your worksheet data using a Web browser. After you publish or save your *Excel* worksheet data as a Web page, you can rearrange the items on the Web page, add more text or graphics, or add other features by using a Web page authoring program such as Microsoft® *FrontPage*®.

In setting up her nutrition unit, Shelly decides that the Internet is an important resource to communicate data effectively. She can use the World Wide Web for both acquiring and publishing information and resources related to her nutrition unit. She decides to construct an Internet resource page that provides a list of Web sites for students to surf in order to acquire information about nutrition and their nutritional profile in order to complete the activities and exercises in the nutrition unit.

LESSON 7.3: TUTORIAL

Inserting Hyperlinks in a Worksheet

You can create hyperlinks in workbooks, by using either text or graphics that link to charts, workbooks, Web pages, or other files.

1. To prepare a worksheet with a list of Web sites for students to surf and acquire nutrition information, insert hyperlinks in the worksheet cells. Open a new workbook and set the width of Column **A** to **60.** In Cell **A1** center and bold the title for the worksheet **Internet Resources for Nutrition.**

2. To enter a hyperlink, select Cell **A3** and select **Insert | Hyperlink.** A dialog box is displayed similar to the example on the following page.

3. Click in the **Text to display** box and type **Calorie Control Council Calorie Calculator.**

4. Click in the **Type the file or Web page name** box and type the URL **http://www.caloriescount.com/cgi-bin/calorie_calculator.cgi** and click **OK.**

5. Repeat steps 2–4 to insert hyperlinks with the following Web page names and hyperlinks in cells **A5, A7, A9, A11,** and **A13,** respectively:

   Cyberdiet Nutritional Profile
   http://www.cyberdiet.com/profile/profile.html
   KRAFT On-Line Nutrition Guide
   http://www.kraftfoods.com/html/nutrition/nutrition.index.html

Nutriquest-Cornell's Nutrition Q&A Service
http://www.nutrition.cornell.edu/nutriquest/nqhome.html
USDA Kids Pages
http://www.usda.gov/news/special/kidpg.htm
USDA Nutrient Database for Standard Reference
http://www.nal.usda.gov/fnic/cgi-bin/nut_search.pl

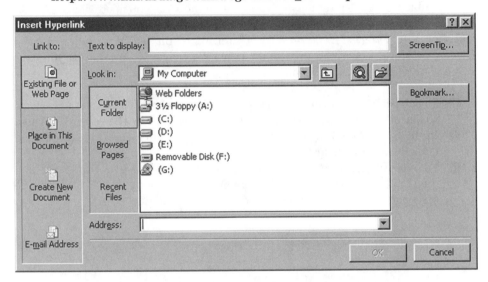

⑥ Save the worksheet as **Ch7WWWNutritionResource.xls.** Your worksheet should look similar to the following example:

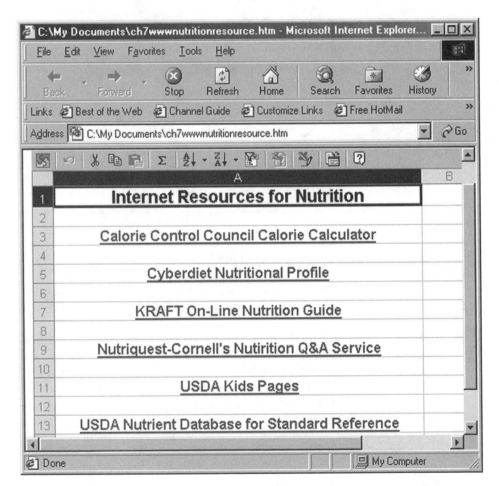

Publishing an Interactive Worksheet on a Web Page

If you want users to be able to interact with data on a Web page, you can put a worksheet on a Web page that is interactive. With interactive worksheets Web surfers can perform such actions as filtering, entering new values for calculations, or summarizing and analyzing data.

To publish and use interactive *Excel* data on the Web, you need Microsoft® *Office Standard, Professional* or *Premium*, the Microsoft® *Office* Web Components, and Microsoft® *Internet Explorer 4.01* or later. Microsoft® *Office* includes *Internet Explorer.* Before you save or publish data on a Web page, be certain that you have saved your workbook as an .xls file.

❶ To publish the Internet Resources for Nutrition worksheet in an interactive form so that additional resources can be added to it, select **File | Save as Web Page.**

❷ In the **Save As** dialog box, select the radio button **Selection: Sheet** and click the **Add interactivity** check box.

❸ For the File name enter **ch7wwwnutritionresource.htm** (no caps), and then click **Publish.** The **Publish as Web Page** dialog box displays on the screen and should be similar to the following example:

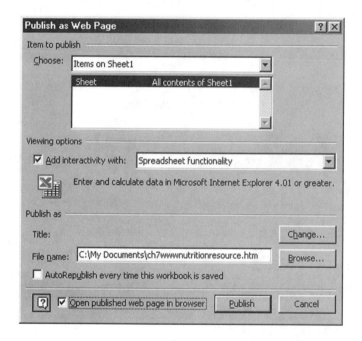

❹ In the dialog box make sure that **Items on Sheet1** is selected in the **Choose** box and **Sheet : All contents of Sheet1** is selected in the list.

❺ Under **Viewing options** make sure that the **Add interactivity with** check box is selected and **Spreadsheet functionality** appears in the window.

❻ Since you placed a title on the worksheet it is not necessary to publish a title on the Web page.

❼ In the **File name** box, make sure that the file name **ch7wwwnutritionresource.htm** is displayed. Notice the file will be saved to your default folder for *Excel* files. If you can publish directly to a Web server either through your local area network or FTP, you can enter the location here. For this exercise you will publish on your local computer and view through the File Open feature of the Web browser on your computer.

❽ Since you will view the Web page in your browser after you publish it, select the **Open published Web page in browser** check box, and click **Publish.** You should see the worksheet displayed in your Web browser similar to the example on the following page:

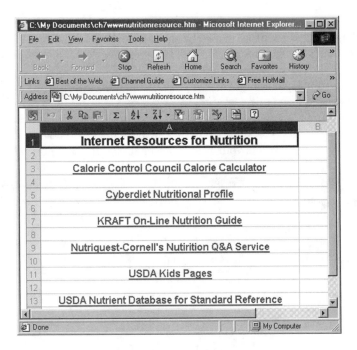

⑨ From your Web browser, navigate the active cell up and down in the worksheet. Notice that you have some *Excel* functionality through your Web browser. If your computer is connected to the Internet, select one of the hyperlinks and surf the Web site.

⑩ Some formatting and features of your worksheet may not be retained when you save it as a Web page. After you save your worksheet as a Web page, you should use a Web page authoring application such as Microsoft® *FrontPage®* and not *Excel* to modify the .htm file. You can republish *Excel* data that you have already put on the Web only by saving or republishing the data again.

⑪ Close your Web browser application and close the **Ch7WWWNutritionResource.xls** file.

Publishing a Noninteractive Chart on a Web Page

Usually the *Excel* data you publish in a Web page is static or noninteractive data, which means that you want others to view the data without making changes to it. To put noninteractive *Excel* data on the Web, you need Microsoft® *Office Standard*, *Professional*, or *Premium*. Microsoft® *Office* includes *Internet Explorer*, but you can use any Web browser to view noninteractive Web pages. Before you publish data on a Web page, be sure you have saved your workbook as an *Excel* file. If saved correctly, it will have an ".xls" extension on the file name.

❶ Open the *Excel* workbook **Ch7NutritionSurveyGr.xls** from your hard disk or diskette, and select the sheet named **Chart2**. To publish Ms. Edwards Nutrition Survey chart in a noninteractive form select **File | Save as Web Page.**

❷ In the **Save As** dialog box, select the radio button **Selection: Chart** and make sure the **Add interactivity** check box is cleared.

❸ For the file name enter **ch7nutritionsurveygr.htm** (no caps) and then click on the **Publish** button. The **Publish as Web Page** dialog box is displayed on the screen.

❹ Make sure that **Items on Chart2** is selected in the **Choose** box and **Chart sheet (Column)** is selected in the list.

❺ Under **Viewing options** make sure that the **Add interactivity with** check box is cleared.

❻ Since you placed a title on the chart it is not necessary to publish a title on the Web page.

❼ In the **File name** box, make sure that the file name **ch7nutritionsurveygr.htm** is displayed. Notice the file will be saved to your default folder for *Excel* files. If you can publish directly to a Web server either through your local area network or FTP, you can enter the location here. For this exercise you will publish on your local computer and view through the **File | Open** feature of the Web browser on your computer.

❽ Since you will view the Web page in your browser after you publish it, select **Open published Web page in browser,** and click **Publish.** You should see the worksheet displayed in your Web browser similar to the following example:

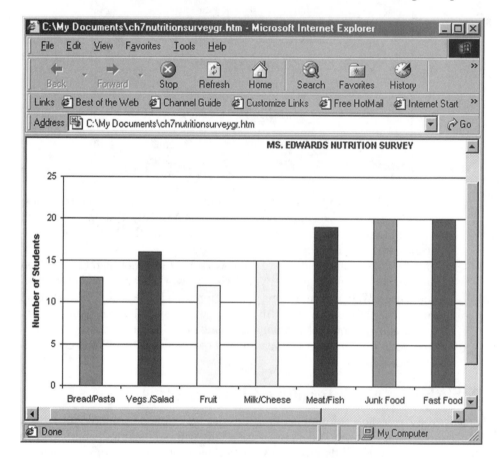

❾ When you publish a noninteractive chart, the chart is saved as a Graphics Interchange Format (.gif) image file in a supporting files folder with the same name as the Web page. For example, in this case a supporting files folder is created named ch7nutritionresource_files and it contains a graphics file named **ch7nutritionresource.gif.**

❿ After you save your worksheet as a Web page, you should use a Web page authoring application such as Microsoft® *FrontPage*® rather than *Excel* to modify the .htm file. You can republish *Excel* data that you have already put on the Web only by saving or republishing the data again.

⓫ Close your Web browser application and close the **Ch7NutritionSurveyGr.xls** file.

Browsing Web Pages

You can view and work with Web pages from *Excel* by using the **Web Toolbar.**

❶ To open the **Web Toolbar** in the *Excel* window, select **View | Toolbars** and select **Web.**

2 If your computer is connected to the Internet, test the various options on the toolbar.

3 To open a Web page you have created, click **Go,** select **Open,** and click **Browse.** Select and open the file **ch7nutritionsurveygr.htm** or **ch7wwwnutritionresource.htm.**

4 Select some of the links on the Web page.

FOLLOW-UP PRACTICE PROJECTS

To expand your skills and allow you more practice on printing *Excel* worksheets, perform each of the following practice exercises. Open *Excel* and the workbook, **Ch7CalorieCalc.xls** that you loaded previously from the **T3 Practice CD** to your own disk or hard drive. Perform each of the following practice exercises using this workbook. When you have completed the practice exercises, close and save the workbook and exit *Excel*.

1 The Healthy Meal Calorie Calculator worksheet allows you to enter certain nutritional data about food items, and it will calculate the approximate number of calories. Try entering data and see how the calculation works. It also includes a print macro assigned to **CTRL+p** that previews and prints the worksheet. Does the macro operate properly when printing through the Web browser?

2 Use the procedure in this lesson to publish an interactive worksheet to a Web page using the *Excel* file name (.xls) for the Web page file name (.htm). Select a range of cells (for example, A1:F12) to save as a Web page, and do not forget to add interactivity to the Web page. Your published Web page should look similar to the following sample Web page:

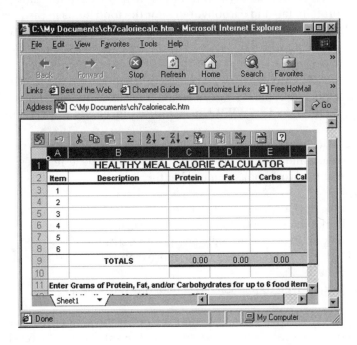

3 Develop a lesson idea or plan related to the activity you just completed that describes using a science or math theme (or subject or theme of your own choosing) for performing calculations and publishing information on the Web. It should be targeted for the grade level you teach or plan to teach. Add it to the **Lesson Plans ePortfolio.**

EXERCISES TO REVIEW AND EXPAND YOUR SKILLS

Set 1: Reviewing Terms and Concepts—For each question below, provide a term on the blank that matches the description.

_____ **1.** A chart saved as part of the worksheet on which it is created.

_____ **2.** A chart saved on a separate sheet within your workbook that has its own sheet name.

_____ **3.** Text or graphics data that link to charts, workbooks, Web pages, or other files.

_____ **4.** Programs that allow you to view and interact with files that store information as Web pages.

_____ **5.** Simplifies the procedure for creating a chart by prompting you to enter the proper information to construct it.

Set 2: Expanding Your Skills—Expand on the skills you learned in this chapter with these activities.

1. Use **Ch7CalorieCalc.xls** for this activity. *Excel* provides tools to use different types of buttons with macros. Click **View | Toolbars | Forms** to display the **Forms Toolbar.** Click **Button** and then click a cell in the worksheet to create a button. Assign the button to the macro named **PrintSheet;** click **OK.** Right-click on the button when the pointer becomes a four-headed arrow, click **Edit Text,** and type **Print** for the name of the button. Test the button to see if it works properly. Save the worksheet.

2. Use **Ch7CalorieCalc.xls** for this activity. Create an embedded chart of an appropriate type (bar or pie) to show the total calories from protein, fat, and carbohydrates for the food items in the meal. Create an embedded chart that shows the total calories for each food item (some may be 0 if you have fewer than 6 food items). Create a macro that prints the menu worksheet, the chart of calories by nutritional element, and the chart of calories by food item. Save the worksheet.

3. Find additional resources on the Internet about nutrition and add them to the **Ch7WWWNutritionResource.xls** worksheet.

Set 3: Use Microsoft® Help—Look up the following features to get further information and tips, and then practice each of these features with one or more of the workbooks you used in this lesson.

• Look up **Controls** to describe various controls, such as buttons and check boxes, that can be added to a worksheet.
• Look up **Print** a help topic and printing to a file.
• Look up **Charts** to learn about more features of charts and various types of charts.
• Look up **Web** to publish *Excel* data on Web pages.

Set 4: Create Your Own Lesson—After reviewing the lessons in this chapter, develop and describe a lesson targeted for the grade level you teach or plan to teach that makes effective use of each of the following *Excel* features. Describe the workbook you or the students would need to create to complete the lesson. Enter your lesson idea or plan into the **Lesson Plans ePortfolio.**

- Students create a data entry form in a workbook that allows them to record survey information and then automatically stores the data on another sheet in the workbook. Use forms, macros, and charts to collect and analyze the survey data.
- Students select a variety of foods based on the Food Pyramid and create a chart and reports analyzing their nutritional values for the nutrients including protein, vitamins, minerals, carbohydrates, and fats.
- Students bring in the wrappers of common snack foods and use a worksheet to record fat grams and other nutritional information. Then they calculate calories and prepare a chart comparing the various snack foods or snack food categories (candy bars, chips, packaged pastries, etc.).
- Students create a classroom Web site with a number of Web pages to publish information and interactive worksheets about nutrition on the Internet.

INTEGRATING TECHNOLOGY IN THE CLASSROOM WITH MICROSOFT® *POWERPOINT®*

OVERVIEW

Dave Johnson is a fifth-grade teacher at Lincoln Elementary School. This year the school installed one computer equipped with Microsoft® *Office* in each classroom for the teacher to use for classroom management, e-mail, and whatever instructional uses the teacher can design and develop.

Dave wants to do more with his computer than just create handouts and tests using word processing. He recently attended a conference where the speaker was using an electronic slide show while he spoke, and Dave noticed that the slide show was helpful for reinforcing the main points of the discussion. Additionally, the speaker provided a handout of the slides used in the electronic slide show and the handout was useful for taking notes.

After the conference Dave began to think about using electronic slide shows in his classroom. Dave conducted a search on the Internet of "electronic slide shows" and found out that they could provide an alternative to printed communication and could actually provide a multimedia presentation that incorporates sound, graphics, animation, video, and text (Morrison, Lowther, & DeMeulle, 1999). Additionally, he discovered that one of the most widely used presentation programs was Microsoft® *PowerPoint®* and it was included in Microsoft® *Office.*

Dave has decided to begin developing presentations for instructional activities in several of the subjects he teaches. Sometimes he wants the presentation to provide structure and organization to his instructional presentation through the use of handouts and lecture notes, and sometimes he wants his instructional presentation to include sound and graphics that will impact his students and motivate them to expand their understanding of a topic.

One of the main reasons that Dave wants to learn to use presentation software is because he thinks that presentations will provide an excellent communication tool for his fifth graders to use to develop communication skills and reinforce learning across the curriculum. Dave has in mind that he wants his students to use presentations in the classroom to present book reports, research reports, science projects, or other types of "electronic reports." Dave decides to become proficient in the use of Microsoft® *PowerPoint*®.

In Part 3 you will learn how to use the Microsoft® *Office* multimedia presentation tool, *PowerPoint*®, to create documents called presentations. Most multimedia presentation programs combine the capability to create and present information on-screen that incorporates sound, graphics, video, and hyperlinks with text. Although multimedia authoring and presentation programs were originally designed to be electronic slide shows (Roblyer, 2003), these programs eventually incorporated powerful design features capable of importing sound and graphics into a presentation document.

Microsoft® *PowerPoint*® possesses the capabilities of designing and developing a presentation as well as presenting the information on the computer monitor screen or projection device or television attached to a computer. Presentation documents are useful for enhancing instruction in traditional lecture discussion formats and are especially effective in a distance learning environment (Roblyer, 2003). Although presentations are often used for large-group lectures, in the classroom multimedia presentation programs increase teacher productivity and enrich classroom teaching and learning activities.

Each presentation document in Microsoft® *PowerPoint*® is organized into a series of on-screen slides. Each slide may contain various types of objects, such as text, graphics, video, sound, and hyperlinks. *PowerPoint*® manipulates the sequence and way in which objects are presented as well as the transition from slide to slide.

Microsoft® *PowerPoint*® presentations make it possible to organize your information or content and visually enhance your message (Morrison, Lowther, & De-Meulle, 1999). When you create a presentation, it is important to determine what information needs to be included or excluded from the presentation. The best presentations provide a concrete reference for your ideas by incorporating a few words with relevant graphics (Morrison, et al.) Microsoft® *PowerPoint*® gives you many ways to deliver your presentation including on-screen presentations, Web presentations, overhead transparencies, 35 mm slides, or paper:

- **On-Screen Presentations.** Most *PowerPoint*® presentations are delivered as on-screen presentations. All *PowerPoint*® special effects and features are available in this mode. You can use slide transitions, timings, movies, sounds, animation, and hyperlinks. Several alternatives can be used to deliver a presentation as an on-screen presentation:

  - **Presentation with a Live Speaker.** If you are presenting in a classroom or meeting room using a large monitor or projection unit, *PowerPoint*® will automatically set and restore correct screen resolution for the target projection system.
  - **Self-Running Presentation.** You might want to set up a presentation to run unattended in a booth or kiosk at a conference or convention. A self-running presentation can be set so that most menus and commands are unavailable and it restarts automatically after each showing.
  - **Online Meeting.** You can use *PowerPoint*® as an online collaboration tool where you share a presentation and exchange information with people at different sites in real time as if everyone were in the same room.

- **Presentations on the Web.** You can design and publish a presentation for the World Wide Web. You can publish a complete presentation, a custom show, a single slide, or a range of slides. You can choose to present in *PowerPoint*® itself, or you can save the presentation in Hypertext Markup Language (HTML) format and use a Web browser application as your presentation tool. *PowerPoint*® presentations in HTML format include a navigation bar you can use to move through the slides by using the outline pane.

- **Broadcast Presentations.** You can broadcast a presentation, including video and audio, over the Web. You can use broadcasting for an online meeting, for presenting to remote groups, or for holding a team meeting whose participants are at several different locations. The presentation is saved in HTML format, so all that a viewer needs in order to see the presentation is a Web browser application. The broadcast can be recorded and saved on a Web server where it will be available for playback at any time.
- **Overhead Transparencies.** You can create a presentation that uses overhead transparencies by printing your slides as black-and-white or color transparencies. You can design these slides in either landscape or portrait orientation.
- **35mm Slides.** Photo processing shops and services can transform your *PowerPoint*® electronic slides into 35mm slides.
- **Paper Printouts, Notes, Handouts, and Outlines.** You can design a presentation so that it looks right when printed in black on a laser printer. Additionally, *PowerPoint*® provides the capability to support your presentation with printed handouts, printed speaker notes, or an outline. You can also send your slide images and notes to Microsoft® *Word* and then use *Word* features to enhance their appearance.

THE TOP TEN MISTAKES MADE BY USERS OF PRESENTATION SOFTWARE

All of the following are qualities that can interfere with readability and/or communicating content during a Microsoft® *PowerPoint*® presentation.

1. **Type too small**—Use at least a 32-point font; use larger type if audience is larger and further away from the presenter.
2. **Text and background don't contrast**—The audience cannot see text too similar in hue to the background. Use text with high contrast to background (e.g., dark blue on white, black on yellow).
3. **Too much text on one frame**—The purpose of text is to focus attention on main points, not present a large amount of information. Ideas should be summarized in brief phrases.
4. **Too many different items on one frame**—Too many items on a frame interfere with reading, especially if some items are in motion. Frames design should be simple, clear, and free of distractions.
5. **Too many fancy fonts**—Many fonts are unreadable when projected on a screen. Use a plain sans serif font for titles and a plain serif font for other text.
6. **Gratuitous graphics**—Graphics interfere with communication when used solely for decoration. They should always help communicate the content.
7. **Gratuitous sounds**—Sounds interfere with communication when used solely for effect. They should always help communicate the content.
8. **No graphics, just text**—Well-chosen graphics can help communicate messages. Text alone does not make best use of the capabilities of presentation software.
9. **Presenting in bright room**—Frames can fade away if the room is too bright. Cover windows and turn off lights during a presentation.
10. **Reading text to audience**—Do not read what the audience can read for themselves. Use text to guide main points.

Source: From *Integrating Educational Technology into Teaching* by Roblyer, p. 177, copyright © 2003 by Pearson Education, Inc., Upper Saddle River, NJ. Used by permission.

Technology Standards and Educational Best Practices for Technology

The lessons in this section assist learners in developing skills for the following International Society for Technology in Education (ISTE) National Educational Technology Standards for Students (NETS·S):

1. Basic operations and concepts

   - Students demonstrate a sound understanding of the nature and operation of technology systems.
   - Students are proficient in the use of technology.

2. Social, ethical, and human issues

   - Students practice responsible use of technology systems, information, and software.
   - Students develop positive attitudes toward technology uses that support lifelong learning, collaboration, personal pursuits, and productivity.

3. Technology productivity tools

   - Students use technology tools to enhance learning, increase productivity, and promote creativity.
   - Students use productivity tools to collaborate in constructing technology-enhanced models, prepare publications, and produce other creative works.

4. Technology communications tools

   - Students use telecommunications to collaborate, publish, and interact with peers, experts, and other audiences.

   - Students use a variety of media and formats to communicate information and ideas effectively to multiple audiences.

The chapters in Part 3: Integrating Technology in the Classroom with Microsoft® *PowerPoint*® address indicators in four of the NETS·S standards. The tutorials and activities in Part 3 require you to open files from a CD, floppy disk, and/or a hard disk, use a keyboard and mouse, and manage files you create, save, or copy. *PowerPoint*® is a productivity tool for creatively and effectively communicating information. *PowerPoint*® provides a communication platform for facilitating collaboration both in the classroom and at a distance. The tutorials and learning activities in Part 3 will provide learning experiences in which students create multimedia slide shows or presentations that incorporate a variety of media and methods to enhance communication.

The chapters in Part 3 demonstrate how Microsoft® *PowerPoint*® is a powerful technology integration tool in constructing and conducting curriculum-related learning activities and effectively communicating information. All learning activities in Part 3 are designed to promote responsible use of computer technology and help students develop positive attitudes about the use of technology to accommodate lifelong learning.

Chapters in Part 3

The step-by-step lessons in each chapter demonstrate the text and graphics processing features of Microsoft® *PowerPoint*®. Each tutorial consists of guided practice that demonstrates how teachers and students can use *PowerPoint*® features in classroom learning activities. For each chapter, use the practice files in the **PP folder** of the **T3 Practice CD** to complete the step-by-step lessons.

Several exercises follow each lesson that may also include activities using files from the **T3 Practice CD** and the **Lesson Plans ePortfolio.** Complete these exercises to reinforce the learning activities demonstrated in the tutorial and to expand your skills.

The tutorials in the following lessons do not include every feature of Microsoft® *PowerPoint®* but are designed to address those features that will allow you to perform text and graphics processing tasks that support classroom instruction and student learning. The tutorials also provide activities that encourage you to investigate other features of *PowerPoint®* not specifically included in these lessons.

Chapter 8:   Designing Presentations and Handouts Using *PowerPoint®*

Chapter 9:   Delivering Multimedia Presentations Using *PowerPoint®*

DESIGNING PRESENTATIONS AND HANDOUTS USING *POWERPOINT*®

NEW TERMS

AutoLayout	Normal View	slide layouts
color schemes	Outline View	slide master
Comments Pane	placeholder	title master
design templates	presentation	views

OVERVIEW

The use of multimedia slide shows or presentation for organizing and communicating information is based on the capability of combining text and graphics in a format that is interesting and compelling. Each of the tutorial lessons in this chapter consists of guided practice that demonstrates how to construct, create, and design sets of multimedia slides into presentations.

The lessons in this chapter demonstrate how *PowerPoint*® features can be used in constructing classroom learning activities to present to students or to be prepared by students. Practice files for the tutorials are located in the **PP folder** on the **T3 Practice CD.** Several exercises follow each lesson, and some include activities from the **Lesson Plans ePortfolio.** Complete these exercises to reinforce the learning activities demonstrated in the tutorials and to build your collection of technology-based lesson plans and ideas.

Lesson 8.1: Opening and Saving *PowerPoint*® Presentations
Lesson 8.2: Designing a Presentation Using *PowerPoint*®
Lesson 8.3: Creating and Formatting Slides Using *PowerPoint*®

FIGURE 8–1

The Microsoft®
PowerPoint® Window
with Standard,
Formatting, and
Drawing Toolbars
Source: Screen captures of
Microsoft® *PowerPoint*®
used in the chapters in Part
3 are reprinted by
permission from
Microsoft® Corporation.

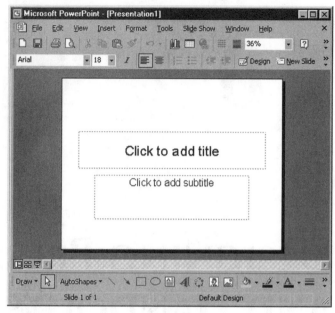

LESSON 8.1: OPENING AND SAVING *POWERPOINT*® PRESENTATIONS

Lesson 8.1: Learning Activities

Opening a presentation document
Saving a presentation document
Changing the default working folder
Closing the presentation document
Exiting *PowerPoint*®

Since Dave wants to teach his students to use presentations in the classroom, he needs
to understand how to manipulate presentation files and navigate the *PowerPoint*® window. The following tutorial demonstrates how to use *PowerPoint*® to open and save
an existing presentation file. Figure 8-1 shows the standard *PowerPoint*® window.

In the following *PowerPoint*® window a slide is under construction that combines
the use of text and graphics to enhance the presentation of the information. The *Power-
Point*® window is using the **Standard** and **Formatting Toolbars** at the top of the window and the **Drawing Toolbar** at the bottom of the window. The window is displayed
in **Normal** view with the **Outline** pane on the left, the **Notes** pane on the bottom, and
the **Slide** pane in the middle (some Macintosh® versions may not have **Normal** view):

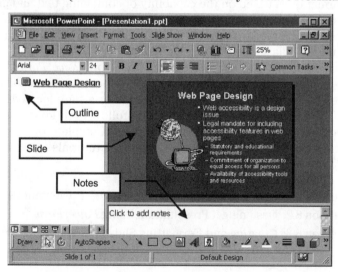

Opening a Presentation Document

The **T3 Practice CD** contains a file called **Ch8Sentences.ppt**. Insert the CD in the CD drive for this procedure.

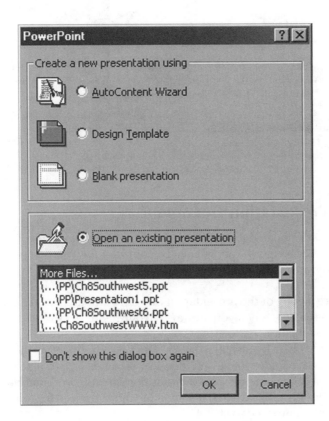

❶ Open the *PowerPoint*® program by double-clicking on the *PowerPoint*® icon or by selecting **Microsoft PowerPoint** from the **Start | Programs** menu on the Windows® screen. When the opening dialog box is displayed, click the radio button for **Open an existing presentation** and click **OK.**

❷ The **Open** dialog box displays the default working folder, the folder that is automatically selected by *PowerPoint*®. For computers using the Windows® operating system, the default working folder is **My Documents.** To select the CD drive, make sure the **T3 Practice CD** is in the CD drive, and then click the down arrow on the **Look in** box and select the appropriate location from the list.

Macintosh®: Using the Microsoft® *Office* Manager icon, select **Microsoft PowerPoint.** When the opening dialog box is displayed, click the radio button for **Open an existing presentation.**

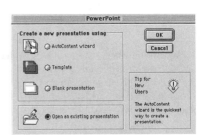

❸ Select the **PP Folder** on the CD drive and open it by double-clicking on it or by pointing at it with the mouse and then clicking **Open.**

❹ From the file list select the presentation document file named **Ch8Sentences1.ppt** by double-clicking it or selecting it and then clicking **Open.** (The .ppt file extension may not appear on the file name based on the hardware platform and system settings of your computer.)

❺ The *PowerPoint*® screen should look similar to the example at the top of the following page:

Macintosh®: To select the CD drive, make sure the **T3 Practice CD** is in the CD drive. In the Macintosh® **File | Open** dialog box, select the CD drive from the Desktop folder and then select the **PP folder** by double-clicking on the folder name.

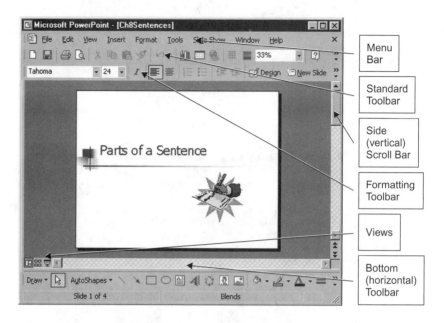

Saving a Presentation Document

The *PowerPoint*® document was loaded from the CD, and a copy of it currently resides in computer memory. You will need a copy of it on your computer to perform the procedures and exercises in this tutorial.

❶ To save a copy of the presentation on your computer, select **File | Save As.** (Use **Save** only when you are saving your file to the same location with the same file name.)

> **Macintosh®:** Macintosh® may remember the last folder you selected, especially with **Open** or **Save As.** You should verify the folder in which you are opening or saving your file each time you perform these operations.

❷ Windows® usually displays the **My Documents** folder as the default working or active folder for saving files. For now it is a good place to store word processing documents, presentation documents, presentations, databases, and other files. To save to the default location, proceed to step 5. For our purposes here, proceed to step 4.

❸ In the **Save As** dialog box select an appropriate folder to locate the presentation file. To save the file in a location other than the hard disk (for example, a floppy disk drive), make sure the disk is in the drive, click the down arrow on the **Save in** box, and select the appropriate location from the list.

> **Macintosh®:** In the Macintosh® **File | Save** dialog box, select an appropriate folder and click the **Save** button. You can also close the document by clicking on the □ in the upper left-hand corner of the document window.

❹ In the **File name** box enter an appropriate file name for the presentation file. The file name **Ch8Sentences1.ppt** is already entered as the file name, which you can use. Therefore, click **Save.**

❺ When the file is saved, the **Save As** dialog box closes and the program returns to the presentation window.

Changing the Default Working Folder

You can specify the default working folder to which *PowerPoint*® automatically saves files.

❶ To change the default working folder, select **Tools | Options | Save.**

❷ In the Default file location: window, type the path for the folder you want to display as the default working folder. For example, you could type **C:\My Presentations** and click **OK.** (To change the default working folder, you must first create the folder. (For purposes of this tutorial, DO NOT change the default file location.)

> **Macintosh®:** Macintosh® may remember the last folder you selected, especially with **Open** or **Save as.** You should verify the folder in which you are opening or saving your file each time you perform these operations.

Closing the Presentation Document

Although the presentation file has been saved, the presentation document still resides in computer memory allocated to the *PowerPoint*® program.

❶ To close the presentation document, select **File | Close.** If you have not already saved your presentation document in a file or saved your document since you made modifications to it, you will be prompted to save the presentation in a file before closing it. You may also close the presentation by clicking on the **X** on the upper right-hand corner of the presentation window (just below the **X** on the top right of the *PowerPoint*® program window).

❷ When you close the presentation document, the *PowerPoint*® program remains in computer memory and you may open another presentation document or exit the program.

> **Macintosh®:** You can also close the presentation document by clicking on the ☐ in the upper left-hand corner of the presentation window.

Exiting *PowerPoint*®

Closing the presentation is not the same as exiting *PowerPoint*®.

❶ To exit *PowerPoint*® and remove it from computer memory, select **File | Exit.** If you have not already closed your presentation document, you will be prompted to save the presentation in a file before quitting the program if you have made modifications to it.

❷ You can also quit the program by clicking on the **X** on the top-right of the *PowerPoint*® program window.

> **Macintosh®:** To exit *PowerPoint*® and remove it from computer memory, select **File | Quit.** If you have not already closed your presentation document, you will be prompted to save the presentation in a file before quitting the program if you have made modifications to it.

FOLLOW-UP PRACTICE PROJECTS

In the following lessons in this chapter and the following chapters of Part 3, you will use several practice files from the **T3 Practice CD.** The following projects allow you to practice the skills you learned in this lesson.

Insert the **T3 Practice CD,** Open *PowerPoint*®, and complete the projects below.

❶ From the **PP folder** of the **T3 Practice CD,** open the presentation file named **Ch8BookReport1.ppt.** Save it to the hard drive of your computer or a personal disk then close it. Repeat the entire procedure with **Ch8Sentences1.ppt**

❷ Expand your skills. Use the Open and Save procedures of *PowerPoint*® to save each of the following files on the hard drive of your computer or a personal disk, or use the Windows® or Macintosh® operating system to copy or drag each of the following files to the hard drive of your computer or a personal disk: **Ch8Southwest1.ppt, Ch8Graphics.ppt.**

LESSON 8.2: DESIGNING A PRESENTATION USING *POWERPOINT*®

Lesson 8.2: Learning Activities

Using design templates to create a new presentation
Using slide layouts
Using the slide master
Using color schemes

You can create a new presentation in several ways. You can design a presentation by working with the AutoContent Wizard, which provides you with prompts and supplies suggested content and design for your presentation. You can also start with an existing presentation and change it to suit your needs. Both of these design approaches use sample presentations that are provided with the *PowerPoint*® program.

You can also design a presentation using an outline that you import from another application or that you enter into *PowerPoint*® as a blank presentation that has neither suggested content nor design. A final way to design a presentation is by selecting a design template that establishes the layout, format, and look of the presentation but does not include content. This final approach is used in this tutorial.

PowerPoint® is designed to give your presentation a consistent appearance and provides several design tools to help you control the look of your slides: design templates, slide masters, color schemes, and slide layouts.

In preparing to teach his students how to create a presentation using *PowerPoint*®, Dave wants to be skilled himself in using the design features of *PowerPoint*® that control the look of a presentation and establish a consistent appearance. Open *PowerPoint*® and follow the tutorial steps for designing a presentation.

LESSON 8.2: TUTORIAL

Using Design Templates to Create a New Presentation

Design templates contain color schemes, slide and title masters with custom formatting, and styled fonts, all designed to create a particular look. When you apply a design template to your presentation, all features of the new template replace the design features of the original presentation. After you apply a design template, each slide you add has the same custom look. *PowerPoint*® has a wide variety of professionally designed templates. In addition, you can create your own templates. If you create a special look for one of your presentations, you can save it as a template.

 **Macintosh®:** Select **Presentation Designs.**

❶ To select a design template for a new presentation, select **File | New | Design Templates.**
❷ Select **Soaring** from the list of design template and click **OK.** The **New Slide** dialog box now appears on the screen.

Using Slide Layouts

When you create a new slide, you can select from many predesigned slide layouts, including layouts for title slides, slides containing tables, slides containing charts or graphs, slides containing text boxes, slides containing clip art, or blank slides. The containers for each of these types of information are called placeholders. After you create a slide you can change its layout or apply a new layout.

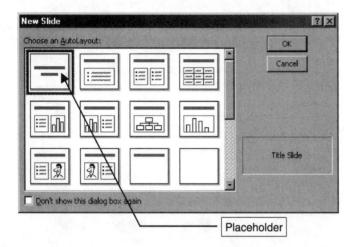

Placeholder

❶ Select the first AutoLayout called **Title Slide** and click **OK**. (In *Office*® *XP* click **X** in the upper right corner of the **Task Pane** to close it.) The first slide for the presentation is created. Your screen should look similar to the following example in **Normal** view:

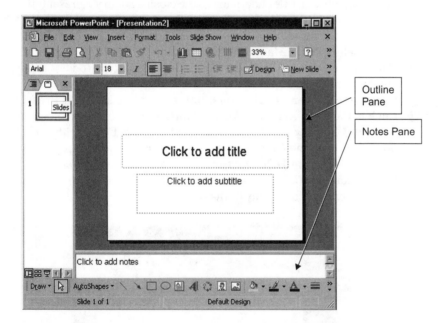

Outline Pane

Notes Pane

❷ For this tutorial you will use **Normal View** without the **Outline Pane** for designing presentations. To close the **Outline Pane,** click the **X** on the upper right corner of the pane. Creating and formatting slides in this way allows you to enter your content directly into placeholders and see what the slide will look like as you construct it. Your screen should look similar to the example at the top of the following page.

Using the Slide Master

The **Slide Master** controls the format and placement of the titles and text you type on slides. You can also have masters that control the format of title slides, notes, and

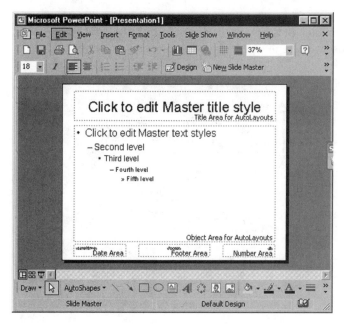

handouts. Masters hold background items, such as graphics you want to appear on every slide. Any change you make to a **Slide Master** is reflected on each slide.

❶ The **Title Master** controls the format of the title slide and any other slide you designate as a title slide, such as the closing slide of a presentation. Since you selected a title slide from the **AutoLayout** dialog, use the **Title Master** to control the formatting of the current slide. To modify the master for title slides, select **View | Master | Title Master.**

❷ Click in the Date Area box on **<date/time>,** and type today's date (for example, **June 2, 2002**).

❸ Click in the **Footer Area** box on **<footer>** and type **My First Presentation.**

❹ Click in the **Title Area for AutoLayouts** box, and use the mouse to select the text. Click to edit **Master title style.** Select **Format | Font,** click the down arrow on the **Color** box select the **red** box, and click **OK.** After you click outside of the **Title Master,** your screen should look similar to the following example: (You may need to close the slide miniature if it appears on your screen and covers any of the boxes.)

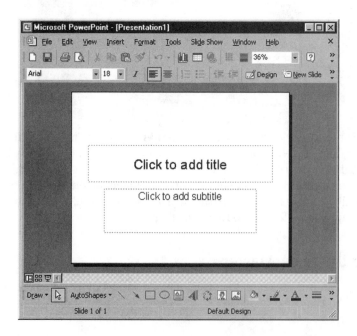

⑤ Now click **Slide View** and your blank title slide will reflect the modifications you made to the **Title Master.** Any other title slides that you add to your presentation will reflect this same style and formatting.

⑥ The title and text placeholders follow the formatting of the slide master for your presentation. If you want an individual slide to look different from the master, you can make changes to that slide without changing the master. You can move, resize, or reformat the placeholders so that they vary from the slide master.

⑦ Click in the **Subtitle** box of the title slide directly on text. Select **Format | Font,** click on the down arrow for the **Color** box, select the **cyan** box, and click **OK.**

⑧ Click outside the Subtitle box to see how the font color applies. Now select **View | Master | Title Master.** (You will notice that the font color for the subtitle on the **Title Master** is still white.)

⑨ Click **Slide View** to return to Slide View.

Using Color Schemes

Color schemes are sets of eight balanced colors designed for use as the main colors of a slide presentation. Color schemes affect text, titles, lines, background, fill, accents, and hyperlinks. Each color in the scheme is used automatically for a different element on the slide.

When you apply a design template to a presentation, you can choose from a set of color schemes predesigned for that design template. This makes it easy to change color schemes uniformly for a slide or an entire presentation.

① To choose a color scheme, select **Format | Slide Color Scheme.** The first color scheme in the list is the default color scheme for the design template you have selected.

② You can apply a color scheme to an individual slide or for an entire presentation. Select the **brown** color scheme, and click **Apply to All.** The color scheme for all the slides in the presentation is now changed.

③ Apply color schemes again to set the color scheme back to the default for the **Soaring** design template.

④ Exit *PowerPoint*® but do not save the presentation file.

FOLLOW-UP PRACTICE PROJECTS

For more practice on designing a presentation, perform each of the following projects. Open *PowerPoint*® and the presentation file **Ch8BookReport1.ppt** that you previously loaded onto your own disk or hard drive. Perform each of the following projects using this presentation. When you have completed the projects, exit *PowerPoint*®.

① **AutoContent Wizard:** You can use AutoContent Wizard to quickly create and organize your presentation. To create a new presentation file using AutoContent Wizard, open *PowerPoint*® and click **File | New.** Then click **Auto-Content Wizard** and **OK.** Click **Next.**

Select **General** under Presentation type, **Generic,** then **Next.** Select **On-screen presentation** for Presentation style, then click **Next.** Enter **Writing a Book Report** in both the **Presentation title** and **Footer** boxes, then click **Next** button. Then click **Finish** and see the ready-made presentation.

a. Scroll through the slides of the presentation by clicking the down arrow on the vertical scroll bar on the right side of the window or by pressing **PGDN** and **PGUP.** You can also click on one of the slide numbers on the outline on the left side of the screen.

b. Change the slide color scheme and apply it to all slides. Then, change the slide color scheme back to the original color scheme.

c. Change the font color on the **Title** area on the **Slide Master** to a bright yellow. (You may have to select **More Colors** on the color palette to find a bright **yellow.**)

❷ *PowerPoint*® **Views:** *PowerPoint*® provides several views of your presentation to help you while you are creating a presentation. The two main views you will use are **Normal** and **Slide View.** To easily switch between views, click the buttons at the lower left of the *PowerPoint*® window. **NOTE:** Macintosh® versions may not contain **Normal** view. In that case, the **Slide View** icon is on the extreme left and the other view icons are in the same order from left to right as shown below.

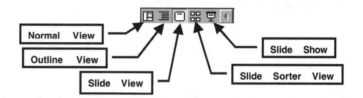

a. **Normal** view contains three panes: the **Outline Pane,** the **Slide Pane,** and the **Notes Pane.** Use the **Outline Pane** to organize and develop the content of your presentation, including titles, bullet points, paragraphs, and slides. Use the **Slide Pane** to see how features look on each slide, including graphics, movies, sounds, hyperlinks, and animations to individual slides. In the **Notes Pane** you can add speaker notes or information that you want to share with an audience. You can adjust the size of the different panes by dragging the pane borders.

b. **Slide Sorter** view allows you to see all the slides in your presentation at the same time in miniature. This view facilitates the ordering of your slides, adding timings, and selecting animated transitions for moving from slide to slide.

c. **Slide Show** runs the presentation for full-screen display.

d. **Slide Show** view allows you to present the presentation. How do you move from slide to slide in **Slide Show** view?

e. Click on each of the view icons to see how the view displays the presentation.

❸ Save the presentation and exit *PowerPoint*®.

LESSON 8.3: CREATING AND FORMATTING SLIDES USING *POWERPOINT*®

Lesson 8.3: Learning Activities

Creating a new slide
Adding text to a placeholder on a slide
Formating text in a placeholder on a slide
Adding a WordArt drawing object in a placeholder on a slide
Adding Clip Art in a placeholder on a slide

Slides can contain several kinds of objects, including text, graphics, video, sound, and hyperlinks. The easiest way to add text to a slide is to type it directly into a placeholder on the slide. You can add text outside a placeholder by using the **Text Box** button on the **Drawing** toolbar to create a text placeholder. You can also add text to an AutoShape or add a WordArt drawing object for a special text effect.

Now that Dave has learned the basics for operating *PowerPoint*®, he is ready to begin creating slides for his first classroom presentation. He is going to start with a simple presentation he will use for direct instruction and discussion in a sentence structure unit his language arts class is currently working on.

Open *PowerPoint*® and the **Ch8Sentences1.ppt** presentation that you previously loaded onto your own disk or hard disk. Close the Outline Pane if it is displayed.

LESSON 8.3: TUTORIAL

Creating a New Slide

To add new content to a presentation, you must create a slide to contain the text, graphics, video, sound, or hyperlink objects that you want to place on the slides.

1 To insert a new slide immediately after the current slide and select **Insert | New Slide** or click **New Slide** on the **Standard Toolbar.**

2 In the **New Slide** dialog box, select the **Bulleted List** AutoLayout (the second one in first row) and click **OK.** The **Bulleted List** Autolayout has two placeholders: a title place holder and a bulleted list placeholder.

Adding Text to a Placeholder on a Slide

The easiest way to add text to a slide is to type it directly into any placeholder on the slide. When you use AutoLayout, you are provided with placeholders in which you can directly enter text or objects. You can change the size and position of a text placeholder or apply a different AutoLayout to an existing slide at any time without losing the information on your slide.

If all your lines of text do not fit in the placeholder, *PowerPoint*® automatically tries to fit the text in the placeholder by reducing the font size of the text. If your text starts to run off the bottom of the slide, you probably need to insert a new slide and enter the text into that slide. Remember that text added to placeholders is the only text displayed in the outline pane, and it can be exported to *Word* to create handouts, study guides, or tests.

1 To add text to the title placeholder, click in the placeholder that says **Click to add title** and type **Types of Sentences.**

2 To add a bulleted list, click in the placeholder that says **Click to add text** and type the following list of text. Press **ENTER** at the end of each sentence to create the next bulleted item on the list (do not press **ENTER** after the last item on the list).

- **Declarative sentence tells something and ends with a period.**
- **Interrogative sentence asks something and ends with a question mark.**
- **Imperative sentence gives a command or order and ends with a period.**
- **Exclamatory sentence expresses strong feeling and ends with an exclamation point.**

Formatting Text in a Placeholder on a Slide

You can reformat the text in a placeholder to differ from the **Slide Master** format.

❶ To reformat the first two words of each item, first select the words and click **Format | Font.** Click the down arrow on the **Color** box, select the **red** box, click **Shadow,** set the font size to **28** or **32,** and click **OK.**

❷ Repeat step 1 for each bulleted item. (You can highlight the text and then select **Edit | Repeat Font** to repeat the settings for each text selection.) Your slide should look similar to the following example:

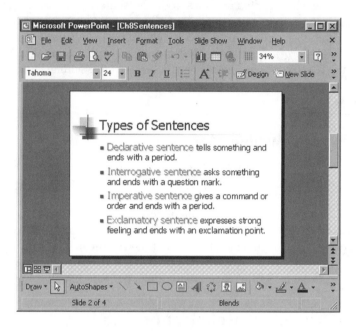

Adding a WordArt Drawing Object in a Placeholder on a Slide

You can insert a WordArt drawing object into a placeholder to create special text effects such as shadowed, skewed, rotated, and stretched text, or text in different shapes. Since WordArt is a drawing object and is not treated as text, you will not see the text effect in the outline pane and you cannot check its spelling as you would ordinary text.

❶ Insert a new slide immediately after the current slide by selecting **Insert | New Slide** or clicking **New Slide.**

❷ In the **New Slide** dialog box, slide the scroll bar down and select the **Object over Text** AutoLayout then click **OK.**

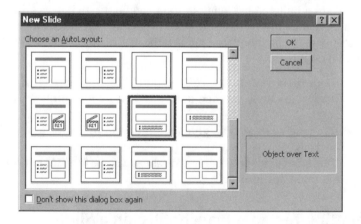

❸ To add text to the title placeholder, click in the placeholder that says Click to add title and type **Declarative Sentences.**

❹ To add WordArt to the object placeholder, double-click in the placeholder that says **Double click to add object. NOTE:** This feature may not be available on some Macintosh® versions. If this feature is not available in your *PowerPoint*® program, skip to step 12.

❺ In the **Insert Object** dialog box, slide the scroll bar down and select **Microsoft WordArt.** Click **OK.**

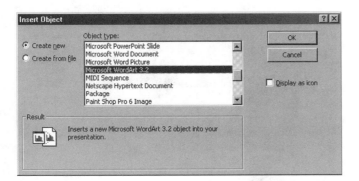

❻ In the **Enter Your Text Here** dialog box, enter **Some examples** and click **Update Display.**

❼ In the **Shape** box click the down arrow, then select **/Slant Up** to make the WordArt text flow from lower left to upper right.

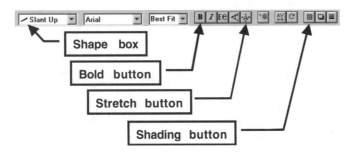

❽ Click the **Bold** button to make the WordArt text bold, and click the **Stretch** button to stretch the WordArt text to the ends of the box.

❾ To change the color of the WordArt text, click the **Shading** button. On the **Foreground** drop-down list, select **Aqua** and click **OK.**

❿ To exit WordArt, click where you want to work next. Be sure to click outside the **Enter Your Text Here** dialog box, **WordArt Toolbar,** and the WordArt itself.

⓫ Resize the object placeholder with the WordArt text by clicking on the placeholder and dragging the appropriate sizing handles until the object placeholder is about the length of the title placeholder.

Dave plans to introduce types of sentences by showing each type on a *PowerPoint*® slide and giving one example. Then he will ask his students to give examples, which he will then type on the screen. Then he will present all the sentence types and examples, asking his students to tell what defines each type. Dave will finish the lesson by presenting another slide show with practice examples, and ask his students to identify the sentence type of each example.

⑫ Click in the placeholder that says Click to add text, and type the following list of text. Press **ENTER** at the end of each sentence to create the next bulleted item on the list (do not press **ENTER** after the last item on the list).

- **Vegetables are good for you.**
- **It is cold outside.**
- **Brazil is in South America.**
- **He likes to go fishing.**

Your slide should look similar to the following example:

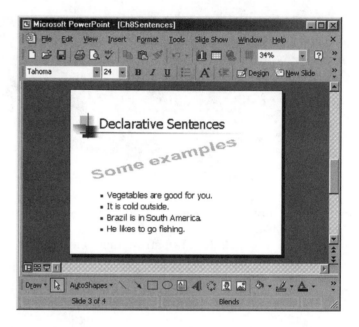

Adding Clip Art in a Placeholder on a Slide

To add text to an AutoShape, just click the shape and type the text. The text attaches to the shape and moves or rotates with the shape as the shape moves or rotates. You can add text to all AutoShapes except for lines, connectors, and freeforms.

❶ Insert a new slide immediately after the current slide by selecting **Insert | New Slide** or **New Slide.**

❷ In the **New Slide** dialog box, slide the scroll bar down and select the **Text and Clip Art** AutoLayout, then click **OK.**

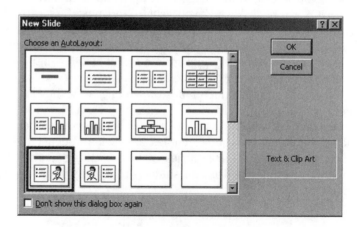

❸ To add text to the title placeholder, click in the placeholder that says **Click to add title** and type **Interrogative Sentences.**

❹ To add clip art to the clip art placeholder, double-click in the placeholder that says **Double click to add clip art.**

❺ In the **Microsoft Clip Gallery** dialog box, enter **question** or **question mark** in the **Search for clips** box and press **ENTER.**

❻ When a set of clips have been found for the search criteria, click the clip you want to add to your document. On the pop-up menu, click **Insert clip.** If you do not have a question mark in your Clip Art database, select another picture.

❼ Use the sizing handles to resize the clip art placeholder so that it does not extend to the edge of the slide. Use the corner sizing handles of the placeholder box to resize in order to maintain the proportion of the clip art object. Your screen should look similar to the following:

Macintosh®: Click the **Find** button and enter **question** or **question mark** in the **Keywords** box. Then click **Find Now.**

❽ Click in the placeholder that says **Click to add text,** and type the following list of text. Press **ENTER** at the end of each sentence to create the next bulleted item on the list (do not press **ENTER** after the last item on the list).

- **Do you like vegetables?**
- **How cold is it outside?**
- **When will she return?**
- **Where did he go?**

❾ Save the presentation as **Ch8Sentences2.ppt** and exit *PowerPoint*®.

FOLLOW-UP PRACTICE PROJECTS

To expand your skills and practice creating and formatting *PowerPoint*® slides, complete the projects below.

❶ Open *PowerPoint*® and the file **Ch8Sentences2.ppt**. When you have completed the practice exercise, close and save the presentation and exit *PowerPoint*®.

a. Create two additional slides with the following title and bulleted lists. Use different AutoLayouts with clip art or WordArt and bulleted lists for the sentence examples.

Exclamatory Sentences

- **How cold it is today!**
- **What a good student she is!**
- **What a beautiful day it is!**
- **How delicious the food was!**

Imperative Sentences

- **Eat all your vegetables.**
- **Read the first sentence.**
- **Put on your coat before going outside.**
- **Close the door when you leave.**

b. Create a third new slide with the following text, and change the list to a numbered list. Save the presentation when you complete the modifications.

Name the type of sentence

- **She likes to use computers.**
- **Get the paper out of the printer.**
- **What a good job you did!**
- **Why did he leave the room?**

c. Change to **Slide Sorter View** and drag the Imperative Sentences slide in front of the Exclamatory Sentences slide.

d. View the presentation in **Slide Show View** to determine that it runs properly and make any necessary revisions.

e. Use the file named **Ch8SentencesFinal.ppt** in the **PP folder** on the **T3 Practice CD** to compare with your solution.

f. Develop a lesson idea or plan that is targeted for the grade level you teach or plan to teach related to the activity you just completed. It should describe using a language arts, social studies, science, or math theme (or subject or theme of your own choosing) for communicating information. Add it to the **Lesson Plans ePortfolio.**

❷ One of Dave's primary objectives for using *PowerPoint*® is to teach his students to communicate information effectively by presenting electronic reports using *PowerPoint*®. Therefore, Dave wants to create a presentation that he can use both as a lesson on book reports and that students can use as a template for preparing book reports using *PowerPoint*® presentations.

a. Open the presentation named **Ch8BookReport1.ppt.**

b. Modify the presentation by following the instructions given below and by replacing the existing content with the following content where given. For example, you would enter a new title on a slide by deleting the existing title and typing the new one.

Title Slide:
Delete any subtitle placeholders. Resize and move the title placeholder so the title text does not wrap and is placed above the red line. Insert an interesting and relevant clip art object on the slide and size it appropriately.

Introduction Slide:
Delete

Discuss Slide:
Change title to **Parts of a Book Report**

Add the following bulleted items:

- **Title and Author**
- **Introduction**
- **About the Book**
- **My Opinion of the Book**

Topic One Slide:
Change title to **Title and Author**
Add the following bulleted items:

- **Write the author's full name.**
- **Capitalize important words in the title.**

Topic Two Slide:
Change title to **Introduction**
Add the following bulleted items:

- **Identify book as fiction or non-fiction.**
- **Say something to get reader interested.**
- **Provide a short summary of the book.**

Topic Three Slide:
Change title to **About the Book**
Add the following bulleted items:

- **Explain the setting of the book.**
- **List the main characters and their role in the story.**
- **Choose part of the story to share.**

Real Life Slide:
Change title to **My Opinion of the Book**
Add the following bulleted items:

- **Tell what you think of the book.**
- **Would classmates enjoy the book?**
- **Explain why or why not.**

What Means Slide:
Delete

Next Steps Slide:
Change the title to **Other Activities**
Add the following bulleted items:

- **Write another chapter to the story.**
- **Present a PowerPoint presentation about the book.**
- **Create a future for one of the characters.**
- **Use the Internet to find out more about the author.**

c. Save the presentation as **Ch8BookReport2.ppt**.
d. View the presentation in **Slide Show View** to determine that it runs properly and make any necessary revisions.
e. Use the file named **Ch8BookReportFinal.ppt** in the **PP folder** on the **T3 Practice CD** to compare with your solution.
f. Develop a lesson idea or plan that is targeted for the grade level you teach or plan to teach. It should describe using a language arts, social studies, science, or math theme (or subject or theme of your own choosing) for creating a template students can use to present electronic reports. Add it to the **Lesson Plans ePortfolio**.

EXERCISES TO REVIEW AND EXPAND YOUR SKILLS

Set 1: Reviewing Terms and Concepts—For each question below, provide a term on the blank that matches description.

_____ 1. The containers on predesigned slide layouts to hold various types of information.

_____ 2. Controls the format and placement of the titles and text you type on slides.

_____ 3. Allows you to see all the slides in your presentation, on the screen at the same time.

_____ 4. A *PowerPoint*® tool used to quickly create and organize a presentation.

_____ 5. Sets of eight balanced colors designed for use as the main colors of a slide presentation.

Set 2: Expanding Your Skills—Expand on the skills you learned in this chapter with these activities. Load the **Ch8Sentences2.ppt** presentation, and select **Normal View** to perform the following activities. Save the presentation file when you have completed the exercises.

1. **Type Notes While Working on a Presentation.** Go to the last slide of the presentation and enter an answer key for the slide into the **Notes Pane.** To see more of the **Notes Pane,** point to the top border of the **Notes Pane** until the pointer becomes a double-headed arrow, then click and drag upward until the pane is the size you want. Click the **Notes Pane,** and type the following answer key:

   1. **Declarative Sentence**
   2. **Imperative Sentence**
   3. **Exclamatory Sentence**
   4. **Interrogative Sentence**

   (After you press **ENTER** the first time, the items way number automatically.) To view the Notes page, click **View I Notes Page.** You can add drawing objects and pictures to Notes pages in **Notes Page View.** Drawing objects and pictures are not displayed in the **Notes Pane,** but appear when you work in **Notes Page** view or when you print slides with notes.

2. **Create and Print Handouts of Slides. View I Master I Handout Master.** To preview the layout you want, click the buttons on the **Handout Master Toolbar.** You can add art, text, headers or footers, dates, times, or page numbers on the handout master. Click **<header>** in the header placeholder and replace it with **Parts of a Sentence.** Items you add appear only on the handouts; no changes are made to the **Slide Master.** Close the **Handout Master Toolbar.** Click **File I Print.** In the **Print what** box, click **Handouts.** In the **Slides per page** box select **3.** Click **OK.**

3. **Send Notes, Handouts, or an Outline to Microsoft**® *Word.* Click **File I Send To I Microsoft Word.** In the write-up dialog box select **Outline only** and click **OK.** When *Word* opens the document, add any formatting and save it as **Ch8SentencesOutline.doc** (Save as type: **Word Document**). Repeat the **Send To** and try some other views.

Set 3: Use Microsoft® Help—Look up the following features to get further information and tips. Then, practice each of these features with one or more of the presentations you used in this lesson.

- Look up **Print** to print slides, notes, or handouts.
- Look up **Autoshape** to add or change an Autoshape.
- Look up **Resize** to resize or crop an object.
- Look up **Clip Gallery,** which contains a variety of pictures, photographs, sounds, and video clips.

Set 4: Create Your Own Lesson—After reviewing the lessons in this chapter, develop and describe a lesson targeted for the grade level you teach or plan to teach that makes effective use of each of the following *PowerPoint*® features. Describe the presentation you or the students would need to create to complete the lesson. Enter your lesson idea or plan into the **Lesson Plans ePortfolio.**

- Create a presentation about how to use *PowerPoint*® so students can create their own presentations.
- Students create a presentation of an original story using text support with clip art.
- Students create a presentation to present the results of a science experiment.
- Students work in teams and create a presentation about a state or region of the United States or a historical event.

DELIVERING MULTIMEDIA PRESENTATIONS USING *POWERPOINT*®

NEW TERMS

action setting   hyperlink   timing

animation   publish   transition

effect   self-running

OVERVIEW

Presentations are a more engaging teaching and learning experience when the full capability of Microsoft® *PowerPoint*® is employed to provide a multimedia teaching and learning experience. *PowerPoint*® provides tools for animating slide content and transitions from slide to slide. Additionally, it is a useful tool for developing and publishing Web pages. Each of the tutorial lessons in this chapter consists of guided practice that demonstrates how to construct sets of multimedia slides and make them into presentations.

Each tutorial consists of guided practice that demonstrates how teachers and students can use Microsoft® *PowerPoint*® features in preparing classroom learning activities. Practice files for the tutorials are located in the **PP folder** on the **T3 Practice CD.** Following each lesson are several exercises, which include activities from the **Lesson Plans ePortfolio.** Complete these exercises to reinforce the learning activities demonstrated in the tutorials and to build your collection of technology-based lesson plans and ideas.

Lesson 9.1:   Creating Multimedia Slides Using *PowerPoint*®

Lesson 9.2:   Controlling Slide Transitions and Hyperlinks Using *PowerPoint*®

Lesson 9.3:   Publishing a Presentation on the Web Using *PowerPoint*®

LESSON 9.1: CREATING MULTIMEDIA SLIDES USING *POWERPOINT*®

Lesson 9.1: Learning Activities

Inserting new slides on an existing presentation
Animating text on a slide
Editing a text or object animation
Animating a graphic object on a slide
Animating the elements of a chart
Previewing animation effects on a slide
Inserting music or sound on a slide
Inserting video on a slide
Setting options for a sound or video to play during a slide show

In Microsoft® *PowerPoint*®, animations are special sound or visual effects used with text or graphic objects to emphasize important points, control the flow of information, and add interest. With animation you can set up the way you want text or objects to appear on your slides. For example, you might specify that:

- Text flies in from the left,
- Lines of text appear by the letter, word, or paragraph, or
- Text or objects dim or change color after the next item appears.

Dave wants to use a Microsoft® *PowerPoint*® slide presentation to introduce a social studies unit on the American Southwest. He plans to create a presentation that not only delivers certain information, but one that his students can use as a model or template for developing their own electronic reports on a state in the American Southwest.

To make his presentation more interesting and engaging, Dave is going to insert multimedia objects and events that will reinforce the presentation content. Open *PowerPoint*® and **Ch9Southwest1.ppt** that you previously loaded onto your own disk or hard disk. Display the slides in **Normal View** (you may close the **Outline Pane** if you do not want it displayed on the screen.)

LESSON 9.1: TUTORIAL

Inserting New Slides on an Existing Presentation

Complete the Southwest presentation by adding two more slides.

1. Move to the last slide in the presentation and insert a new slide. Select **Insert | New Slide** or click **New Slide,** then select the **Object & Text** AutoLayout and click **OK.**

2. To add a picture object to the slide, click once in the object placeholder (do not double-click) and select **Insert | Picture | From File.** Select the file named **Nmpic.gif** from the **PP folder** of the **T3 Practice CD** and click **Insert.** A picture of the state of New Mexico is inserted in the placeholder. Click, drag, and resize the picture as necessary to properly position it in the placeholder on the slide.

3. To add a bulleted list, click in the text placeholder and type the following list of text. Press **ENTER** at the end of each line to create the next bulleted item on the list (do not press **ENTER** after the last item on the list).

- **Nickname: Land of Enchantment**
- **Statehood: January 6, 1912**
- **47th State in the Union**

- **Border States: Arizona, Colorado, Oklahoma, Texas, Utah**
- **Population: 1,819,046 (36th)**
- **Land Area: 121,593 square miles (5th)**

You may need to increase the size of the text placeholder slightly and decrease the size of the object placeholder for the text to fit properly on the slide.

4 To repeat this process for an Arizona slide, first select **Insert | New Slide** or click **New Slide.** Then select the **Object & Text** AutoLayout and click **OK.**

5 To add a picture object to the slide, click once in the object placeholder (do not double-click) and select **Insert | Picture.** Then select **From File** the file Arizpic.gif from the PP folder of the T3 disk, and click **Insert.** A picture of the state of Arizona is inserted in the placeholder. Click drag, and resize the picture as necessary to properly position it in the placeholder on the slide.

6 To add a bulleted list, click in the text placeholder and type the following list of text. Press **ENTER** at the end of each line to create the next bulleted item on the list (do not press **ENTER** after the last item on the list).

- **Nickname: Grand Canyon State**
- **Statehood: February 14, 1912**
- **48th State in the Union**
- **Border States: California, Colorado, Nevada, New Mexico, Utah**
- **Population: 5,130,632 (20th)**
- **Land Area: 113,642 square miles (6th)**

You may need to increase the size of the text placeholder slightly and decrease the size of the object placeholder for the text to fit properly on the slide.

7 Use the built-in chart feature of *PowerPoint*®. Add a slide with a chart illustrating the population of each Southwest state. Select **Insert | New Slide** or click **New Slide** and select the **Chart** AutoLayout. To add a chart object to the slide, double-click in the chart object placeholder. A Microsoft® *Graph* datasheet is displayed on the screen with sample chart information. Clear the existing data from the datasheet (select it and press **DELETE**) and add the population data as shown in the following illustration:

Ch9Southwest1 - Datasheet		A	B	C	D
		Arizona	New Mexico	Oklahoma	Texas
1	Population	5130632	1819046	3450654	20851820
2					
3					
4					

8 Once you have entered the new data in the datasheet, click on the legend for the chart on the slide behind the datasheet to select it, then delete it.

9 To stop updating the datasheet, click on the slide outside of the chart area, and the finished chart is displayed on the slide. Add a title to the slide, **Population by State.**

10 Reorder the slides in the presentation using **Slide Sorter View** so that the state slides (slides 5–8) are in alphabetical order: Arizona, New Mexico, Oklahoma, Texas.

11 Save the presentation as **Ch9Southwest2.ppt.** Use the completed **Ch9Southwest2.ppt** file in the **PP folder** on the **T3 Practice CD** to compare with your solution.

NOTE: Applying animation effects and animation schemes in *Office*® XP *PowerPoint*® 2002 is significantly different than in older versions of the program. In the next several exercises, additional instructions for using *Power-Point*® 2002 are provided.

Animating Text on a Slide

Animation of text allows you to evoke movement and control the timing of movement of animated text on a slide. Move to the third slide in the presentation entitled Land Forms and Climate. Click **Normal View,** and close the **Outline Pane.**

Macintosh®: Select the **Timing** tab and under **Slide Objects Without Animation** point at **Text 2** to highlight and select it. Under **Start animation** click the **Animate** radio button and then click the **On mouse click** radio button. Repeat for **Text 3.**

❶ Select **Slide Show | Custom Animation,** and then click the **Effects tab.**
❷ Under the **Check to animate slide objects** box, click the **Text 2** and **Text 3** check boxes.

In *Office*® XP (*PowerPoint*® 2002):

Animating Text on a Slide

(for step 2)
Select the left text box by pointing and clicking on it. In the **Task Pane** click **Add Effect,** select **Entrance,** and select **Fly In.** Click the down arrow on the **Direction** box and select **From Left.** Repeat for the right text box.

(for steps 3 and 4)
Select the left text box and click the down arrow on the **Start** box and select **On click.** Select the right text and click the down arrow on the **Start** box and select **After Previous.** Click the down arrow on the **Speed** box and select **Medium.**

(for step 5)
On the slide objects list in the **Task Pane,** select the object you want to change and then click the **Re-Order** up-arrow or down-arrow to move the object up or down in the animation order.

(for step 7)
Select **Slide Show | Animation Schemes** and select **Dissolve in** from the list of animation schemes.

❸ Select the **Effects** tab and then under **Entry animation and sound** select **Fly** in the first window and **From Left** in the second. For **Introduce text** select **All at once.**
❹ Click the **Order & Timing** tab, select **Text 2** under Animation order: then select **On mouse click** below start animation. Select **Text 3 Automatically,** and then enter **00:02** seconds to elapse between the previous bulleted time and the current one.

Macintosh®: **Text 2** and **Text 3** are already set to **On mouse click.** To start animation automatically for **Text 3,** highlight **Text 3** under **Animation Order.** On the **Timing** tab click the **Automatically** radio button under **Start animation** and enter **2** seconds to elapse between the previous bulleted time and the current one.

❺ To change the order of animation, select the object you want to change under **Animation order** and then click one of the move arrows to move the object up or down in the list. (DO NOT change the animation order for this slide.) Click **OK** and close the **Animation Effects Toolbar.**
❻ Click **Slide Show | Animation Preview** (menu bar) to view the slide with the selected animation (view it in the pop-up window called **Animation Preview**). Press the mouse button for each of the bulleted items in the text box on the left side of the slide. When all of the bulleted items in the left text box have been displayed, the bulleted items in the right text box will be displayed automatically with a two-second pause between each bulleted item.

7 Using preset animate schemes is a quick way to create basic animation on a slide. Select the object you want to animate and use the **Preset Animation** scheme feature. In **Slide View** move to the next slide, Industry and Economy. Point at and click the bulleted text to select the text box. Select **Slide Show | Preset Animation | Dissolve.** Click **Slide Show | Animation Preview** to view the slide with the selected animation.

Editing a Text or Object Animation

You can modify the animation settings you have applied to a slide element or place-holder.

1 To change the animation setting on the Industry and Economy slide, in **Normal View** select **Slide Show | Custom Animation.**

2 Under **Check to animate slide objects** click **Text 2** to select it. (You can remove the animation from the object by clearing the check box next to the object name, but for our purposes here do not clear the check box.)

Macintosh®: Select the **Timing** tab and under **Animation Order** click **Text 2** to select it. (You can remove the animation from the object by clicking the **Don't animate** radio button under **Start animation.**)

In *Office*® *XP* (*PowerPoint*® 2002):

Editing a Text or Object Animation

(for step 2)
Select the text box by pointing and clicking on it. (You can remove the animation from the object by clicking on **Remove** in the **Task Pane**, but for our purposes here do not remove the animation.)

(for step 3)
Select **Text 2** from the objects list in the **Task Pane** and click **Change.** Select **Entrance** and select **More Effects.** In the **Change Entrance Effect** box drag the scroll bar down to the **Exciting** category and select **Spiral In** and click **OK.**

(for step 4)
Click the down arrow on the **Text 2** box and select **Effect Options.** Click the down arrow beside **After animation** and select the **light blue** box to change the bulleted item to **light blue** (You may have to select **More Colors** and find a **light blue** on the color palette) and click **OK.**

(for step 5)
Click **Play** in the **Task Pane** to preview the changes you made.

---

3 Select the **Effects** tab and click the down arrow under **Entry animation and sound** and select **Spiral.**

4 Click the down arrow under **After animation** and select the **light blue** box to change the bulleted item to **light blue** when the next bulleted item appears.

5 To preview the changes you made, click **Preview.** Then click **OK.**

Animating a Graphic Object on a Slide

Animation of graphics allows you to evoke movement and control the timing of movement of the graphic element on a slide. Move to the slide entitled Oklahoma in the presentation and display the slide in **Normal View.**

1 Select **Slide Show | Custom Animation** and then click the **Effects** tab.

In *Office*® XP (*PowerPoint*® 2002):

Animating Graphics on a Slide

(for step 2)
Select the Oklahoma state graphic by pointing and clicking on it.

(for step 3)
In the **Task Pane** click **Add Effect**, select **Entrance**, and select **Dissolve In** from the **Change Entrance Effects** box and click **OK.**

(for step 4)
Click the down arrow on the **Start** box and select **With Previous.**

(for step 5)
Click **Play** in the **Task Pane** to preview the animation setting.

(for step 6)
Select the left text box by pointing and clicking on it. In the **Task Pane** click **Add Effect**, select **Entrance**, and select **Checkerboard.**

(for step 7)
Click **Play** in the **Task Pane** to preview the animation setting.

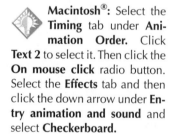

Macintosh®: Select the **Timing** tab under **Slide Objects Without Animation.** Click **Picture Frame 4** to select it. Under **Start animation** click the **Animate** radio button and then click the **Automatically** radio button.

Macintosh®: Select the **Timing** tab under **Animation Order.** Click **Text 2** to select it. Then click the **On mouse click** radio button. Select the **Effects** tab and then click the down arrow under **Entry animation and sound** and select **Checkerboard.**

➋ Under **Check to animate slide objects** click the **Picture Frame 4** check box to animate the Oklahoma state graphic.

➌ Select the **Effects** tab and click the down arrow under **Entry animation and sound** and select **Dissolve.**

➍ Select **Order & Timing** and under **Start animation** select **Automatically.** (This step has already been completed for Macintosh®.)

➎ To preview the animation setting, click **Preview.**

➏ Now animate the bulleted list on the slide. Under **Check to animate slide objects** click **Text 2.** Select the **Effects** tab and then click the down arrow under **Entry animation and sound** and select **Checkerboard | across.**

➐ Click **OK** and click **Slide Show | Animation Preview** to present the slide with the selected animation.

Animating the Elements of a Chart

To increase interest in a chart, you can animate the individual elements of a chart created with Microsoft® *Graph* or Microsoft® *Excel.* In the following steps you will animate the population chart so that each bar appears in sequence when the slide is displayed. Move to the slide entitled Population by State and display the slide in **Normal View.**

Macintosh®: Select the **Timing** tab under **Slide Objects Without Animation.** Click **Chart 2** to select it. Under **Start animation** click the **Animate** radio button and then click the **Automatically** radio button. Click the **Chart Effects** tab.

➊ Select **Slide Show | Custom Animation** and then click the **Chart Effects** tab.

➋ Under **Check to animate slide objects** click the **Chart 2** check box to animate the population chart.

➌ Click the down arrow under **Introduce chart elements** and select **by Element in Series.**

➍ Click the down arrow under **Entry animation and sound** and select **Wipe | Up.**

➎ Select **Order & Timing** and under **Start animation** select **Automatically** (for Macintosh® this action has already been performed).

➏ To preview the animation setting, click **Preview.** Then click **OK.**

In *Office*® *XP* (*PowerPoint*® 2002):

Animating the Elements of a Chart

(for step 2)
Select the chart by pointing and clicking on it.

(for step 3)
In the **Task Pane** click **Add Effect,** select **Entrance,** and select **Wipe** from the **Change Entrance Effects** box and click **OK.**

(for step 4)
Click the down arrow on the **Chart 2** box and select **Effect Options.** Click the **Chart Animation** tab, click the down arrow after the **Group chart** box and select **By series** from the list, uncheck **Animate grid and legend** and click **OK.**

(for step 5)
Click the down arrow on the **Start** box and select **After Previous.**

(for step 6)
Click **Play** in the **Task Pane** to preview the animation setting.

Previewing Animation Effects on a Slide

You can preview the animation settings on any slide using a menu command, as you have already done. The slide must have custom animation settings in order to preview. Move to the slide entitled Population by State and display the slide in **Normal View.**

➊ Select **Slide Show | Animation Preview.** The animation plays in the **Animation Preview** window that appears. To replay the effects, click the **Animation Preview** window.

➋ To preview the animations for multiple slides in the slide show, switch to **Slide Sorter View.** Select slides **2–9** by clicking slide **2,** pressing and holding **SHIFT,** pointing at slide **9,** then click **Animation Preview.**

Macintosh®**:** You cannot perform **Animation Preview** from **Slide Sorter View**.

In *Office*® *XP* (*PowerPoint*® 2002):

Previewing Animation Effects on a Slide

(for step 1)
Select **Slide Show | Custom Animation** and click **Play** in the **Task Pane** to preview the animation on the selected slide.

(for step 2)
Switch to **Slide Sorter** view. Select slides **2–9** by clicking slide **2,** pressing **SHIFT,** pointing at slide **9,** then click **Play** in the **Task Pane** to preview the animation on the selected slides.

Inserting Music or Sound on a Slide

PowerPoint® slide presentations will play audio files. Audio objects may be controlled by mouse clicks or play automatically when a slide is presented. *PowerPoint*®

allows the audio file to continue while the slide show is presented or to stop when the slide show transitions to the next slide. Move to the first slide in the slide show and switch to **Normal View.**

❶ Select **Insert | Movies and Sounds | Sound from File,** and then select the file named **SWmusic.mid** from the **PP folder** of the **T3 Practice CD** by double-clicking on the file name.

❷ A message is displayed asking if you want the sound to play automatically when you run the slide. Click **Yes.** A sound icon appears in the middle of the slide. Drag the icon down to the right hand corner of the slide, and you will hide it later.

❸ To preview the sound in **Normal View,** double-click the sound icon. To stop the audio, press **ESC.**

❹ Now play the presentation using **Slide Show** view and after it has played a few seconds, click the mouse button or **ENTER** to advance to the next slide in the presentation. Notice the music stops when you advance to the next slide. (You may have to click the mouse button or press **ENTER** twice to stop the music and advance to the next slide.)

Inserting Video on a Slide

PowerPoint® slide presentations will play animated graphics and movie files. Movie presentations may be controlled by mouse clicks or play automatically when a slide is presented.

❶ Move to the first slide in the slide show and display it in **Normal View.** Change the color scheme of the presentation by selecting **Format | Slide Color Scheme** and select the color scheme with the **black** background and click **Apply to All.** The new color scheme will also adjust the colors of the chart on the last slide of the presentation.

❷ To improve the appearance of the video graphic on the slide, you need to change the slide color scheme.

In *Office*® *XP* (*PowerPoint*® 2002):

Inserting Video on a Slide

(for step 2)
Select **Format | Slide Design** and then select **Color Schemes** in the **Task Pane.** Select the color scheme with the **black** background. The new color scheme will also adjust the colors of the chart on the last slide of the presentation.

---

❸ Select **Insert | Movies and Sounds | Movie from File** and then select the file **Globe.avi** from the **PP folder** of the **T3 Practice CD** by double-clicking on the file name.

❹ A message is displayed asking if you want the movie to play automatically when you run the slide. Click **Yes.** A movie object appears in the middle of the slide.

❺ To preview the movie in **Normal View,** double-click the movie icon. The movie runs for about four seconds (the globe spins) and then stops.

❻ Drag the object down underneath the title on the slide so that it is centered in the lower half of the slide.

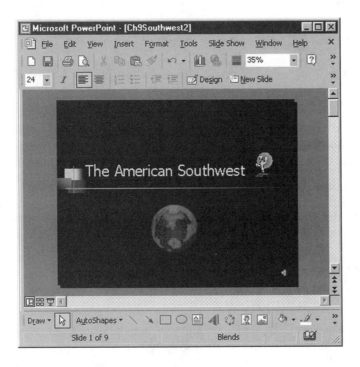

❼ Play the presentation using **Slide Show** view. You may need to click the mouse button (or press **ENTER**) to start the sound and/or start the movie. Then click the mouse button (or press **ENTER**) again to advance to the next slide. Press **ESC** to return to **Normal View.** In the next step you will change the settings of both slide elements to cause them to play simultaneously when the slide is displayed.

Setting Options for a Sound or Video to Play During a Slide Show

You can modify the options of audio clips and movies to set the order and timing of play, cause them to continue when you advance to subsequent slides, cause them to play with a mouse click, and set animation effects. Suppose you want to take advantage of the multimedia capabilities of *PowerPoint*® to increase student interest prior to starting the presentation. You want the title slide to be displayed on the screen with the globe spinning and the music playing until you actually begin your instruction or presentation.

❶ Move to the first slide; display it in **Normal View.** Select **Slide Show | Custom Animation.** Notice that all slide elements that can be animated are listed on the **Custom Animation** dialog box in numerical order in the order that they were added to the slide. The sound clip is labeled **Media 3** and the movie clip is labeled **Media 4.** The **Order & Timing** for both elements is set to **Automatically,** so this requires one element to complete its animation before the next element begins. Since animation for each slide element is set in relation to the other elements, you need to set options for each multimedia element.

In *Office*® *XP* (*PowerPoint*® 2002):

Setting Options for a Sound or Video to Play During a Slide Show

(for step 1)

Move to the first slide; display it in **Normal View.** All slide elements that can be animated are listed in the **Task Pane** by the actual file names in the order they were added to the slide. The **Start** for both elements is set to **After Previous,** so this requires one element to complete its animation before the next element begins.

(for step 2)

Select **Slide Show | Custom Animation** and click the down arrow on the **SWMusic.mid** object listed in the **Task Pane** and select **Effect Options.**

(for new step 3)

Click the **Effect** tab and click the **After current slide** radio button under **Stop Playing** and click **OK.**

(for step 5)

Select **Slide Show | Custom Animation** and click the down arrow on the **Globe.avi** object listed in the **Task Pane** and select **Effect Options.** Click the **Effect** tab and click the **After current slide** radio button under **Stop Playing.** Click the **Timing** tab, click the down arrow on the **Repeat** box, and select **Until End of Slide** and click **OK.** (Be certain that the **Start** box is set to **After Previous.**)

(for step 8)

Select **Slide Show | Custom Animation** and click the down arrow on the **SWMusic.mid** object listed in the **Task Pane** and select **Effect Options.** Under **Sound Settings** click in the check box, **Hide while not playing,** and click **OK.**

Macintosh®: Select the **Timing** tab and under **Slide Objects Without Animation** click **Media** to select it. Under **Start animation** click the **Animate** radio button and then click the **Automatically** radio button. Click the **Play Settings** tab.

② To cause the music to continue to play while the movie plays, select **Slide Show | Custom Animation** and select **Media 3** from the slide objects list and then select the **Multimedia Settings** tab.

③ Click the **Continue slide show** option and click **OK.** Now the movie will play while the audio clip is playing. Play the presentation using **Slide Show View** and after it has played a few seconds, click the mouse button to start the movie. Notice that the music continues when you play the movie.

④ Click the mouse button again and the slide show advances to the next slide and the music stops. Press **ESC** to return to **Slide View** and go back to the title slide (the first slide).

⑤ To cause the movie (and the music) to continue to play until you advance to the next slide, select **Slide Show | Custom Animation** and select **Media 4** from the slide objects list and then select the **Multimedia Settings** tab (**Play Settings** on Macintosh®) Click **More Options** and select both **Loop until stopped** and **Rewind movie when done playing.** Now the movie will rewind and continue to play until you advance to the next slide. (Be certain that **Automatically** is selected for **Start Animation** for both multimedia elements.) Click **OK** and **OK** again.

⑥ Play the presentation using **Slide Show View.** Notice that the music continues when you play the movie and the movie continues to rewind and play. Let the slide run for a few seconds, and then click the mouse button again and the slide show advances to the next slide and the music and movie stop.

7 Press **ESC** to return to **Slide View,** and go back to the title slide (the first slide).

8 You can also hide multimedia elements so they are not displayed until played. Select **Slide Show | Custom Animation.** Select **Media 3** from the slide objects list and then select **Multimedia Settings** (**Play Settings** on Macintosh®) Click in the **Hide while not playing** check box.

9 Play the presentation using **Slide Show View.** Notice that the music icon is now hidden while playing. Let the slide run for a few seconds, and then click the mouse button again and the slide show advances to the next slide and the music and movie stop.

10 Press **ESC** to return to **Slide View,** and go back to the title slide.

11 Save the presentation as **Ch9Southwest3** and exit *PowerPoint*®. Use the file **Ch9Southwest3.ppt** found in the **PP folder** on the **T3 Practice CD** to compare with your solution.

FOLLOW-UP PRACTICE PROJECTS

For more practice on adding multimedia features to a presentation, start *PowerPoint*® and open the presentation file **Ch9Southwest3.ppt** that you created in this lesson. Perform each of the following practice projects using this presentation. When you have completed the projects, exit *PowerPoint*®.

1 **Animate Slides using Slide View.** You can use **Slide Sorter View** to animate the remainder of the slides in **Ch9Southwest3.ppt.** View the presentation using **Slide Sorter View.** The Slide Transition icon indicates if a transition is present on the slide. (Slide transitions are demonstrated in the next lesson.) The Preset Animation icon indicates if animation effects are present on the slide. Click the **Preset Animation** icon under slide **3.** The animation effects on the slide are previewed.

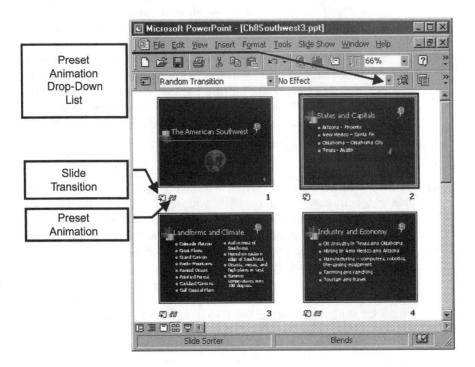

Notice that some slides have animation effects and some do not. Select slide **2** by clicking on it and select **Slide Show | Preset Animation.** Select an animation effect from the list. The animation effect is previewed when you select it. If you do not like the effect, select another one from the **Preset Animation** drop-down list. Repeat this process for each of the slides that do not have animation effects. Save the presentation as **Ch9Southwest4.ppt** then close it. Use **Ch9Southwest4.ppt** in the **PP folder** on the **T3 Practice CD** to compare with your solution.

②   OPTIONAL: Insert a CD Audio Track on a Slide. Add interest to your presentation by preceding it with music that is appealing to the audience viewing the presentation. You can set the stage for your presentation by putting the title slide on the screen and set it to launch a song on an audio CD. This procedure works best with an audio CD so you can test if it is working correctly, but you do not need to insert an audio CD in the CD-ROM drive to perform this procedure. If you have an audio CD with several song titles on it, choose a song to use and then determine the track the song is on, then insert the CD into the CD-ROM drive.

a. Open **Ch9Southwest4.ppt** and view the title slide (the first slide) using **Slide View.**

b. Delete the existing audio effect from the slide by clicking on the sound icon in the right-hand corner of the slide to select it and then press **DELETE.**

c. Select **Insert | Movies and Sounds** and select **Play CD Audio Track.**

d. In the **Movie and Sound Options** dialog box, enter the track number in the **Start** field and one track higher in the **End** box of **Play CD audio track.** Click **OK.**

e. When the message displays asking if you want the CD to play automatically in the slide show, click **No** so the CD will play only when you click the CD icon during a slide show. A CD icon appears on the slide.

f. Run the slide show and click the CD icon to start playing the song. When the music starts, click the slide one more time to start the movie effect (the spinning globe). When you click the mouse button, the presentation will advance to the next slide and the music will stop playing. (You may have to click more than once to get the slide show to advance to the next slide.)

g. To change play settings, for example, to change the tracks you want to play, select **Slide Show | Custom Animation | Multimedia Settings.** Click the **More Options** button. **NOTE:** When you remove the audio CD from the CD-ROM drive or when you close the presentation, it may cause the presentation to lose the track settings. You can force the CD effect to find the track setting by increasing the End track and then setting it back.

③ Develop a lesson idea or plan that is targeted for the grade level you teach or plan to teach related to the activity you just completed. It should describe teaching students how to use the multimedia features of *PowerPoint*® for communicating information. Add it to the **Lesson Plans ePortfolio.**

④ Develop a lesson idea or plan that is targeted for the grade level you teach or plan to teach on a subject of your own choosing. It should describe developing a *PowerPoint*® presentation to be used as a template or model for students to use for communicating information for an electronic report on a particular subject or theme. Add it to the **Lesson Plans ePortfolio.**

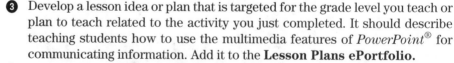

LESSON 9.2: CONTROLLING SLIDE TRANSITIONS AND HYPERLINKS USING *POWERPOINT*®

Lesson 9.2: Learning Activities

Adding transitions to a slide show
Creating a hyperlink to a location in the current presentation
Inserting action buttons on a slide
Creating a hyperlink to a Web page
Setting actions on text or object hyperlinks

To increase the potential for effectively communicating the information in his American Southwest lesson, Dave is going to insert slide transitions that build interest and maintain attention in the lesson. Additionally, he plans to add hyperlinks that will provide additional information resources for students to research when they create their own electronic reports.

Transitions are special effects used to introduce a slide during a slide show or presentation. Transitions cause slides to be displayed using various effects including dissolves, fades, wipes, uncovers, and several other effects. You can control the speed at which transitions occur and other multimedia features, such as the inclusion of sound and automatic execution. You can change the transition effect to indicate a new section of a presentation or to emphasize a certain slide.

You can add hyperlinks to a presentation to automatically advance to a variety of locations, including a subsequent or previous slide in the current presentation, a slide in a different presentation, a Microsoft® *Word* document or Microsoft® *Excel* worksheet, or an Internet, intranet, or e-mail address. Hyperlinks can be created from any slide element including text, shapes, tables, graphs, and pictures. Hyperlinks become active when you run your slide show. Text that represents a hyperlink appears underlined and in a color that coordinates with the color scheme. Like a Web browser, the color of the hyperlink changes after you click it and advance to a new location. Thus, you can tell which hyperlinks you have already selected.

Microsoft® *PowerPoint*® contains several ready-made action buttons to insert in a presentation for which you can define hyperlinks. Action buttons consist of graphic shapes such as right and left arrows that you place on a slide and use when you want to include commonly understood symbols for going to next, previous, first, and last slides. These buttons are especially useful for a self-running presentation at a kiosk or for a presentation used for individualized or self-paced instruction. *PowerPoint*® also has action buttons for playing movies or sounds.

Open *PowerPoint*® and the **Ch9Southwest4.ppt** presentation document. Click **Slide Sorter View** to display all the slides in this presentation.

LESSON 9.2: TUTORIAL

Adding Transitions to a Slide Show

Animations relate to the elements of a particular slide, while transitions relate to movement from slide to slide. Since transitions occur at the presentation level, one good way to add transitions is in **Slide Sorter View.**

❶   Select **Edit | Select All** to create transitions for all the slides in the presentation.
❷   Select **Slide Show | Slide Transition** to establish slide transitions for the presentation.

❸ In the **Effect** box, click the down arrow and scroll to the bottom of the drop-down list and select **Random Transition.** Click the **Apply to All** button to place a transition on all slides in the presentation.

In *Office*® *XP* (*PowerPoint*® *2002*):

Adding Transitions to a Slide Show

(for step 3)
In the list underneath **Apply to selected slides** in the **Task Pane,** click the down arrow, scroll to the bottom of the drop-down list, and select **Random Transition.** Click the **Apply to All** button to place a transition on all slides in the presentation.

(for step 4)
While still in **Slide Sorter** view, select all the slides in the show and view the transitions by clicking the **Play** button in the **Task Pane.**

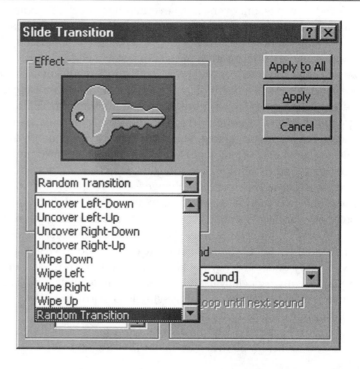

❹ While still in **Slide Sorter View,** select all the slides in the show and view the transitions by selecting **Slide Show I Animation Preview.** The preview plays the slide show with the transition and animations applied to each slide.

Creating a Hyperlink to a Location in the Current Presentation

You can add a hyperlink to an object or element on a slide to allow you to navigate through a presentation with hyperlinks. Set Slide 2 (States and Capitals) of the presentation to **Slide View** by double-clicking on it in **Slide Sorter View.**

❶ Select the first bulleted line of text on the slide Arizona-Phoenix, to represent the hyperlink.

2   Select **Insert | Hyperlink** and select the button **Place in This Document** on the left side of the **Insert Hyperlink** dialog box.

3   From the list select the **Arizona** slide and click **OK**.

Macintosh®: Click **Select** beside **Named location in file (optional)** in the **Insert Hyperlink** dialog box.

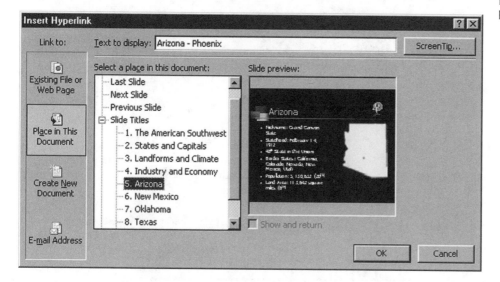

4   To preview how a hyperlink will appear in the slide show, click **Slide Show** at the lower left of the *PowerPoint*® window.

5   Create a hyperlink to the corresponding state slide for each of the states listed on the States and Capitals slide, then test each link to determine that it works correctly.

6   A problem you may notice with these hyperlinks is that after you make the link there is no way to return to where you were. In the next step you will learn to add ready-made action buttons with hyperlinks to the next, previous, first, and last slides.

Inserting Action Buttons on a Slide

Action buttons are ready-made buttons that appear to be "pressed" when you click them during a slide show. Action buttons are useful for navigational purposes. You can place buttons on every slide by placing buttons on the **Slide Master.**

Macintosh®: Select **Last slide viewed** from the list of action buttons.

1   You can insert a **Return** button on each of the state slides to return to the slide with the hyperlink source. To insert a **Return** Action Button on the Arizona slide, move to slide **5** (Arizona) and select **Normal View.**

2   Select **Slide Show Action Buttons** and then select the **Return** button. When you click the **Action Button: Return** a cross-hatch cursor will be displayed. Place the cross-hatch on the slide and click the slide.

3   In the **Action Settings** dialog box, click in the **Play Sound** check box and select **Chime** from the drop-down list of sounds to accompany the mouse action of clicking the **Return** button. Next, select the **Mouse Over** tab, click in the **Play Sound** check box, and select **Whoosh** from the drop-down list of sounds to accompany the mouse action of dragging the mouse over the **Return** button without clicking it. Click **OK** to accept the button action settings. Please see the **Action Settings** dialog box on the following page.

4   Drag the button down near the lower right corner of the slide and resize the button to a smaller size. To maintain the shape's width-to-height ratio, hold down **SHIFT** as you drag the shape.

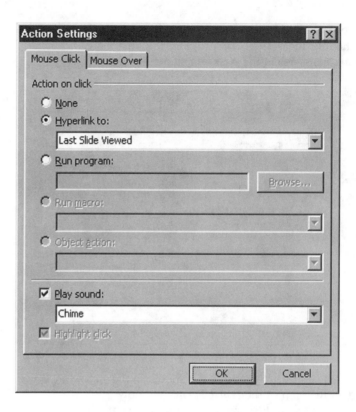

⑤ To format the button further, double-click on the button. In the **Format AutoShape** dialog box select **Gold** for the **Fill Color** and **No Line** for the **Line Color.** Click **OK.**

⑥ Test the button by moving to the States and Capitals slide and running the slide show. Click the mouse button to display the first item of the bulleted list and click the link to the Arizona slide. Display the items on the bulleted list of the Arizona slide by clicking the mouse button, and then click the **Return** button.

⑦ When the button works correctly, select it and copy and paste it on the New Mexico, Oklahoma, and Texas slides.

⑧ Save the presentation as **Ch9Southwest5.ppt.**

Creating a Hyperlink to a Web Page

You can create a hyperlink to any type of existing file, such as a Microsoft® *Word* document, Microsoft® *PowerPoint*® presentation, Microsoft® *Excel* workbook, Microsoft® *Access* database, or Web page.

❶ Create a hyperlink to a Web page from the state graphic on each of the state slides. To link to the home page of the State of Arizona (http://www.state.az.us) from the Arizona slide, move to slide **5** (Arizona) and select **Normal View.**

Macintosh®**:** In the field Link to file or URL enter **http://www.state. az.us.**

❷ Select the Arizona graphic by clicking on it, and then click **Insert | Hyperlink.** Click **Existing File or Web Page.** In the **Type the file or Web page name** box enter **http://www.state.az.us.**

❸ To assign a tip to be displayed when you rest the mouse pointer on the hyperlink, click the **Screen Tip** button and type **State of Arizona Home Page.** Click **OK** and **OK** again.

❹ Test the hyperlink by running the slide in **Slide Show View.** Rest the mouse pointer on the Arizona graphic, and the mouse pointer changes to a hand and a screen tip should be displayed. If your computer is connected to the Internet, click on the graphic and test the hyperlink to determine if it accesses the Web page. Close the browser window to return to *PowerPoint*®. Press **ESC** to return to **Normal View.**

5 Attach each of the following hyperlinks to the state graphics for each of the state pages and insert a screen tip: **New Mexico: http://www.state.nm.us; Oklahoma: http://www.state.ok.us; Texas: http://www.state.tx.us.**

6 Save the presentation as **Ch9Southwest5.ppt.**

Setting Actions on Text or Object Hyperlinks

Action settings can help you emphasize hyperlinks in your presentations using Action Settings on the Slide Show menu. With action settings you can specify that a sound should play when the pointer rests on the text or object during a slide show. If the hyperlink is an object, you can also specify that the object be highlighted when the pointer rests on it.

1 To create action settings on the hyperlinks you created in the previous step, move to slide **5** (Arizona) and Click **Normal View.** Click on the Arizona graphic to select it and then select **Slide Show | Action Settings.**

2 Click in the **Play Sound** check box and select **Chime** from the pop-up list of sounds to accompany the mouse action of clicking the object. To highlight the object when the mouse clicks on it, click in the **Highlight click** check box.

3 Select the **Mouse Over** tab, click in the **Play Sound** check box, and select **Whoosh** from the pop-up list of sounds to accompany the mouse action of dragging the mouse over the object without clicking it. To highlight the object when the pointer rests on it, click in the **Highlight when mouse over** check box. Click **OK** to accept the object action settings.

4 Do not specify a hyperlink in the **Hyperlink to** box on the **Mouse Over** tab, because it is possible to go to a link when you really do not want to by accidentally resting the pointer on a hyperlink during your slide show. It is better to assign hyperlinks only on the **Mouse Click** tab or by clicking **Insert Hyperlink** and then using **Mouse Over** primarily for feedback.

5 Save the presentation as **Ch9Southwest5.ppt** and exit *PowerPoint*®. Use the completed **Ch9Southwest5.ppt** in the **PP folder** on the **T3 Practice CD** to compare with your solution.

FOLLOW-UP PRACTICE PROJECTS

For more practice on slide transitions, open *PowerPoint*® and the presentation file **Ch9Graphics.ppt** that you previously loaded onto your own disk or hard drive. The presentation file consists of 12 slides with graphics that include a one-minute audio file that automatically runs when the presentation starts. Perform each of the following projects using this presentation. When you have completed the practice exercise, exit *PowerPoint*®.

Self-running presentations are commonly used for presentations that are highly graphical. For example, a self-running presentation may consist of photographs from a class field trip set to a musical theme. Self-running presentations are a great way to communicate information without having to have someone available to run a slide show. For example, you might want to set up a presentation to run unattended at an open house or in a booth or kiosk at a conference. With self-running presentations you can make most controls unavailable so that users cannot make changes to the presentation. A self-running presentation restarts when it is finished and also when it has been idle on a manually advanced slide for longer than five minutes.

When creating a self-running presentation, there are two ways you can set the length of time a slide appears on the screen. One way is to set a time manually for each slide, and then run the slide show and view the timings you set. The other way is to use the rehearsal feature, where you can record timings automatically as you rehearse. You can also adjust the timings you have already set and then rehearse the new ones. For this exercise you will set all slides to be displayed for the same amount of time and continue to recycle until the presentation is manually stopped.

You can set timings for your slides before you rehearse, or you can set them automatically while you rehearse. If you set them before you rehearse, you will find it easiest to work in **Slide Sorter View** where you see miniatures of each slide in your presentation. You can set the timing for one or more selected slides by clicking **Slide Transition** on the **Slide Sorter Toolbar** and then entering the number of seconds you want the slides to appear on the screen.

❶ To set up the presentation as a self-running show, begin by selecting **Slide Show | Set Up Show** and then click **Browsed at a kiosk (full screen).** When you click this option, **Loop continuously until Esc** is automatically selected.

   a. To set timings for all the slides in the presentation, select **Slide Show | Slide Transition.** Since there are 12 slides and the time of the audio file is one minute, you can set each of the slides to show for five seconds to get through the presentation one time per each play of the audio file. On the **Slide Transition** dialog box set the **Effect** to **Random Transition** and **Advance Automatically after 00:05** seconds and click the **Apply to All** button.

   b. Run the slide show and see how the slide transition timings synchronize with the length of the audio file. If the audio finishes before all the slides have cycled through, you can use **Slide Show | Slide Transition** and lower the timing on some of the slides.

❷ Another way to set the timings on slides is to rehearse your timings. Select **Slide Show | Rehearse Timings.** You can use the buttons in the **Rehearsal** dialog box to advance to the next slide, pause between slides, and repeat a slide. *PowerPoint*® keeps track of how long each slide appears and sets the timing accordingly. When you finish, you can accept the timings or you can try again.

a. When you have the timings set for the presentation, you are ready to save it as a slide show. The file extension for a presentation is .ppt. The extension for a file saved as a slide show is .pps. When you open this type of file from your desktop, it will automatically start as a slide show. *PowerPoint*® closes when the show ends, and you return to the desktop. If you start the show from within *PowerPoint*®, the presentation opens and can be edited. To set the presentation to automatically open as a slide show, select **File | Save As** and enter the file name **Ch9GraphicsAutoRun.**

b. In the **Save as type** list, click the down arrow and select *PowerPoint*® **Show,** and click **Save.**

c. To run the slide show, exit *PowerPoint*® and then locate the file name **Ch9GraphicsAutoRun.pps** and double-click it. The slide show should run and then recycle and start over again until you press **ESC** to stop the show. Use **Ch9GraphicsAutorun.pps** in the **PP folder** on the **T3 Practice CD** to compare with your solution.

❸ Develop a lesson idea or plan that is targeted for the grade level you teach or plan to teach. It should describe teaching students how to design and create a self-running *PowerPoint*® show for communicating information for an electronic report on a particular subject or theme. Add it to the **Lesson Plans ePortfolio.**

LESSON 9.3: PUBLISHING A PRESENTATION ON THE WEB USING *POWERPOINT*®

Lesson 9.3: Learning Activities

Preparing a presentation for Web publication
Publishing a presentation to the Web
Updating a Web presentation after you publish it

To publish a presentation on the Web means to create a copy of a presentation as Web pages in Hypertext Markup Language (HTML) format and place it on a computer that hosts Web pages on the Internet. You can publish copies of the same presentation to different locations (or Web servers). You can publish a complete presentation, a custom show, a single slide, or a range of slides as Web pages.

PowerPoint® provides a simple and easy way to create Web pages either from one or more slides in a presentation that are ready and available for posting on a Web server. Even if you do not publish a presentation on a Web server, it is still viewable with a Web browser program such as Microsoft® *Internet Explorer*, and saving it as Web pages makes it more transportable to other computers and available for viewing on a computer that does not have *PowerPoint*® installed on it.

Dave has put a lot of time and effort into creating this social studies unit on the American Southwest using a *PowerPoint*® slide presentation. Since this introductory unit contains a considerable amount of content and hyperlinks to several Web sites that students will use to create their electronic reports, he wants this unit available to students after he has finished presenting the lesson so they can access the information in the lesson to prepare their electronic reports on the American Southwest.

Dave decides to publish his presentation on the Web so students will have access to it at home or during class. Open *PowerPoint®* and the **Ch9Southwest5.ppt** presentation. Click **Slide View** to display the slides in this presentation in **Slide View,** and move to the first slide in the presentation by using the slide scroll bar.

Lesson 9.3: Tutorial

Preparing a Presentation for Web Publication

When preparing a presentation for Web publication, some design and formatting issues must be considered concerning why you are publishing the presentation on the Internet. If your purpose for publishing includes limited access by yourself (or other experts in the content area) to use it as a presentation to a group using a Web browser program instead of *PowerPoint®*, then you may want to retain the multimedia and animation features of the presentation in the Web pages. If your purpose for publishing is to provide content for others to browse for informational, instructional, or research purposes, then you may want to remove some of the multimedia or animation features from the presentation that may cause confusion or slow processing when to others are navigating your Web presentation.

Since Dave's purpose for publishing the American Southwest presentation is to make the information available to his students on the Web, he will need to eliminate some of the multimedia features. (When you save a presentation as a Web page, *PowerPoint®* gives you the option to retain or eliminate animation.) Most of the multimedia effects and navigation features you placed in the American Southwest presentation will not be useful and may be confusing to students browsing the presentation for information or research purposes. For example, you would not want Web surfers to have to click the mouse for each item in a bulleted list; you would want the bulleted list to be displayed all at once.

The Web page version of the presentation will create its own form of navigation, so internal navigation links or buttons are not necessary. Additionally, backgrounds and text colors used in the presentation may not be appropriate for Web pages.

❶ To remove the multimedia effects on slide **1,** click on each multimedia object (the globe and the CD icon) to select it and press **DELETE.**

❷ To remove the internal navigation links on slide **2,** click each bulleted item on the slide, click **Insert Hyperlink** on the **Standard Toolbar,** and then click **Remove Link** in the **Edit Hyperlink** dialog box. You will know the link is removed when the underline disappears.

❸ To remove the action (**Return**) button on slide **5** (Arizona), click **Return** to highlight it then press **DELETE.** Do not remove the hyperlinks to Web pages attached to each of the state graphics. Remove the **Return** action button on each of the other state slides (New Mexico, Oklahoma, and Texas).

❹ Since Web pages are usually viewed on a computer monitor and not projected on a large screen, a light colored or white background is more pleasing to the Web surfer. To set the background color of the presentation to a more appropriate color for Web pages, select **Format | Slide Color Scheme** and select a color scheme with a **white** background. Then click **Apply to All** to change all slides in the presentation.

❺ Save the presentation as **Ch9Southwest6.ppt.**

Publishing a Presentation to the Web

Once the presentation has been prepared for Web publication, publishing a presentation as a Web page is as simple as saving the file as a Web page.

❶ To publish a prepared presentation as a Web page, select **File | Save as Web Page.**

❷ In the **File name** box, enter **Ch9SouthwestWWW** for the name of the Web page, and save it in an appropriate folder (the folder where your presentation files are located).

❸ Change the page title by clicking on the **Change Title** button and naming the presentation as **The American Southwest Home Page.** Click **OK.**

Macintosh®: Select **File | Save as HTML.** A Web page design wizard appears and prompts you for information about the Web page(s). Accept all the defaults by clicking the **Next** button, except on the information page window enter your e-mail address. On the **Finish** page select an appropriate location on your computer for the Web page folder and enter **Ch9SouthwestWWW** as the folder name. After the presentation has been published to the folder, select the **Ch9Southwest-WWW** folder and double-click on the **index.htm** file to view the presentation. Continue at step 3.

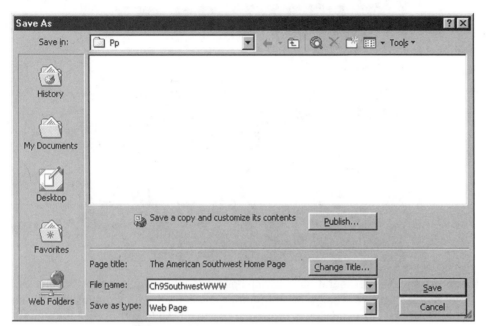

❹ To save the presentation as a Web page, click **Publish.** In the **Publish as Web Page** dialog box, click the **Complete presentation** check box and click the **Open published Web page in browser** check box (see example on the following page). With these settings all the slides in the presentation will be published. A source file named **Ch9SouthwestWWW.htm** is created for the Web presentation.

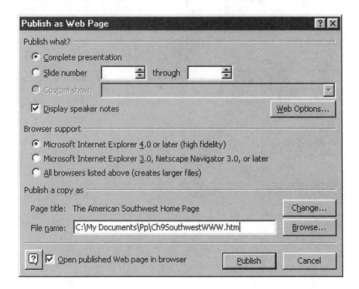

❺ The default setting for publishing Web presentations is to create a folder with the file name plus "_file" (for example, **Ch9SouthwestWWW_file**). The folder contains a Web page for each slide and the associated multimedia files. The default browser will be opened when you publish the page so you can view the Web presentation.

6 To select additional Web page formatting and display options, click **Web Options.** Deselect **Show slide animation while browsing** to turn off animation features of the presentation.

7 In the drop-down list of the **Colors** box, select **Presentation colors (text color)** to match navigation control colors with the text colors on the slides (see the following example). Click **OK.**

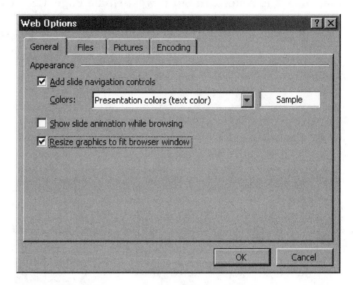

8 To save the presentation as a Web page using the settings you have selected, click **Publish.** The Web presentation is created with a navigation frame down the left-hand side in order to move to any slide in the presentation. Additionally, a navigation bar at the bottom of the Web page allows you to move sequentially, slide by slide, through the presentation. The Web formatting settings you have selected are preserved with the source file. See the example below.

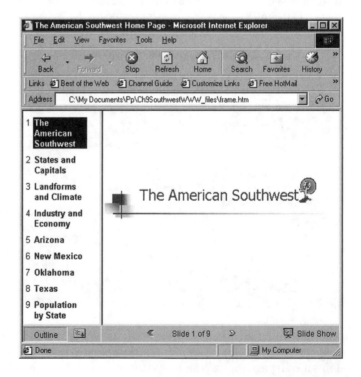

❾ Close the Web browser window and save the presentation source file as **Ch9Southwest6.ppt,** and exit *PowerPoint*®. Use the completed **Ch9Southwest6.ppt** in the **PP folder** on the **T3 Practice CD** to compare with your solution.

Updating a Web Presentation After You Publish It

You can use *PowerPoint*® like a Web page editor to update the Web presentation source file (.htm), or you can update the *PowerPoint*® presentation file and re-publish the presentation. When you publish the source file again, all of the original **Publish as Web Page** dialog box settings for that source file are preserved. The best method is to update the *PowerPoint*® presentation file and republish it.

❶ To make updates to the Web page, open the source presentation file **Ch9Southwest6.ppt.**

❷ On slide **1** (the title slide) click in the title placeholder, and change the title to **The American Southwest Home Page** (press **ENTER** between the words "Southwest" and "Home", and increase the size of text box to format it appropriately on the slide).

❸ Republish the presentation by selecting **File | Save as Web Page.** Use the same file name, **Ch9SouthwestWWW,** so that your Web page file will always be the latest update. Click **Publish** and then **Publish.**

❹ View your Web presentation in the Web browser window.

❺ Close the Web browser window and save the presentation source file, **Ch9Southwest6.ppt,** and exit *PowerPoint*®.

FOLLOW-UP PRACTICE PROJECTS

For more practice on publishing a presentation on the Web, open *PowerPoint*® and the presentation file **Ch9Southwest6.ppt.** You will add text links to your

Macintosh®: Before re-publishing the presentation, delete the **Ch9SouthwestWWW** folder by dragging it to the trash can. Then select **File | Save as HTML** and proceed through the Web page design wizard again. Save the presentation in a folder named **Ch9SouthwestWWW,** so that your Web page file will always be the latest update. View the presentation by double-clicking on the **index.htm** file in the **Ch9SouthwestWWW** folder. Continue with the Follow-up Practice Projects at the end of this Lesson.

Web presentation using the presentation file and learn a procedure for uploading a Web presentation to a Web server. When you have completed the project, exit *PowerPoint®*.

❶ **Add a Text Link to an Existing Presentation:** Since it is not clear that there is a hyperlink to the state page attached to the state graphic, you need to insert text boxes.

    a. In the presentation go to the Arizona slide and insert a text box underneath the state graphic. In the text box type the text **State of Arizona Home Page** into the text box. You may have to resize the font to make it fit in the text box. (You can either select the box or the text inside the box to resize the font)

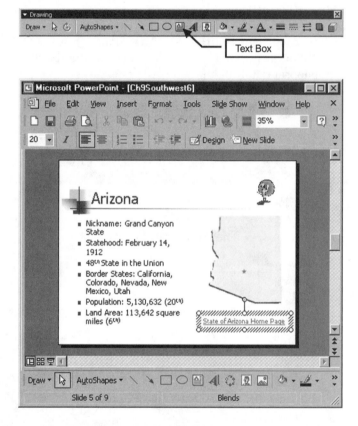

    b. Select the text inside the text box, and click the hyperlink icon on the **Standard Toolbar** to establish the hyperlink for the highlighted text. Since you have used this hyperlink before, it will be in the **Inserted Links** list in the **Insert Hyperlink** dialog box. Choose it and click **OK.** See the dialog box on the top of the following page.

    c. Now repeat steps a and b for each of the state slides, then republish your Web presentation. If your computer has an Internet connection, test the link in the browser to determine that it connects to the linked page.

❷ **Uploading a Web Presentation to a Web Server:** To upload a Web presentation to a Web server, it is important to explain to your Webmaster the names of the files and folders in the presentation and their organization or relative placement to each other.

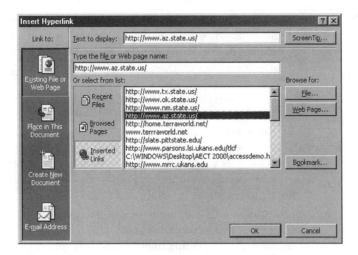

a. For example, if you published the **Ch9SouthwestWWW** Web presentation in a folder named, **My Presentations,** your Web presentation would be organized like the following:

My Presentations (folder)
Ch9SouthwestWWW.htm (file)
Ch9SouthwestWWW_files (folder)

b. To post or publish your Web presentation on a Web server, provide your Webmaster with the Web presentation source file **Ch9Southwest WWW.htm** and the folder with the individual slide Web pages and graphics, **Ch9SouthwestWWW_files.** The .htm file should be at the same path level as the _files folder. The link to your Web presentation would contain the source file **Ch9SouthwestWWW.htm.** This page will provide appropriate links and associations to all the other pages and graphics in the **Ch9SouthwestWWW_files** folder.

❸ Develop a lesson idea or plan that is targeted for the grade level you teach or plan to teach. It should describe teaching students how to design and publish a *PowerPoint*® presentation on the Web for communicating information for an electronic report. Add it to the **Lesson Plans ePortfolio.**

EXERCISES TO REVIEW AND EXPAND YOUR SKILLS

Set 1: Reviewing Terms and Concepts—For each question below, provide a term that matches the description.

_____ 1. Create a copy of a presentation as a Web page in HTML format and place it on a computer that hosts Web pages on the Internet.

_____ 2. Presentations requiring little or no human intervention and automatically start over at the end of the show.

_____ 3. Special effects used to introduce a slide during a slide show.

_____ 4. Used to automatically advance to a variety of locations, including another slide or Internet or e-mail address.

_____ 5. Special sound or visual effects added to text or other slide objects to add emphasis or interest to a slide.

Set 2: Expanding Your Skills—Expand on the skills you learned in this chapter with these activities. Load the **Ch9Southwest5.ppt** file, and select **Slide View** to perform the following activities. Save the presentation file when you have completed the exercises.

1. **Write or Draw on Slides During a Slide Show:** You can annotate slides during a slide show using the mouse. Run the presentation in **Slide Show View.** To make the mouse pointer work like a pen, right-click the mouse, select **Pointer Options,** and click **Pen.** Press the mouse button as you write or draw on your slide. The pointer remains a pen until you choose another Pointer Option. To erase annotations during a presentation, press the letter **E.**

2. **Check Spelling in a Presentation:** You can check the spelling of text in a presentation anytime you want by selecting **Tools | Spelling.** You cannot check spelling in embedded objects such as charts, WordArt, or inserted objects such as *Word* documents.

Set 3: Use Microsoft® Help—Look up the following features to get further information and tips, and then test each of these features with one or more of the presentations you used in this lesson.

- Look up **Pack and Go** to transport a presentation to another computer.
- Look up **Viewer** to run slide shows on computers without *PowerPoint*® installed.
- Look up **Broadcast** for information on a presentation through the Internet.

Set 4: Create Your Own Lesson—After reviewing the lessons in this chapter, develop and describe a lesson targeted for the grade level you teach or plan to teach that makes effective use of each of the following *PowerPoint*® features. Describe the presentation you or the students would need to create to complete the lesson. Enter your lesson idea or plan into the **Lesson Plans ePortfolio.**

- Create a presentation about how to design *PowerPoint*® presentations using various animations, transitions, colors, and fonts. Demonstrate both good and bad examples.
- Students create a presentation of an original story using animation of text and clip art supported with slide transitions.
- Students create a scrapbook using digital pictures from a class field trip or class project and create a self-running slide show set to music.
- Students work in teams and create a presentation about a state or region of the United States or a historical event and publish it to Web pages.

PART

4

INTEGRATING TECHNOLOGY IN THE CLASSROOM WITH MICROSOFT® *OUTLOOK*®

OVERVIEW

The Cedar Valley School District has recently undertaken a major technology initiative to create a district wide area network. The network is designed to distribute file services to each school site and provide centralized e-mail services from a Microsoft® Exchange server in the district administrative offices. Each teacher has a desktop computer with Microsoft® *Office* installed and will use Microsoft® *Office* for messaging, collaboration, and other personal productivity tasks. In this unit you will share in the experiences of several Cedar Valley teachers who are learning to use *Outlook*® to enhance their professional work.

In this part you will meet Yolanda Adams, a first-year teacher at Cedar Valley Intermediate School. Yolanda is excited about getting a computer at her desk because she wants to use the productivity features of Microsoft® *Outlook*® to communicate with colleagues, share lesson plans and ideas, schedule meetings and events, and organize and manage classroom tasks and learning activities. She also wants to have her students do the kinds of e-mail projects with other schools she has been reading about in her professional journals.

Microsoft® *Outlook*® is a productivity tool that manages e-mail messages, address books, individual and group calendars, projects, and tasks for personal and professional purposes. With *Outlook*® users can perform these functions using a common interface. *Outlook*® is designed to be a powerful collaboration tool that allows users to communicate, plan, and manage work activities and projects cooperatively. When *Outlook*® is used as an *Exchange* network client, you can take advantage of collaboration features such as group scheduling and public folders.

While Microsoft® *Outlook*® has these powerful collaboration features, it can also be used as a simple e-mail program and stand-alone productivity tool. In Part 4 you will learn to use *Outlook*® as a basic e-mail program, address book, and productivity tool. If you use *Outlook*®, all the tasks you learn in the lessons in Part 4 will be applicable and transferable to an advanced computing and network environment where all the features of *Outlook*® can be used fully.

Technology Standards and Educational Best Practices for Technology

The lessons in this section assist learners in developing skills for the following International Society for Technology in Education (ISTE) National Educational Technology Standards for Students (NETS·S):

1. Basic operations and concepts

    *   Students demonstrate a sound understanding of the nature and operation of technology systems.
    *   Students are proficient in the use of technology.

2. Social, ethical, and human issues

    *   Students practice responsible use of technology systems, information, and software.
    *   Students develop positive attitudes toward technology uses that support lifelong learning, collaboration, personal pursuits, and productivity.

3. Technology productivity tools
    *   Students use technology tools to enhance learning, increase productivity, and promote creativity.

4. Technology communications tools

    *   Students use telecommunications to collaborate, publish, and interact with peers, experts, and other audiences.
    *   Students use a variety of media and formats to communicate information and ideas effectively to multiple audiences.

The chapters in Part 4: Integrating Technology in the Classroom with Microsoft® *Outlook*® address indicators in four of the NETS·S standards. The tutorials and activities in Part 4 require you to open files from a CD, floppy disk, and/or a hard disk, use a keyboard and mouse, and manage files you create, save, or copy. *Outlook*® is a productivity tool for creatively and effectively communicating and storing information. *Outlook*® provides a communication platform for facilitating collaboration both in the classroom and at a distance. The tutorials and learning activities in Part 4 will provide learning experiences that allow you to use communication features of *Outlook*® to enhance learning and increase productivity. *Outlook*® provides productivity tools that facilitate communication with peers, students, parents, experts, and others in a variety of formats. All learning activities in Part 4 are designed to promote responsible use of computer technology and help students develop positive attitudes about the use of technology to accommodate lifelong learning.

Differences Between Windows® and Macintosh® Versions of *Outlook*®

The Macintosh® version of Microsoft® *Office* is not packaged with Microsoft® *Outlook*®. When *Outlook*® is used in a Macintosh® computing environment, it is generally to connect a Macintosh® computer to a Microsoft® *Exchange* server to use the e-mail and collaboration features of *Outlook*®. While there are some differences in the way *Office* runs on a Macintosh® and the way it runs in Windows®, most of these differences can be attributed to the differences between Mac OS and Windows® and their respective user interfaces.

The tutorials in this unit present Microsoft® Outlook® from a Windows® perspective and then identify processing steps for Macintosh® when significant differences occur in the way the program operates in Mac OS and Windows®. Minor differences in the processing steps are noted in parentheses immediately following the corresponding Windows® processing step.

Chapters in Part 4

The step-by-step lessons in each chapter demonstrate the e-mail, scheduling, and project management features of Microsoft® Outlook®. Each tutorial consists of guided practice that demonstrates how teachers and students can use Outlook® features to improve professional productivity, including communicating and sharing information with colleagues, scheduling meetings and events, and organizing and managing tasks and activities. For each chapter use the practice files in the OL folder of the T3 Practice CD to complete the step-by-step lessons.

Several exercises follow each lesson that may also include activities using files from the T3 Practice CD as well as the Lesson Plans ePortfolio. Complete these exercises to reinforce the learning activities demonstrated in the tutorial and to expand your skills.

The tutorials in the following lessons do not include every feature of Microsoft® Outlook® but are designed to address those features that will allow you to perform text and graphic processing tasks that support classroom instruction and student learning. The tutorials also provide activities that encourage you to investigate other features of Outlook® not specifically included in these lessons.

Chapter 10:   Messaging and Collaboration Using Outlook®

Chapter 11:   Scheduling and Project Management Using Outlook®

MESSAGING AND COLLABORATION USING *OUTLOOK*®

NEW TERMS

address book	e-mail flag formats	read receipts
attachments	HTML mail	rules
AutoPreview	hyperlinks	Shortcut
Card view	Mail Merge to Contacts	signature
digital security	Personal Distribution List	Table view
drafts	Preview Pane	

OVERVIEW

Microsoft® *Outlook*® is a messaging, collaboration, and scheduling tool. This chapter contains three lessons with step-by-step tutorials to build skills in messaging and collaboration using *Outlook*®. Each tutorial consists of guided practice that demonstrates how teachers and students can use *Outlook*® for personal and professional productivity and classroom learning activities.

The lessons in this chapter demonstrate how teachers and students can use Microsoft® *Outlook*® features to communicate and share information with friends or colleagues. Practice files for the tutorials are located in the OL folder on the T3 Practice CD. Following each lesson are several exercises. Some exercises include activities from the Lesson Plans ePortfolio. Complete these exercises to reinforce the learning activities demonstrated in the tutorials and to build your collection of technology-based lesson plans and ideas.

Lesson 10.1: Navigating the *Outlook*® Window
Lesson 10.2: Keeping an Address Book with Contacts in *Outlook*®
Lesson 10.3: Sending and Receiving E-mail Using Inbox in *Outlook*®

LESSON 10.1: NAVIGATING THE *OUTLOOK*® WINDOW

Lesson 10.1: Learning Activities

Opening the *Outlook*® window
Navigating the *Outlook*® window
Customizing Folders on the Shortcuts Bar
Modifying groups on the *Outlook*® Bar
Using *Outlook*® Today
Closing the *Outlook*® Window

Microsoft® *Outlook*® is a productivity program that coordinates multiple functions for managing various personal and professional tasks. *Outlook*® allows users to create and view these tasks using a common interface. Transactions for each of these tasks or items can be journalized. As a stand-alone program, *Outlook*® provides you with capability to perform the following functions or tasks:

- Send and receive e-mail
- Maintain an address book of contact information
- Schedule appointments, meetings, and events
- Maintain a to-do list of projects and activities
- Keep a journal of activities and e-mails
- Post and save notes
- Access Web pages

Yolanda Adams currently uses her home computer with a modem to e-mail her colleagues and share information. Yolanda wants to set up and start using *Outlook*® for e-mail and maintain an address book. Since Yolanda uses a different e-mail program on her home computer, she must first become familiar with the *Outlook*® window and environment before using it to send e-mail and set up a new address book.

LESSON 10.1: TUTORIAL

Opening the *Outlook*® Window

The *Outlook*® program opens like other *Office*® programs. If your computer is connected to a local area network or the Internet, *Outlook*® will try to make a connection to an e-mail account. Typically *Outlook*® is open and the window is minimized while you are working in other programs.

❶   Open *Outlook*® by double-clicking on the *Outlook*® icon or by selecting Microsoft® *Outlook*® from the **Start | Programs** menu on the Windows® screen. Your screen should look similar to that shown in Figure 10-1.

❷   Click the **Minimize** button in the top right corner on the title bar of the active window. The *Outlook*® window will minimize to a button on the Windows® taskbar.

❸   Maximize the *Outlook*® window by clicking on the *Outlook*® button on the Windows® taskbar.

Macintosh®: Using the Microsoft® *Office* Manager icon, select **Microsoft Outlook.** The *Outlook*® window generally defaults to the **Inbox** (e-mail folder).

Navigating the *Outlook*® Window

Outlook® has the look and layout of other *Office*® programs. *Outlook*® has a Title bar, a Menu Bar, Status Bar, and Minimize, Maximize/Restore, and Close buttons. The default view for *Outlook*® is to display the **Inbox,** listing any e-mail messages you have received. On the left side of the *Outlook*® window is the *Outlook*® Shortcuts Bar. (A Shortcut is an icon that provides quick access to a program or folder.)

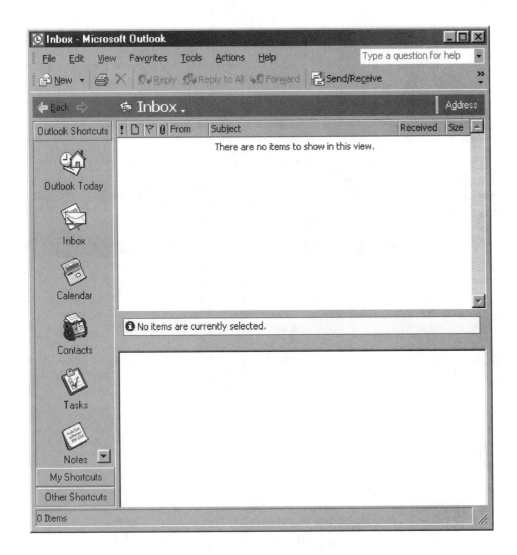

FIGURE 10–1

The Microsoft®
Outlook® Window
Source: Screen captures of
Microsoft® *Outlook*® used
in the chapters in Part 4 are
reprinted by permission
from Microsoft®
Corporation.

The *Outlook*® Shortcuts Bar contains three default groups of common *Outlook*®
folders and features: *Outlook*® **Shortcuts, My Shortcuts,** and **Other Shortcuts.**

Shortcuts bars include a number of shortcuts to programs or folders. Shortcuts
may be moved, added, or deleted on a bar. The Shortcuts on Yolanda's computer are
organized in the following way:

Outlook Shortcuts
Outlook Today: displays appointments, messages, and tasks for the day
Inbox: displays an e-mail message list
Calendar: displays appointment and event information
Contacts: displays address book list
Tasks: displays a task list
Notes: displays a list of active notes and reminders
Deleted Items: displays items that have been deleted from other folders
My Shortcuts
Drafts: displays a list of unfinished or unsent e-mail messages
Outbox: temporarily stores messages that have been sent
Sent Items: displays a list of e-mail messages you have sent
Journal: automatically tracks specified *Outlook*® items
Outlook Update: automatically accesses Microsoft® Web site to update *Office*®

Other Shortcuts

My Computer: displays the Windows® environment folders and drives
My Documents: displays folders and files in the My Documents folder
Favorites: displays links from the Favorites menu in *Internet Explorer*

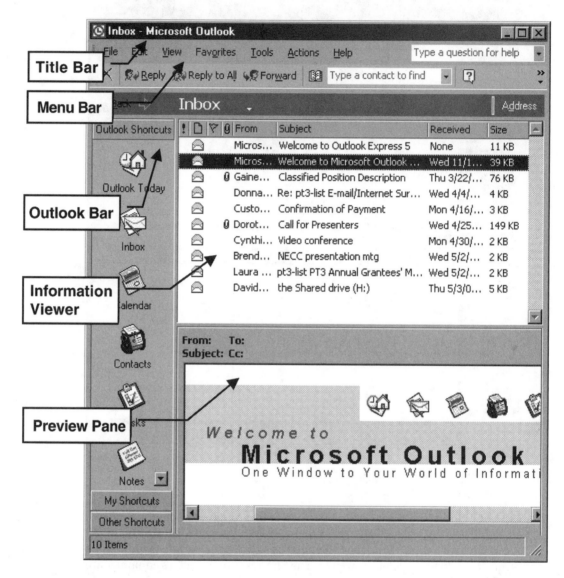

Title Bar

Menu Bar

Outlook Bar

Information Viewer

Preview Pane

Macintosh®: The *Outlook* Bar does not contain additional groups. The **Outbox** is by default included on the *Outlook* Bar. To include the Journal folder on the *Outlook* Bar, select **Edit | Preferences,** select **Microsoft Outlook,** and then select **General.** Click the **Show folders containing journal items** check box and click **OK.**

Macintosh®: To display all folders, select **View | Folder List.** You can then drag any folder to the *Outlook* Bar.

❶ Click *Outlook* **Shortcuts** at the top of the *Outlook* **Bar.** The shortcut icons are displayed for each of the standard *Outlook*® folders.

❷ Click **My Shortcuts** at the bottom of the *Outlook* **Bar.** The button moves to the top of the *Outlook* **Bar,** and several shortcut icons for several *Outlook*® folders are displayed.

❸ Click **Other Shortcuts** at the bottom of the *Outlook* **Bar.** The button moves to the top of the *Outlook* **Bar,** and shortcut icons for **My Computer, My Documents,** and **Favorites** are displayed.

❹ To open an item on the *Outlook* **Bar,** click the icon for the type of item you want to open. Click *Outlook* **Shortcuts | Calendar** to display the Calendar window. The example at the top of the following page shows the Calendar window in **Day View.** If your screen does not display Calendar like this example, select **View | Day.** Please see the dialog box at the top of the following page.

❺ Sometimes you may want to see all the *Outlook*® folders at one time. To view the Folder List, select **View | Folder List.** A list of all the *Outlook*® folders (*Outlook* **Shortcuts** group and **My Shortcuts** group) is displayed. (The

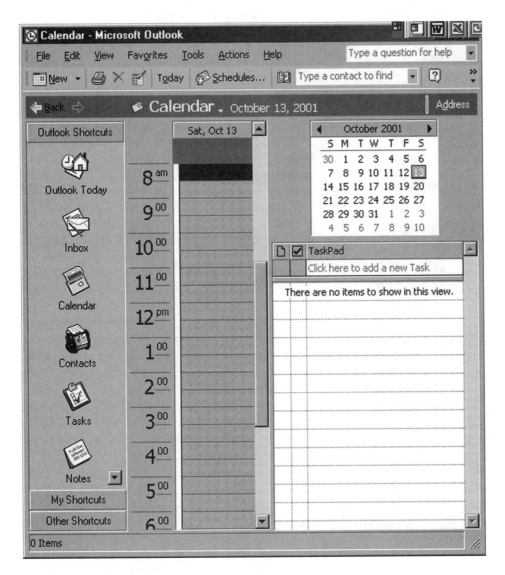

folder list may be slightly different on your computers due to configuration and version differences among computers running Microsoft® *Office.*) To remove the Folder List from the Information Viewer, click the **X** in the top right corner of the Folder List or deselect the Folder list by selecting **View | Folder List** again. Please see the example at the top of the following page.

Customizing Folders on the Shortcuts Bar

You can create additional folders for storing *Outlook*® documents. For example, you can create a folder to store e-mail messages of communications and collaborations on a specific topic of interest or research.

❶ Select **File | New | Folder.** In the **Name** window of the **Create New Folder** dialog box, enter **Teaching Ideas** as the name for the folder. In the **Folder contains** box, click the down arrow and select **Mail Items** to create a folder that could be used for e-mail collaborations. In the **Select where to place the folder** list, click **Personal Folders** to place the new folder inside **Personal Folders.** Click **OK.**

❷ In the **Add shortcut to *Outlook* Bar?** message box click **Yes.** A shortcut is added to the **My Shortcuts** group. Click **My Shortcuts** to view the shortcut for the new folder.

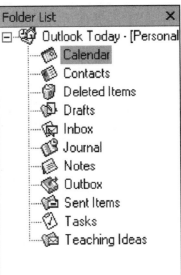

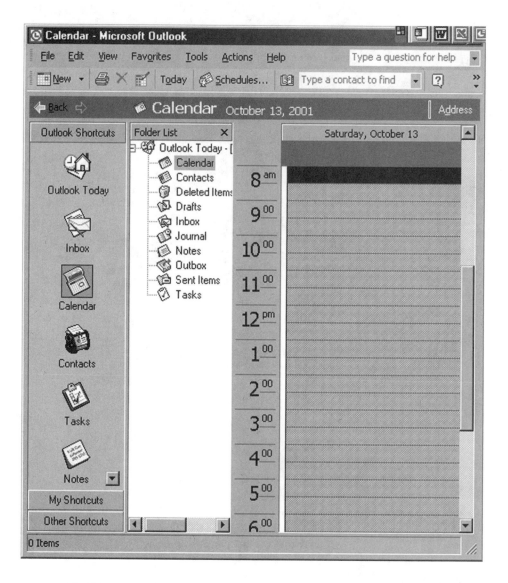

③ Notice the **Teaching Ideas** folder is now displayed on the Folder List. It should be displayed at the same level as the *Outlook*® folders.

④ To move the **Teaching Ideas** folder under the **Inbox** folder (make it a subfolder of **Inbox**) in the Folder List, click **Teaching Ideas** and click **File | Folder** and select **Move "Teaching Ideas."** In the **Move Folder** dialog box click **Inbox** and then click **OK.**

Modifying Groups on the *Outlook*® Bar

The default ***Outlook*** **Bar** provides access to standard *Outlook*® and Windows® folders. The ***Outlook*** **Bar** can be customized to fit your individual needs. (**NOTE:** This is a feature of computers that use the Windows® operating system.)

❶ While the three groups of shortcut icons—***Outlook*** **Shortcuts, My Shortcuts,** and **Other Shortcuts**—may provide sufficient groupings for all the *Outlook*® items you create, you can have up to 12 groups. To add a new group, right-click on **My Shortcuts** and click **Add New Group** from the submenu. A new group bar is added at the bottom of the *Outlook* Bar. Change the name to **More Shortcuts** and press **ENTER.**

② To delete a group, right-click **More Shortcuts** and click **Remove Group.** Click **Yes** in the confirmation box to remove the group.

③ To make the *Outlook* **Bar** narrower or wider, move the mouse pointer onto the right border of the *Outlook* **Bar.** When the mouse pointer becomes a pair of vertical lines with left and right pointing arrows, hold down the mouse button and drag the border to the right or left to make it wider or narrower.

④ To change the size of the icons on the *Outlook* **Bar,** select the *Outlook* **Shortcut** group by pointing at it. When the mouse pointer changes to a pointing hand, right-click the mouse and from the submenu select **Small Icons.**

⑤ You can have up to 12 groups on the *Outlook* **Bar.** To add a group to the *Outlook* **Bar,** point at any existing group and when the mouse pointer changes to a pointing hand, right-click the mouse and from the submenu select **Add new group.** A group bar is displayed at the bottom of the *Outlook* **Bar** with the temporary name, **New Group,** highlighted. Type in a new group name, **My New Group** and press **ENTER.**

⑥ You can rename a group by right-clicking on the group and selecting **Rename Group**, typing the new name at the bottom of the *Outlook* **Bar,** and pressing **ENTER.** (Do not rename the new group you created.) To delete **My New Group,** right-click **My New Group,** click **Remove Group** from the submenu, and select **Yes** from the confirmation box.

Using *Outlook*® Today

(**NOTE:** This is a feature of computers that use the Windows® operating system.) *Outlook*® Today provides a preview of the current day. This preview provides a summary of appointments, a list of your tasks, and a count of new e-mail messages received. It can be set to be the first page that opens when you start *Outlook*®. Additionally, the appearance of *Outlook*® Today can be customized to fit your needs.

❶ To make *Outlook*® Today the default page when you start *Outlook*®, on the *Outlook* **Bar** click once on the *Outlook* **Today** icon. At the top of the *Outlook*® Today window, click once on **Customize *Outlook* Today.** Click the **When starting, go directly to *Outlook* Today** check box to select it.

❷ To change the **Inbox** folders that are displayed on the *Outlook*® Today page, in the **Messages** area click on the **Choose Folders** button, and select the check box next to **Drafts, Inbox,** and **Sent Items** to display these folders on the *Outlook*® Today page. (To deselect a folder, click on the checked box.) Click **OK.**

❸ To change how many appointments appear, in the **Calendar** area, click the down arrow and in the drop-down list select **7.**

❹ To change the tasks that are displayed on the *Outlook*® Today page, in the **Tasks** area click the **Today's tasks** radio button and click the **Include tasks with no due date** check box. To change the order in which the Tasks are listed in the **Tasks** area, click the down arrow of the **Sort my task list by** drop-down box, select **Start Date,** and click the **Ascending** radio button directly underneath it. To sort tasks by a second criterion, click the down arrow of the **then by** drop-down box, select **Importance,** and click the **Descending** radio button.

❺ To change the background and layout of the *Outlook*® Today page, in the **Styles** area, click the down arrow of the **Show *Outlook* Today in this style** drop-down box and select **Standard (one column).** The graphic below the drop-down box shows how the *Outlook*® Today page will appear with your selection. Click **Save Changes** and then **Outlook Today** to display the customized layout of the *Outlook*® Today page.

Exiting the *Outlook*® Window

The *Outlook*® program exits like other Microsoft® *Office* programs. Typically, *Outlook*® is open and minimized while you are working in other programs.

❶ Exit *Outlook*® by clicking the **Close** button in the top right corner on the title bar of the *Outlook*® window or by selecting **File | Exit**.

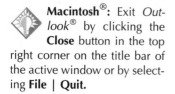

Macintosh®: Exit *Outlook*® by clicking the **Close** button in the top right corner on the title bar of the active window or by selecting **File | Quit**.

FOLLOW-UP PRACTICE PROJECTS

❶ **Viewing Information in the *Outlook* Window.** To perform the following exercises and activities, open *Outlook*®. After completing the practice projects, close *Outlook*®. The practice activities demonstrate the default view and other views for each type of *Outlook*® item.

Each *Outlook*® folder, such as Inbox and Calendar, displays its items in a default layout, called a view. Views consist of a view type, fields, a sort order, colors, fonts, and other settings. Each view puts the items or files in a folder in different arrangements and layouts. An example of a common view is viewing the Contacts folder in the Address Cards view, which displays names and addresses in blocks like business cards. Different views are useful for obtaining different types of information. You can use views to control the amount of detail that appears for items and files, to help you emphasize or analyze details. You can also create custom views. You can choose from the following view types:

a. **Table View:** Click the **Inbox** icon to open the **Inbox folder**. Select **View | Current View | Define Views**. Notice in the **Define Views for Inbox** dialog box that **Table View** is the default view for all Inbox views, except for **Message Timeline View**. In a table items are in a grid of rows and columns. Each row contains one item. Details about items are in columns. Table view is best for viewing messages, tasks, and details about any other item.

b. **Card View:** Click the **Contacts** icon to open the Contacts folder. Select **View | Current View | Define Views**. In **Card View** items are listed in the form of a business card, best for viewing Contacts.

c. **Timeline View:** Click **My Shortcuts** and click the **Journal** icon to open the **Journal folder**. If a dialog box displays asking if you want to turn the Journal on, click the check box that says **Do not show me this dialog again** and then click **No**. **Timeline View** is the default view for Journal, and items appear as icons arranged in chronological order from left to right on a time scale. **Timeline View** is best for viewing journal entries and other items such as tasks that you want to plot in relation to time.

d. **Day/Week/Month View:** Click *Outlook* **Shortcuts** and click the **Calendar** icon to open the **Calendar folder**. Select **View | Current View | Day/Week/Month**. **Day/Week/Month View** is the default view for Calendar. In **Day/Week/Month View** items are arranged on the calendar similar to a day planner. You can view items in blocks of time for days, weeks, or for a month. **Day/Week/Month View** is best for viewing appointments, meetings, or tasks.

e. **Icon View:** Click **Notes** to open the **Notes folder**. Select **View | Current View | Icons**. **Icon View** is the default view for Notes. In **Icon View** items and files are represented by individual icons arranged on an invisible grid. Select **Views | Current View | Notes List**. The view is changed from **Icon View** to **Notes List View**. Now change the view back to **Icon view**. **Icon view** is best to view notes and files as large icons, small icons, or in a list of icons.

❷ Begin a lesson idea or plan that is targeted for the grade level you teach or plan to teach. You can find ideas in articles from ISTE's *Learning and Leading with Technology.* For example:

> Baugh I. & Baugh, J. (1997). Global classrooms: e-mail learning communities. *Learning and Leading with Technology, 25*(3), 38–41.
>
> Boehm, D. (1997). I lost my tooth! *Learning and Leading with Technology, 24*(7), 17–19.
>
> Harris, J. (1994). Information collection activities. *The Computing Teacher, 21*(6), 32–33.

It should describe using a language arts, social studies, science, or math theme (or subject or theme of your own choosing) in which students e-mail friends or peers to share information and ideas. Add it to the **Lesson Plans ePortfolio.**

LESSON 10.2: KEEPING AN ADDRESS BOOK WITH CONTACTS IN *OUTLOOK*®

Lesson 10.2: Learning Activities

Creating a new contact
Importing a contact list into *Outlook*®
Maintaining a contact list
Customizing the look of Contacts

The Contacts folder stores e-mail addresses and mailing address and telephone information for the people with whom you communicate and share information. Use the Contacts folder to store the e-mail address, street address, multiple phone numbers, and other personal and business information that relates to a contact. *Outlook*® can address a meeting request, e-mail message, or task request to the contact, and you can link any *Outlook*® item or *Office*® document to a contact to help you track your activities associated with a contact. You can sort, group, or filter Contacts by any part of the name or any part of the address you want.

You can file contact information under a last name, first name, company name, nickname, or any word that helps you find the contact quickly. *Outlook*® gives you several naming choices under which to file the contact, or you can enter your own choice. You can enter up to three addresses for each contact, designate one address as the mailing address, and use the information for mailing labels, envelopes, or mail merge letters.

Since Yolanda currently uses her home computer with a modem to e-mail, she has built an address book of contacts with e-mail addresses. The first thing she needs to do in preparing to e-mail from her computer at school is to transfer the address book on her home computer to her computer at school.

Open *Outlook*® and then click **Contacts** to open the **Contacts folder.**

LESSON 10.2: TUTORIAL

Creating a New Contact

When you enter a name or address for a contact, *Outlook*® separates the name or address into parts and puts each part in a separate field. You can enter a name and e-mail address only, or you can enter complete work and home address and phone information for a new contact.

❶ To create a new contact, select **File | New | Contact** or click on the **New Contact** icon. A window with a form to enter contact information is displayed. In the **Full Name** box type **Greg Gregory** for the contact name. In the **Job title** box type **Teacher.** In the **Company** box type **Silverlake School District.** Notice in the **File as** box how Contacts has determined to file this contact in the address book.

❷ Click the down arrow of the drop-down list for the **File as** box, and select the arrangement of first name first or last name first (the default is last name first). In the **Address** box type **1200 Broadway,** press **ENTER,** then type **Silverlake, Texas 76767.** In the Business box type the phone number **(123) 456-7890.** In the e-mail box type **ggreg@sss.k12.tx.us.** Your contact information form window should look similar to the following example:

❸ Click **Save and Close** to save the contact information.

❹ To create a new contact with two names in the **First Name** box, select **File | New | Contact** or click **New Contact.** In the **Full Name** box type **Pat & Patsy Patterson** for the contact name, then press **TAB.** To verify that the parts of a name are identified correctly for sorting, filtering, or mail merge, the **Check Full Name** dialog box pops up (or click **Full Name**). Review the name, make changes as appropriate then click **OK.** Review the **File as** box and select the appropriate order for filing. In the e-mail box type **2pats@myemail.com.**

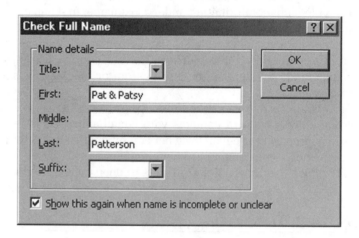

❺ Click **Save and Close** to save the contact information.

Importing a Contact List into *Outlook*®

Yolanda wants to import her address book from her home computer into *Outlook*®. She has exported her Address Book from her home computer into a Personal Folder

File. Personal Folder files have an extension of .pst. Now she needs to import the file into her *Outlook*® Contacts list. To select the CD drive, make sure the **T3 Practice CD** is in the CD drive.

❶ To import an address book stored as a Personal Folder file into the Contacts folder, select **File | Import and Export** to start the **Import Wizard.**

❷ Select **Import from another program or file,** and click **Next.** Scroll down the list of file types and select **Personal Folder File (.pst)** and click **Next.**

❸ In the **OL Folder** on the **T3 Practice CD,** select the file named **Ch9ContactsImport** for the File to import, click the **Do not import duplicates** radio button, and click **Next.**

❹ The final screen of the **Import Wizard** asks you to select the from and to export files and requires some additional explanation. In the **Select the folder to import from** box, point at the file name **Ch9ContactsImport** to highlight and select it. Deselect the **Include subfolders** check box by clicking on it. Select the **Import items into the current folder** radio button and click the **Finish** button.

Macintosh®: Select **Import Contacts from a text file** and click **OK.** In the **OL Folder** on the **T3 Practice CD,** open the file named **Ch9ContactsImportMac.csv.**

Macintosh®: On the **Import Contacts** dialog box, expand the Mailbox folder if necessary and select the **Contacts** folder and click **OK.** The new contacts are imported into your existing **Contacts folder**.

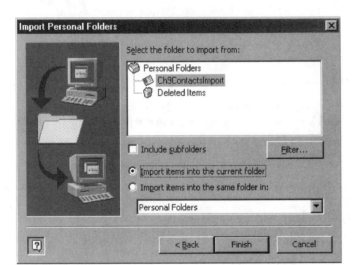

❺ The names and addresses in the imported file are now added to your contact list.

Maintaining a Contact List

There are several tasks you can perform in *Outlook*® to allow you to maintain an up-to-date Contacts list and to view it in various ways.

❶ Notice some of the Contacts in the list are filed in first and last name order and some are filed in last and first name order. To change the way a contact is filed in the contact list, double-click on **Josh Hibley** to select it for maintenance. Click on the down arrow of the **File as** box and select **Hibley, Josh** to view it by last and first name order. Click **Save and Close** and then repeat this process for **Zack Hurley.**

❷ To ensure that new contacts that you add are filed in the Contacts list in last and first name order, select **Tools | Options.** Click **Preferences** then **Contact Options.** Click the down arrow of the Default file as order drop-down list and select **Last, First** (it may already be selected as the default). Click **OK** on the **Contacts Options** dialog box, and then click **OK** on the **Options** dialog box.

Macintosh®: Select **View | Sort,** click the down arrow of the Sort items by drop-down list and select **File As** (it may already be selected as the default), then click the **Ascending** radio button and click **OK.**

Macintosh®: Select **Tools | Find Contact,** type **Stevens** in the **Find Contact** dialog box, and click **Find.** Close the **Eddy Stevens Contacts** form when it is displayed on the screen.

❸ To find a contact in the Address Book, on the toolbar type the name of the contact you want to find in the **Address Book Find** box. To find Eddy Stevens, type **Stevens** in the **Address Book Find** box and press **ENTER.** (You can enter a partial name, a first or last name, or an e-mail alias.)

❹ You can also find a contact in the Address Book by clicking the **Address Book** icon and selecting a name from the list. Double-click on **Marie Montgomery** to display the **Marie Montgomery-Contact** form. Close the **Marie Montgomery-Contact** form when it is displayed on the screen and then close the **Address Book** dialog box.

❺ When you imported the Contacts list, you had an entry for Greg Gregory in the imported file. You had also typed the same contact into your Contacts list. Although the import did not recognize a duplicate contact when one was typed in and one was imported, the import function will prevent duplication of imported Contacts when indicated. To delete the duplicate, select the first card with **Greg Gregory** and select **Edit | Delete** or click **Delete.**

Customizing the Look of Contacts

Outlook® allows you to select different views of the Contacts list. The default view for Contacts is Card View. In Card View, Contacts are listed in the form of a business card. (On Macintosh® all views are in a list format.)

Macintosh®: Select **View | Current View** and select **Address List** to display address information available on each contact.

Macintosh®: Select **View | Current View** and select **Phone List** to display phone information available on each contact.

Macintosh®: Select **View | Sort,** click the down arrow of the **Sort items by** drop-down list, select **Company,** click the **Ascending** radio button, and click **OK.**

Macintosh®: Select **View | Current View** and select **Normal** to display e-mail information available on each contact.

❶ To change the view of the Contacts list, select **View | Current View** and select **Detailed Address Cards** to display all the information available on each contact.

❷ To view the Contacts list as a Phone list, select **Views | Current View** and select **Phone List.** The view is changed from **Card View** to **Table View**.

❸ To sort the order in which the cards are displayed, select **View | Current View** and select **Customize Current View.** Click **Sort,** click the down arrow on the drop-down list for the **Sort items by field,** and drag the scroll bar down until the **Company** box is displayed. Select **Company** and click **OK.** Then, click **OK** on the **View Summary** dialog box to display the Phone List sorted by Company. Now change the **Sort order** back to **File as.**

❹ To filter the cards that are displayed, select **View | Current View** and select **Customize Current View.** Click **Filter** and in the **Search for the word(s)** box, type **Teacher.** Click the down arrow on the drop-down list for the **In** field, select **name fields only,** and click **OK** and click **OK** on the **View Summary** dialog box to display only cards with Teacher in one of the fields. **NOTE:** This is a feature of computers that use the Windows® operating system.

❺ Change the view back to **Address Cards. Card View** is best to view Contacts and any other *Outlook®* items you want to find quickly in alphabetical order.

❻ Close *Outlook®*.

FOLLOW-UP PRACTICE PROJECTS

The following projects provide practice in maintaining and using your Microsoft® *Outlook®* address book. To complete these projects, you will use *Outlook®* and Microsoft® *Word*. In *Outlook®* use the **Contacts** icon to select the **Contacts folder**.

❶ Building Your Address Book: Enter five names, addresses, and e-mail addresses from friends or colleagues into the **Contacts folder**. Be sure to include complete mailing address information for each contact.

❷ Using Contacts for Mail Merge: You can use Contacts as the data source for merged documents, such as form letters, mailing labels, or envelopes in Microsoft® *Word*. The mail merge process can begin from *Outlook*®.

To send a mail merge document to a filtered set of Contacts, you would create a subset of Contacts by using an *Outlook*® view, and then begin your mail merge directly from the view in *Outlook*®. To create labels, mail merge documents, envelopes, or catalogs using names and addresses in Contacts, open Microsoft® *Word*, select **Tools | Letters and Mailings,** and select **MailMerge Wizard.** In the **Wizard** select **Labels** and select a label format. Next, select *Outlook* **Contacts** in the **Contacts folder** to be the recipients of the MailMerge document. Clear all the MailMerge recipients and then go back and select several of the Contacts that have more complete addresses. Replicate or update the layout of the first label to all labels, then preview the labels and complete the merge. Before you complete the merge you can use previous and next to go back and repeat any step and modify your settings.

❸ Create a Custom Contact Field: You can add additional data fields to Contacts. For example, if you wanted to use Contacts to include the parents names and addresses of students in your class, you could add a new field to Contacts called **Student Name**. If there is an entry in the Student Name field, then you know the contact is a parent. You can use this field to filter your data for MailMerge. From Contacts set the current view to **Phone List** because it is a table view. Select **View | Current View** and select **Define View.** To create a new field, on the Define Views for Contacts dialog box, click **Modify,** click **Fields,** and then click **New Field.** Enter a text field named Student Name. The field is added to the view. When you return to the **Phone List** view, the field is added to the table (you may need to scroll to the far right side of the table view to see the field).

❹ Add to the lesson idea or plan you started at the end of the previous lesson to include a procedure for adding names, addresses, and e-mail addresses to the contact list that accompanies your e-mail program. Update your lesson plan or idea in the **Lesson Plans ePortfolio**.

LESSON 10.3: SENDING AND RECEIVING E-MAIL USING INBOX IN *OUTLOOK*®

Lesson 10.3: Learning Activities

Creating and sending e-mail messages
Sending e-mail messages with file attachments
Reading and reply to received messages and saving attachments
Moving an e-mail message to another folder
Creating and sending messages using a personal distribution list
Using signatures in messages
Setting other options for managing messages

You can have e-mail service by adding an e-mail account to Microsoft® *Outlook*® using the information provided to you by your administrator or Internet Service Provider (ISP). Depending on your needs, you can add several e-mail accounts to a single *Outlook*® user profile. For example, you can add a Microsoft® *Exchange* Server account to handle your business e-mail and then add an Internet e-mail account, such as Hotmail, to handle your personal e-mail.

The Inbox folder is the *Outlook*® folder that contains e-mail messages you have received. The Inbox folder allows you to manage e-mail by creating, sending, receiving, reading, responding to, and forwarding messages. The Inbox folder allows you to view a list of received messages. A Preview Pane allows you to preview the contents of a selected message without opening it.

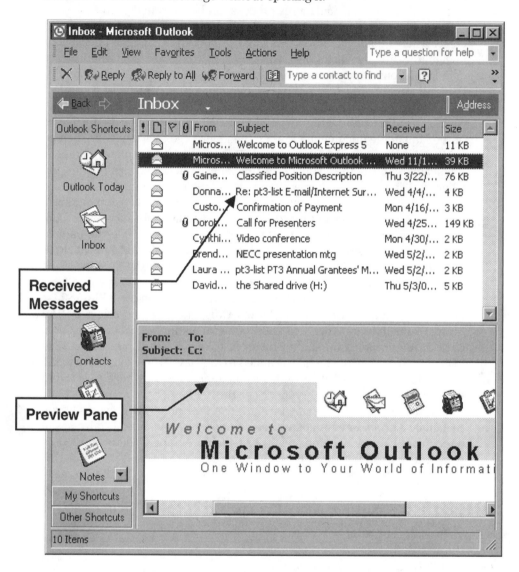

You can adjust the size of the Preview Pane by positioning the mouse pointer on the horizontal line between the message list and the Preview Pane. When the mouse pointer changes to an up and down arrow, click and drag it up or down to increase or decrease the size of the Preview Pane. You can toggle the Preview Pane on and off by selecting **View | Preview Pane.**

E-mail messages in the Inbox are either read or unread. Read messages are listed in normal type, while unread messages are listed in bold type. If you have unread messages in your Inbox, the Inbox folder name will be displayed in bold, and the number of unread messages will be displayed beside the folder name in parentheses. The Inbox works in conjunction with three other *Outlook*® folders for sending e-mail messages:

1. The **Outbox folder** temporarily contains messages you have designated to send but are still waiting to send. This folder is mainly used when you are working offline.

2. The **Sent Items folder** is an archive of all the messages you have sent. It contains a copy of each message you send.
3. The **Drafts folder** contains messages that are unfinished until you are ready to complete them and send at a later time.

Yolanda is now ready to start using her computer at her school to communicate and share information with friends and colleagues. Her Internet connection at school is faster since it works through the school network, rather than through a modem like her connection at home. Therefore, she can send and receive e-mails faster and be more timely and productive in her e-mail communications. Now she can correspond with others all during the work day instead of just the evenings and weekends. Since she has built her address book on her school computer, she now needs to inform many of the persons in her Contacts list of her new e-mail address. Before she can begin e-mail correspondence from school, she needs to learn the features and capabilities of e-mailing with *Outlook*®.

The following learning activities assume that you are on a computer with an Internet connection so you can send and receive e-mail. Exchange e-mail addresses with another student so you can use an active e-mail address for these exercises and add the e-mail address to your Contacts. The tutorial steps will note when to actually send or not send a message. You can complete the tutorial without an Internet connection, because *Outlook*® will work in an offline mode and any sent messages will be retained in the Outbox folder. If you are working offline, just delete all messages from the Outbox folder at the end of the lesson.

To complete the following tutorial steps, open *Outlook*® and click on the **Inbox** icon to open the **Inbox folder**.

LESSSON 10.3: TUTORIAL

Creating and Sending E-Mail Messages

When you create a new message, a message window with a form to enter the message is displayed. The message form allows you to enter the e-mail address information as well as the message content. (The tasks in this step use the active e-mail address you obtained from another student. You may perform this step even if your computer is offline.)

❶ To create a new e-mail message, select **File | New** and select **Mail Message** or click the **New Mail Message** button. Click on the down arrow of the **Message Format** box to display a drop-down list and select **Plain Text** from the list. We recommend you send e-mail messages as **Plain Text** to ensure that it can be displayed by any e-mail program. **NOTE:** This is a feature of computers using the Windows® operating system.

❷ Click the **Address Book** icon beside the **To** box to display your *Outlook*® Contacts list. The **Select Names** dialog box is displayed and provides you with several ways to select a name from the **Contacts folder**. Scroll down the Name list and select the person's name with whom you exchanged e-mail addresses, click the **To** button, and click **OK**.

❸ In the Subject box enter **New e-mail Address.**

❹ Click in the text box and enter the following message:

Hi,

We finally have e-mail set up in our classrooms. Please change my listing in your address book. My new e-mail address is yadams@ssd.k12.tx.us. Thanks.

Yolanda

Your message should look similar to the following example:

Hi,
We finally have E-mail set up in our classrooms. Please change my listing in your address book. My new E-mail address is yadams@ssd.k12.tx.us. Thanks.
Yolanda

❺ Click **Send** to e-mail the message. Check with the other student to see if your message was received. If your computer is offline, the message will be held in the Outbox.

Sending E-Mail Messages with File Attachments

You can attach a file to an e-mail message and send it to a recipient along with a message. When you create a new message, a message window with a form to enter the message is displayed. The message form allows you to enter the e-mail address information and the message content. (You may perform this step even if your computer is offline.) To complete this task, you should place the **T3 Practice CD** in the CD drive of your computer.

❶ To attach a *Word* document to an e-mail message, again create a new e-mail message to the active e-mail account. In the **Subject** box enter **Technology Standards.** In the text box enter the message:

Hi again,

I am serving on a district committee to establish technology standards for teachers. We are beginning this process by reviewing the ISTE Technology Standards. I have attached an MS Word file named ISTE Technology Standards.doc to this e-mail. Please review this document and send me your feedback on using these standards with K–12 teachers. Hope to hear from you soon as we have a meeting next week.

Yolanda

❷ After you have finished entering this message, click **Insert | File** (**Edit | Insert** and select **File** on Macintosh®) or click the **Insert File** icon (the paper clip). In the **OL Folder** on the **T3 Practice CD**, select the file named **ISTE Technology Standards.doc** and click **Insert** (**Open** on Macintosh®). **NOTE:** You should always explain in the body of message the format and name of any file you have attached. Please see the example at the top of following page.

❸ Click **Send** to e-mail the message. Check with the other student to see if your message and attachment were received. If your computer is offline, the message will be held in the **Outbox folder** in the **My Shortcuts** group.

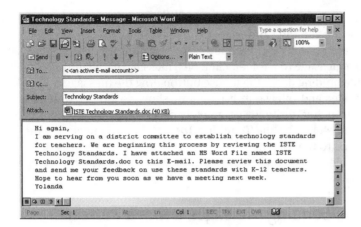

Reading and Replying to Received Messages and Saving Attachments

You can read, reply to, or forward e-mail messages that you receive. When you reply to a message, the sender of the e-mail automatically becomes the recipient of your reply. When you forward a message, you must enter a recipient for the message. (If you are working offline, read this step but do not attempt to perform the tasks in this step.)

1 To read an e-mail message, point at a new message in the information window to highlight it. Point at one of the e-mail messages you received from another student. You can read its contents in the **Preview Pane.** To open the message and view its contents, double-click on the e-mail message.

2 To reply to the sender of the message, with an e-mail message selected in the **Preview Pane** or opened, click **Reply.** Notice that **RE:** is entered in front of the Subject and the e-mail address of the e-mail account from whom you received the message is automatically entered in the **To** box. In the text box enter the message **Message received,** and click **Send.**

3 To forward an e-mail message to another person, with an e-mail message selected in the **Preview Pane** or opened, click **Forward.** Notice that **FW:** is entered in front of the **Subject.** Forward the e-mail message to Eddy Stevens.

4 To save an attachment that you receive in an e-mail, open the e-mail message that contains the file attachment you want to save. When an e-mail message contains an attachment, it is denoted by a paper clip icon beside the Subject in the information window. Right-click the icon for the attachment and from the drop-down list select **Save As.** In the **File name** box, enter a name for the file or keep the existing name of the file and click the **Save** button. **NOTE:** If the e-mail message includes more than one attachment, you can save multiple attachments to the same location. Hold down **SHIFT,** select each attachment by clicking on it and then select **File | Save Attachments.**

Moving an E-Mail Message to Another Folder

You can move a message to another folder for future reference or processing or to archive important information.

Macintosh®: Open the e-mail message and select the attachment file by pointing at it. Select **File | Save As** and then select the folder and file name you want to use for the attached file (you can use the current name of the file that is displayed in the **Save As** dialog box). If the **Save these attachments only** radio button is not selected, then select it and click **Save. NOTE:** If the e-mail message includes more than one attachment, you can save multiple attachments. Hold down **SHIFT,** select each attachment by clicking on it, and then follow the same steps as for a single attachment.

❶ To move one of the messages you have received to the **Teaching Ideas** folder, be certain the **Folder List** is displayed on the screen. If it is not displayed, select **View | Folder List.**

❷ To drag a message to a folder, click on a message in the information window and while holding down the mouse button drag the message to the **Teaching Ideas** folder and release it. It may now show as a deleted item with a line drawn through it, or it may completely disappear from the information window. Double-click on the **Teaching Ideas** folder to check that the message was moved to the folder.

❸ Now double-click **Inbox** to display e-mail messages you have received.

Creating and Sending Messages Using a Personal Distribution List

A personal distribution list is a collection of contacts. A message sent to a distribution list goes to all recipients who are members of the distribution list. A distribution list can be used for a number of *Outlook®* items, including messages, task requests, meeting requests, and even other personal distribution lists.

❶ To create a personal distribution list, select **File | New | Distribution List.** Click **Select Members** (**Address Book** on Macintosh®) and in the **Select Members** box select and add each of the following names to the list by highlighting the name and then clicking **Members: Eddy Stevens, Greg Gregory, Josh Hibley, Susan Adams.** Click **OK** and the **Distribution List** form is displayed with the names you added. If you added a name to the list that should not be included, select it and click **Remove.** In the **Name** box type **Teachers** for the name of the personal distribution list. Click **Save and Close.**

❷ To add an additional name to the **Teachers** personal distribution list, click **Contacts** on the *Outlook* Bar to open the **Contacts folder.** Scroll through the Contacts cards until you find the one labeled **Teachers** and double-click it to open it. Click **Select Members** (**Address Book** on Macintosh®) and scroll through the list and click **Zack Hurley,** then click **Members** to add his name to the list. Click **OK** and the distribution list form is displayed with Zack Hurley added to the list. Click **Save and Close.**

❸ To send an e-mail to the **Teachers** personal distribution list, click **Inbox** and create a new message. Click **Address book** and select **Teachers** as the recipient of the message. Send an e-mail message to the list indicating the change in Yolanda's e-mail address. If your computer is online, you will receive an error message stating the e-mail message was undeliverable. If your computer is offline, a message for each person in the list will be held in the **Outbox folder** in the **My Shortcuts** group.

Using Signatures in Messages

It is appropriate and desirable in e-mail correspondence to include a signature at the end of the e-mail consisting of the name, job title, organization, mailing address, phone number, and e-mail address of the sender. Signatures are helpful to people receiving e-mails because they supply helpful contact information such as mailing address and phone number. You can also use a signature to add boilerplate information to your messages. For example, some people like to include a favorite quote or phrase. You can create multiple signatures and select a signature to insert in a message after you have created the message. When you set up a signature, you must also specify the default format for your e-mail messages.

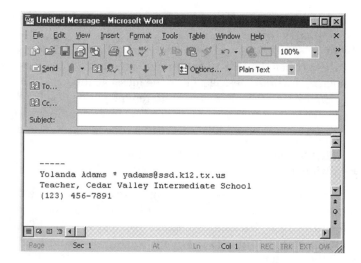

❶ To create a signature for Yolanda, select **Tools | Options | Mail Format.** *Outlook*® can send and receive messages in three formats: HTML, Rich Text, and Plain Text. HTML format allows for text formatting, numbering, bullets, alignment, horizontal lines, backgrounds, HTML styles, and Web pages. Rich Text includes text formatting, bullets, and alignment. Plain Text does not allow formatting of text. If you send much of your mail over the Internet, you should use Plain Text format for your e-mail messages rather than adding formatting that recipients might not be able to view. You can specify one of these as a default message format and override it when necessary for an individual message.

❷ Click on the down arrow of the **Compose in this message format box** to display a drop-down list and select **Plain Text** from the list. **NOTE:** This is a feature of computers that use the Windows® operating system.

❸ Click **Signatures** at the bottom of the **Options** dialog box and click **New.** In the **Enter a name for your new signature box**, enter **Yolanda Adams.** Under **Choose how to create your signature** click the **Start with a blank signature** radio button and click the **Next** button. In the **Signature** text box, enter the following information:

Yolanda Adams * yadams@ssd.k12.tx.us
Teacher, Cedar Valley Intermediate School
(123) 456-7891

❹ Click **Finish** and then click **OK.** On the **Options** dialog box in the **Signature for new messages box**, **Yolanda Adams** should be entered to automatically include signatures on all e-mail messages.(To stop automatically including signatures, select **None** here.) Click **OK.**

❺ On the **Inbox** folder click the **New Mail Message** icon. You should now see the signature added at the bottom of the message. Close the e-mail message without sending it by clicking the **X** in the top right corner of the e-mail form window.

Setting Other Options for Managing Messages

You can set several other options for sending and receiving messages and for managing your Inbox.

❶ To create a draft of a message, create a new message. In the **Subject** line enter **First Draft** and close the email form window by selecting **File | Close** or by clicking the **X** in the top right corner of the e-mail form window. When

Macintosh®: Select **Tools | Signature | New.** In the **Name of signature box**, enter **Yolanda Adams** and in the **Signature** text box enter the information for Yolanda Adams listed above and click the **Save** button. In the **Signatures** dialog box, **Yolanda Adams** should be set as the default signature by selecting it and clicking the **Set as Default** button. Click in the check box for **Add the default signature to the end of the outgoing message** to cause the signature to be added to your e-mail messages. Then click **Close.**

Macintosh®: When you close the e-mail message, click **Save** to save it in the **Drafts folder.** To retrieve the draft message, on the ***Outlook* Bar** click **Drafts** to open the **Drafts folder** and double click the message to open it.

the e-mail is closed with some information entered, it automatically saves it in the **Drafts folder**.

② To retrieve the draft message, on the ***Outlook* Bar** click **My Shortcuts,** click **Drafts** to open the **Drafts folder**, and double-click the message to open it.

③ To delete the draft message, close the message then click **Delete**.

④ You can flag a message or contact to remind yourself to follow up or to set a reminder for the message or contact. The three conditions for a flag are:

- No flag means an item is not flagged.
- A red flag means an item is flagged for action.
- A white flag means an item was flagged and the action was completed.

⑤ When the recipient receives a message with a flag, a comment on the purpose of the flag appears at the top of the message. If you set a reminder, the date will also appear. To flag the message you received for follow-up, select the message on the information window, click **Actions | Flag for Follow Up,** click the down arrow by the Flag to (**Flag** on Macintosh®) box, and select **Follow up** from the drop-down list.

⑥ Click the down arrow (check box on Macintosh®) by the **Due by** box, and use the calendar to find and select the current date. Some versions may have a second box that allows you to select a time. Select a time that is earlier than the current time on the computer and click **OK.**

⑦ Notice that the message is now displayed in red in the information window because flagged items past their due date are displayed in red.

⑧ To denote that action has been taken and completed for the message, highlight the message that is now displayed in red and select **Actions | Flag for Follow Up** and click **Clear Flag.**

⑨ You can mark a read message as unread. Select the message you received in step 2 and select **Edit | Mark as Unread.** Notice that the message is now displayed in bold as other unread messages. To mark the message as read, select **Edit | Mark as Read.**

⑩ Close *Outlook*®.

FOLLOW-UP PRACTICE PROJECTS

The following projects provide practice in maintaining your *Outlook*® Inbox folder. To perform these projects, you will use *Outlook*® and Microsoft® *Word*. In *Outlook*® use the **Inbox** icon to select the Inbox folder.

① **Keeping Track of Messages:** Several settings are available for the Inbox to help you manage your messages. To display a notification on the screen when you receive an e-mail message, select **Tools | Options.** Click **Preferences** and then click **E-mail Options.** Select or clear the **Display a notification message when new mail arrives** check box. To play a sound when you receive an e-mail message, click **Advanced E-mail Options.** Under **When new items arrive** click the **Play a sound** check box, then click **OK.**

② **Tracking When Messages are Delivered or Read:** You can track when messages you send are delivered or read by recipients with a message notification as each message is delivered or read. The contents of the message notifications are then automatically recorded on the **Tracking** tab of the original message in your Sent Items folder. You can automatically delete message notifications in your message list. To automatically process requests and responses to e-mails you receive, select **Tools | Options,** select **E-mail Options,** and select **Tracking Options.** Set one or more of the following options:

- Select the Process requests and responses on arrival check box.
- Select the Process receipts on arrival check box.
- Select the After Processing move receipts to check box.
- Move receipts out of your Inbox after processing
- Select the Delete blank voting and meeting responses after processing check box.

❸ If you use *Outlook*® as a client on a Microsoft® *Exchange* Server, you can use rules to manage your e-mail messages and automatically perform actions on messages. When you create a rule, *Outlook*® applies the rule when messages arrive in your Inbox or when you send a message. You can turn rules on or off and change the order for when rules are applied. You can also run rules manually. When you create a rule, you can specify whether the rule is applied when the message arrives in the Inbox or applied when you send a message. You can specify whether a rule runs automatically or manually in order to apply it to messages already delivered to your Inbox or other folder. Test the rules with one or more of the following options:

- Set up a notification, such as a message or a sound, when important messages arrive.
- Flag messages from a particular person.
- Assign categories to your sent messages based on the contents of the messages.
- Delay delivery of messages by a specified amount of time.
- Redirect a message to a person or distribution list.
- Move messages to a particular folder based on who sent them.

❹ Complete the lesson idea or plan you created in the previous lessons to target the grade level you teach or plan to teach. Relate it to the activity you just completed. It should describe using a language arts, social studies, science, or math theme (or subject or theme of your own choosing) for students to share information with other students who are located in another class or at another school. Update or add your lesson plan or idea in the **Lesson Plans ePortfolio**.

EXERCISES TO REVIEW AND EXPAND YOUR SKILLS

Set 1: Reviewing Terms and Concepts—For each question below, provide a term on the blank that matches the description.

_____ **1.** An icon that provides quick access to a program or folder.

_____ **2.** A collection of selected contacts lists from the Contacts folder.

_____ **3.** To automatically insert personal information or text in messages you send.

_____ **4.** An *Outlook*® folder that contains unfinished and unsent messages.

_____ **5.** View and print Contacts in a format that resembles an address card file.

Set 2: Expanding Your Skills—Expand on the skills you learned in this chapter with these activities.

1. Open an E-mail Attachment: Send a message to your own e-mail address, and attach a Microsoft® *Word* and a Microsoft® *Excel* file to the message. When you receive the message, open the attachments by double-clicking on each. View the file contents for each document.

2. **Save the Contents of an E-mail Attachment:** Save the contents of each attachment in your **My Documents** folder or other folder. After you save the documents in a folder, close *Outlook*® and then open each of the saved files to determine that each of the files is complete and not damaged or corrupted in any way.

Set 3: **Use Microsoft® Help**—Look up the following features to get further information and tips, and then test each of these features with one or more of the learning activities you used in this lesson.

- Look up **Address Book** to learn how to print the contents of your Contacts folder.
- Look up **Preview** and find information about **AutoPreview** to read the first few lines of a message in the information window.
- Look up **Digital Signature** to learn how to sign a message with a secure digital signature.

Set 4: **Create Your Own Lesson**—After reviewing the lessons in this chapter, develop and describe a lesson targeted for the grade level you teach or plan to teach that makes effective use of each of the following *Outlook*® features. Describe the procedure you or the students would need to create to complete the lesson. Enter your lesson idea or plan into the **Lesson Plans ePortfolio**.

- Students organize into teams and identify and research a specific topic or subject related to the curriculum (e.g., social studies, literature, earth science). Each team presents periodic progress reports to the teacher via e-mail, and the teacher provides feedback. Students prepare a final report based on their research and teacher feedback and send it as an attachment to the teacher.
- Students use Contacts and Microsoft® *Word* to develop a database of parents and use MailMerge to send a letter to parents announcing a classroom event or activity.
- Students develop a creative writing (poem, short story, report) and send it to students on a distribution list in another class for critique. Students provide feedback on one another's work and generate a final product.
- Students use e-mail to survey other students about a particular topic or subject related to the curriculum, record the survey data in Microsoft® *Excel,* and use a *PowerPoint*® presentation to report the results.

SCHEDULING AND PROJECT MANAGEMENT USING OUTLOOK®

NEW TERMS

AutoJournal	Notes List	tasks
events	recurring tasks	task timeline view
icons view	task requests	

OVERVIEW

Besides being a communication tool, Microsoft® *Outlook*® is a scheduling and project management tool. The three lessons in this chapter build skills in scheduling, project management, and journaling using *Outlook*®. Each tutorial consists of guided practice that demonstrates how teachers and students can use *Outlook*® for personal and professional productivity and classroom learning activities.

The lessons in this chapter demonstrate how teachers and students can use Microsoft® *Outlook*® features to schedule meetings and events and manage and organize information. Practice files for the tutorials are located in the OL folder on the T3 Practice CD. Following each lesson are several projects. Some exercises include activities from the Lesson Plans ePortfolio. Complete these projects to reinforce the learning activities demonstrated in the tutorials and to build your collection of technology-based lesson plans and ideas.

Lesson 11.1: Scheduling Using Calendar in *Outlook*®

Lesson 11.2: Managing Projects Using Tasks in *Outlook*®

Lesson 11.3: Keeping a Journal and Writing Notes in *Outlook*®

LESSON 11.1: SCHEDULING USING CALENDAR IN *OUTLOOK*®

Lesson 11.1: Learning Activities

Scheduling an appointment or meeting
Scheduling an event
Viewing the Calendar
Setting options for Calendar

Calendar allows you to schedule appointments, meetings, and events. While you use Calendar to schedule all three, each activity has certain characteristics:

- **Appointments** are activities that you schedule in your Calendar that do not involve other people or resources. You can set reminders for your appointments, schedule recurring appointments, and view appointments by day, week, or month. When you select start and end times for an appointment, you can take advantage of the AutoDate function and type text such as "next Tuesday" or "noon" instead of typing an exact date or time.
- **Meetings** are appointments to which you invite people or for which you reserve resources. You can create and send meeting requests and reserve resources for face-to-face or online meetings. When you create a meeting, you can identify the people to invite, the resources to reserve, and a meeting time. You can add people to an existing meeting or reschedule a meeting.
- **Events** are activities that last twenty-four hours or longer. Examples of an event include a conference, a seminar, or a vacation. Annual events occur yearly on a specific date, while standard events occur once and can last for one or more days. Events and annual events appear in banners in Calendar.

Since Yolanda had only a simple e-mail program on her home computer, she was enthusiastic about using some of the other features of Microsoft® *Outlook*®, especially the scheduling feature that would allow her to keep track of meetings and schedule appointments—even using the information in her Contacts list. Yolanda participates in a number of committees, has several duty assignments at her school, attends workshops and seminars, and meets with students and parents. Therefore, she wants to use *Outlook*® to record these activities in her calendar so she can maintain better control over her time and reduce scheduling conflicts.

Open *Outlook*® and click on the **Calendar** icon to open the **Calendar folder**.

LESSON 11.1: TUTORIAL

Scheduling an Appointment or Meeting

An appointment is an activity that you schedule in your Calendar that does not involve other people or resources. A recurring appointment repeats on a regular basis.

1 To schedule an appointment, select **File | New | Appointment** to display the Appointment data entry form.

2 In the **Subject** box enter **District Technology Committee Meeting**. In the **Location** box enter **Administrative Center, Room 201**.

3 Select a starting date that is the first **Thursday** of the first full week of the following month. Select **4:00 PM** for the **Start** time and **5:00 PM** for the **End** time by clicking the down arrow to display the drop-down list beside each of the start and end time fields. When you select the date for the Start time, it will automatically be entered in the date field for the **End** time.

4 Click the **Reminder** check box and select **4 hours** from the drop-down list. Your form should look similar to the following example:

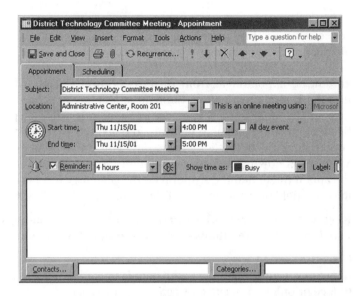

5 Click **Save and Close** to save the appointment, and then view the appointment in **Day/Week/Month View**. You may need to click the day of the appointment in the mini calendar in order to view it.

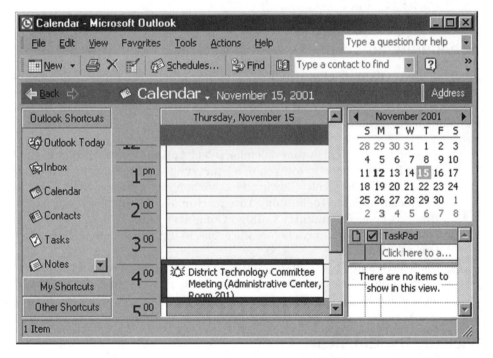

6 Create a new appointment by clicking **New Appointment** or **Actions | New Appointment** for **Wednesday** of the same week as the last appointment. Enter the description for the appointment as **Playground Duty.** The **Start** and **End** time is **7:45 AM** to **8:15 AM** (You must enter the beginning time since selections from the drop-down list are based on the hour and half-hour times.)

7 Click **Save and Close.**

8 Now create a new appointment of your own in the Calendar and save it.

9 To schedule a recurring appointment, select **Actions | New Recurring Appointment.** Enter **3:30 PM** for the **Start** time and **4:30 PM** for the **End** time. For the **Recurrence Pattern** click the **Monthly** radio button and the radio button to specify the **first Monday** of every **1** month. For **Range of recurrence** select the **End by** radio button and select the last day of the month **12** months from the current date and click **OK.** Enter **Faculty Meeting** for the **Subject** and **Faculty Lounge** for the **Location**. Click **Save and Close.**

⑩ To edit an appointment from **Day/Week/Month View** with AutoPreview, find the District Technology Committee Meeting appointment by scrolling through the monthly view calendar to the month with the appointment. Notice that days with appointments are in bold on the monthly calendar.

⑪ On the mini calendar click on the day with the appointment. On the **Day View** scroll down to the starting time of the appointment. Double-click on the appointment and the **Appointment** data entry form is displayed. In the message field near the bottom of the form enter the following text:

Review current technology plan and take copy to meeting.
Provide written feedback on Professional Development section.

⑫ Click **Save and Close.**

⑬ A meeting is an appointment with people invited to it. Meetings can be face-to-face or online. You can only send meeting requests if you use *Outlook*® to send e-mail. You can set up a meeting by setting up an appointment and then adding Contacts to it. Create a new appointment on **Wednesday** of the same week as the other appointments you previously created from **12:00 PM** to **12:30 PM.** The **Subjec**t of the meeting is **Grade Level Team Meeting.** Click **Save and Close.**

Scheduling an Event

An event is an activity that lasts twenty-four hours or more. An annual event occurs yearly on a specific date. Events and annual events appear in banners, rather than occupying blocks of time in your Calendar. Events are created in the same way as appointments, but marked as all-day events.

❶ To schedule an event in your Calendar, select **Actions | New All Day Event.**

❷ In the **Event** data entry form enter a **Start** time and **End** time of **Thursday** and **Friday** of the week following the other appointments you created. In the **Subject** box enter **Technology Integration Workshop** and in the **Location** box enter **Community College Computer Lab.**

❸ Set a reminder for **2 days** before the event. In the **Show time as** box select **Out of Office.**

❹ Click **Save and Close** and view the appointment in **Day/Week/Month View.** Click on one of the days of the Event and notice the Event is displayed as a banner across the **Day View.**

Viewing the Calendar

In order to use your Calendar for planning and scheduling, there are several ways to view the Calendar. The **Day/Week/Month View** of Calendar allows the screen display to include one day, a work week, a week, or a month.

❶ In **Day/Week/Month View** click on **Monday** of the week of the appointments you entered earlier. On the **Standard Toolbar** click **Day,** then **Work Week,** then **Week,** and then **Month** and observe the format and layout of each view.

Macintosh®: Click on the **Change View** icon. A drop-down list is displayed with options for multiple days, week, or month view.

Setting Options for Calendar

There are several options you can set to customize Calendars for your individual needs.

❶ To change the calendar background, select **Tools | Options | Preferences** and select **Calendar Options.** In the **Background color:** field select the color you want. Click **OK** and **OK** again. This color is applied to Day and Work Week views. Week and Month views use white and gray background colors. Additionally, the color you choose is applied to weekday hours and a darker version of the background color you chose is applied to night and weekend hours. **NOTE:** This is a feature of computers that use the Windows® operating system.

❷ To set the days of your work week, select **Tools | Options | Preferences** and select **Calendar Options.** In the **Calendar Work Week** section click each of the check boxes for Monday through Saturday. Click **OK** and **OK** again.

❸ To set the hours of your work day, select **Tools | Options | Preferences,** and select **Calendar Options.** Click on the down arrow of the Start time: field and select **7:30 AM** from the drop-down list. Click on the down arrow of the End time: field and select **4:30 PM** from the drop-down list. Click **OK** and **OK** again.

❹ To load holidays into your calendar, select **Tools | Options | Preferences,** and select **Calendar Options.** In the Calendar Options section click **Add Holidays** and click the check box for **United States.** Click **OK.** If the holidays have not been loaded into the Calendar, they will be loaded. If the holidays have previously been loaded, allow Calendar to reinstall them. (**NOTE:** This is a feature of computers that use the Windows® operating system.) Click **OK** and **OK** again.

❺ Close *Outlook®.*

Macintosh®: On Macintosh® you can set the beginning day of the work week. Select **Edit | Preferences** and under **Calendar** select **General.** Click on the down arrow beside **Week starts on** and select **Monday** from the drop-down list, then click **OK.**

Macintosh®: Select **Edit | Preferences** and under **Calendar** select **General.** Click on the down arrow beside **Work day starts at** and select **7:30 am** from the drop-down list, and then click on the down arrow beside Work day ends at and select **4:30 pm** from the drop-down list. Click **OK.**

FOLLOW-UP PRACTICE PROJECTS

In the following projects you will use *Outlook®* and *Word* in order to practice extending the features of Calendar by publishing your calendar on the Web or distributing it by e-mail. After completing the projects, close *Outlook®.* In *Outlook®* use the Calendar icon to select the Calendar folder.

❶ **Save a Personal Calendar as a Web Page:** (**NOTE:** This is a feature of computers that use the Windows® operating system.) You can save a calendar as a Web page and then share it with others. When you save a calendar as a Web page, you can specify the start and end dates for the calendar and whether to include appointment details that are entered in the text section of the appointment. You can post your calendar to almost any standard Web server.

- To create a Web page of your calendar for a specific period of time, select **File | Save as Web Page.**
- Under **Duration** enter the first and last day of the month for which you created appointments, meetings, and events in the tutorial in this lesson in the **Start date** and **End date** boxes.
- Under **Options** select **Include appointment details.** Under **Save As** for the **Calendar title** enter something like **My Web Calendar.** For the **File name** box enter something like, **MyWebCalendar** (be sure to note the file name and what folder you save it in).
- To view the Web calendar in your browser after you save it, click in the **Open saved Web page in browser** check box. An example calendar Web page is available under the **OL folder** on the **T3 Practice CD** with the file name, **MyWebCalendar.htm.**

② **AutoCreate and Creating New Items from Existing Items:** To quickly create a new item, you can drag an item of one type into a folder of items of another type. For example, to create an appointment from an e-mail message, drag the message into the Calendar folder. Relevant information from the message is added to fields in the new appointment, and the entire message appears in the appointment body.

AutoCreate works only with items of different types such as a message and an appointment. If you drag a meeting request or task request from your Inbox to Calendar or Tasks, the request is automatically accepted and an acceptance reply is sent to the sender. Try this by dragging the e-mail message received in the tutorial to the Calendar folder on the *Outlook* Bar. When the Calendar data entry form is displayed, finish entering information appropriate to make an appointment or event in your e-mail.

LESSON 11.2: MANAGING PROJECTS USING TASKS IN *OUTLOOK*®

Lesson 11.2: Learning Activities

Creating a task
Setting other views and options of Tasks

A task is a personal or work-related activity you want to track from its beginning through completion. A task can occur once or repeatedly. A recurring task can repeat at regular intervals or based on the date you mark the task complete. Recurring tasks are added one at a time to the task list. When you mark one occurrence of the task complete, the next occurrence appears in the list.

If you use *Outlook*® to send e-mail, you can create tasks that you assign to others. You do this by sending a task request to someone. The person who receives the task request becomes the temporary owner of the task. They can decline the task, accept the task, or assign the task to someone else. If they decline the task, it is returned to you. If they accept the task, they become the permanent owner. If they assign the task to someone else, the new assignee becomes the owner.

Since Yolanda is a first-year teacher, she wants to use the project management and journaling features of *Outlook*® to help her track the progress of student projects and learning activities and to maintain a journal of instructional activities that take place in her classroom. Additionally, she wants to track her current work projects to document her progress and facilitate discussions with her mentor teacher. With *Outlook*® it is possible to track and journalize activities as well as coordinate and integrate these activities with the Inbox, Contacts, and Calendar.

Open *Outlook*® and click on the **Tasks** icon to open the **Tasks folder**.

LESSON 11.2: TUTORIAL

Creating a Task

A task is a personal or work-related activity you want to track through completion. It can occur once or repeatedly.

① To create a task that occurs once, select **File | New | Task** to display the **Task** data entry form or click **New Task.** The **Task** data entry form resembles the data entry form for a **New Appointment**. In the **Subject** box enter **Rewrite Professional Development section of District Technology Plan.**

② In the drop-down list for the **Due date** box select a date one month from today's date. In the drop-down list for the **Status** box select **In Progress.**

Select **Reminder** and set a reminder for one day before the due date of the task.

❸ Enter the following text in the message box:

Review and update Professional Development section of the District Technology Plan based on ISTE NETS-T technology standards.

❹ To add people to the task, click the **Contacts.** Select **Susan Adams** then click **Apply,** select **Sharon Shapiro** then click **Apply,** and select **Eddy Stevens** then click **Apply.** Click **OK.** Your form should look similar to the following example:

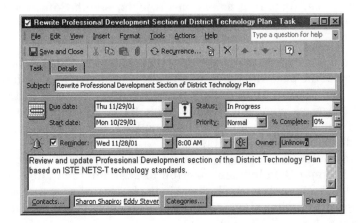

❺ Click **Save and Close** to save the task. Then view the task in **Simple List View**, similar to the following example:

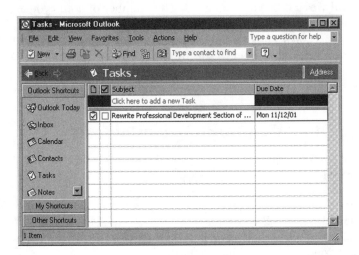

❻ To quickly add a task in the task list, double-click on a blank line in **Simple List View** or point at a blank line and press **ENTER.** In the **Subject** line enter **Studying Early Native Americans Via E-Mail.**

❼ Select a **due date** in about six weeks from the current date.

❽ Click **Save and Close** to save the task.

❾ Now add a Task of your own to the Task list and save it.

❿ To create a task that recurs at regular intervals, select **File | New | Task** to display the **Task** data entry form, select the **New Task** icon, or double-click on a blank line of the **Simple List View**.

⓫ In the **Subject** box, enter **Monthly Vocabulary List.** Select **In Progress** for the Status. Select **Actions | Recurrence** or click the **Recurrence** icon.

For the **Recurrence pattern** select **Monthly** and then select the **first Monday** of every **1** month.

⑫ Select **End by** and enter the next **May 31.**

⑬ Click **OK** then **Save and Close.**

⑭ To edit a task, double-click on the task with the **Subject** entitled **Studying Early Native Americans Via E-mail** (double-click on ▶ on Macintosh®). From the drop-down list for the **Status** box select **In Progress.** Enter the following text in the message box:

Students research topics and share them with audiences throughout the state using e-mail. The unit is developed using a variety of resources, including hands-on projects, simulations, books, local resource people, field trips, Internet Websites, and e-mail.

⑮ Click **Save and Close** to save the edited task.

⑯ To mark a task as complete on the **Task list**, click in the check box on the left of the task with the **Subject** entitled **Rewrite Professional Development section of District Technology Plan.** Notice that the task is now marked as completed on the **Task list** with a check mark and a line through the task. Remove the complete status by clicking again on the check box for the same task.

⑰ To mark a task partially complete, double-click on the task, **Rewrite Professional Development section of District Technology Plan** (double-click on ▶ on Macintosh®) and in the **% Complete** box select **50%.** Click **Save and Close.** On the **Task list** no check mark appears for the task since it is not 100% complete.

⑱ To record time information on a task, select the task **Rewrite Professional Development section of District Technology Plan.** Click the **Details** tab (not on Macintosh®) and in the **Total work** field enter **6 hours.** In the **Actual work** box, you would enter the number of hours you actually spent on the task. Click **Save and Close.**

⑲ To sort tasks, click on the heading label for which you want to sort the **Task list.** Click on **Subject** to sort by subject. Now click on **Due Date** to sort the tasks by due date.

Setting Other Views and Options of Tasks

You can set several options to customize Tasks or change the view to fit your individual needs.

❶ To change to a **Timeline View** of Tasks, select **View | Current View | Task Timeline.** Scroll forward and backward along the timeline. You can select a task by double-clicking on it. **NOTE:** This is a feature of computers that uses the Windows® operating system.)

❷ To change to a detailed table view of tasks, select **View | Current View | Detailed List.**

❸ To change the color of overdue Tasks, select **Tools | Options** and select the **Preferences** tab. Click **Task Options** and select a color in the **Overdue tasks color** box and in the **Completed tasks color** box. Click **OK** and then **OK** again. **NOTE:** This is a feature of computers that uses the Windows® operating system.

❹ To stop the recurrence of a task, edit the **Monthly Vocabulary List** task. In the **Task** data entry form select **Actions | Recurrence** (or click **Recurrence**) and click **Remove Recurrence.** Click **Save and Close** to save the edited task.

❺ Close *Outlook*®.

Macintosh®: To view the task list in various forms such as All Tasks, Active Tasks, Overdue Tasks, or Completed Tasks, select **View | Tasks** and select the form of the **Task list** you want to display.

FOLLOW-UP PRACTICE PROJECTS

To perform the following projects, you will use *Outlook*® in order to provide practice in using Tasks to monitor and track student learning activities and projects. After completing the projects, close *Outlook*®.

In *Outlook*® use the **Tasks** icon to select the **Tasks folder**.

❶ Create a New Project Task: Create a new task that is based on a student assignment. You have assigned your class to e-mail students you have located for them in other countries to exchange information about differences in customs and opinions on events in different parts of the world. After they work in teams to complete their e-mail exchanges, they will summarize their findings and create a report on their region. Create a new project task with the subject **Gathering Information for Different Cultures.** Enter lesson plan information in the message box and **Save and Close** the task.

- Drag the **Task** onto the **Calendar folder** on the *Outlook*® folder list. In **Calendar View** select a beginning date and ending date that is two weeks later. Now view the task in Calendar. Notice the task is recorded in Calendar as an event.
- Use **Plan a Meeting** (on **Actions** menu) to assign members to a team and schedule a meeting. You can add attendees to the meeting by selecting names from the address book. Add three attendees to the task and meeting.

❷ Using Categories to Coordinate Projects: Open the task **Gathering Information for Different Cultures** and click **Categories.** In the top window enter a category name for the item called **Writing and Research Methods** and click **OK.** The **Task** is now assigned to the new category. Now create a new project task following the procedure in the first project above and assign it to the new category, but add three different names on the **Attendee** list. This procedure allows you to create the same project or task for multiple groups. What are some other ways you could organize project teams using Tasks?

❸ Creating Custom Views of Tasks: (**NOTE:** This is a feature of computers that uses the Windows® operating system.) Define a custom view for tasks and name it **Curriculum Projects Report** and select Cards as the type of view. For the available fields select all Task fields and **Add** them from the list on the left to the list on the right with the exception of **Recurring** or **Reminder** fields (and any other fields you may not use). Filter the view by **Category** to display only the tasks for your new category **Writing and Research Methods.** Modify the output of your card view to include only those fields you actually use.

❹ Create a lesson idea or plan to target the grade level you teach or plan to teach related to the activity you just completed. It should describe students using Tasks to plan and organize a science or math project or other complex project conducted with a small group or team of students. Update or add your lesson plan or idea in the **Lesson Plans ePortfolio.**

LESSON 11.3: KEEPING A JOURNAL AND WRITING NOTES IN *OUTLOOK*®

Lesson 11.3: Learning Activities

Activating automatic Journaling
Recording an activity manually in the Journal
Creating a note

You can use Journal to record interactions with important contacts and important items and activities. Activities that can be automatically recorded in Journal include *Outlook*® functions such as e-mail messages, meeting requests and responses, task requests and responses, and Microsoft® *Office* documents created in *Word, Excel,* and *PowerPoint*®.

The Journal folder is a timeline of events and activities. Journal items are stored in the Journal folder in the order in which they occur. By default, Journal is not turned on because journaling will create a link to every item you create. Journaling should be used carefully, because it can increase the size of your mailbox.

Yolanda wants to track activities for certain contacts and tasks using Journal. She wants to track projects she is working on as a part of her first-year teacher/mentor program, meetings she attends, and interactions with certain people on her Contacts list. With *Outlook*® it is possible to track and journalize activities as well as coordinate and integrate these activities with the Inbox, Contacts, and Calendar.

Open *Outlook*®, click on the **My Shortcuts** group (Windows® only), and click on the **Journal** icon to open the **Journal folder**.

Macintosh®: Journaling is not a strong feature of *Outlook*® on the Macintosh®. To use a Journal folder, be sure that you have included the Journal folder on the ***Outlook Bar***. Select **Edit | Preferences,** select **Microsoft Outlook,** and then select **General.** Click in the **Show folders containing journal items** check box and click **OK.** The first two Sections in this lesson cover Journal features that are not included in Macintosh® *Outlook*®.

LESSON 11.3: TUTORIAL

Activating Automatic Journaling

Journal entries can be recorded either manually or automatically. You can set the Journal to automatically record items that reference specific contacts or documents created in any Microsoft® *Office* application. **NOTE:** This is a feature of computers that uses the Windows® operating system.

① To automatically record a document in Journal, select **Tools I Options**, select the **Preferences** tab, and click **Journal Options.** Select the **e-mail** check box in the **Automatically record these items** box. Select the check box for **Eddy Stevens** in the **For these contacts** box to automatically record e-mail transactions in Journal related to this individual. Click **OK** and **OK** again.

② To turn off automatic recording of documents in Journal, clear the check box next to the contact for which you want to stop automatic recording.

Recording an Activity Manually in the Journal

A manual Journal entry can be used to record activities such as phone conversations, work or research activities, and meetings. **NOTE:** This is a feature of computers that uses the Windows® operating system.

① To record a manual Journal entry, select **File I New I Journal Entry.**
② In the **Subject** box enter **District Technology Committee Meeting.** Select **Meeting** from the drop-down list of the **Entry type** field. Select **4:00 PM** as the start time. In the **Duration** field select **1 hour** from the drop-down list.
③ Enter the following text in the message box: **Reviewed Professional development of the District Technology Plan.**
④ Select **Save and Close** to save the manual journal entry.

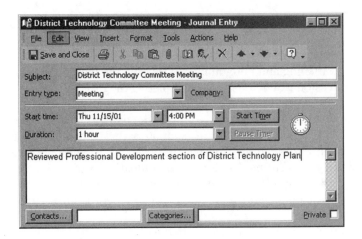

Creating a Note

Notes are the electronic equivalent of paper sticky notes. You can use Notes in the same way as you would write bits of information such as brainstorming ideas, reminders, phone numbers, or directions on a note pad. With Notes you can "stick" the note on your computer desktop. When you change a note, the changes are saved automatically. You can leave Notes open on the screen while you work, or you can close a Note and leave it in the Notes folder. Click **Notes** to open the **Notes folder**.

1 To record a Note, start select **File | New | Note** or click **New Note.**

2 Enter the following text in the **NOTE: Hand out monthly vocabulary list at the end of the day.** The note continues to be displayed on the screen.

3 Minimize *Outlook®* and notice that the note is still displayed on the screen. Then maximize *Outlook®* again.

4 To close the note, click the **X** in the upper right corner of the **Note.**

5 To change the color of a note, open the note by double-clicking on it. Click the **Note icon** in the upper-left corner of the Note window and select **Color.** Select a color that is different than the default color.

6 To show or hide the time and date on Notes, select **Tools | Options** and select the **Other** tab. Click **Advanced Options** and click the **When viewing Notes, show time and date** check box to clear it. Click **OK** and then **OK** again **NOTE:** This is a feature of computers that uses the Windows® operating system.

7 The default view of Notes is **Icons View**. To view Notes in **Notes List View,** select **View | Current View | Notes List.** Now change the view back to **Icons. NOTE:** This is a feature of computers that uses the Windows® operating system.

8 You can assign a note to a category. Select or highlight the note and select **Edit | Categories.** Type **Vocabulary** in the category window, click **Add to list,** and click **OK.** The Vocabulary category should now be indicated for the note on the Notes List. **NOTE:** This is a feature of computers that uses the Windows® operating system.

9 To change the font, font size, or font style on Notes, select **Tools | Options** and select the **Note Options** button. Click **Font** and change the **Size** to **12,** then click **OK.** Click **OK** on the **Notes Options** dialog box, and click **OK** on the **Options** dialog box. View the note and notice the change in the font size.

10 To delete the note, select the note and select **Edit | Delete** or click **Delete.**

11 Close *Outlook®*.

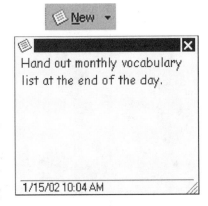

Macintosh®: Select **Actions | Change Color** and select a color that is different from the default color.

Macintosh®: Select **View | Magnify Text** and select **150%.** View the note and notice the change in the font size.

Follow-up Practice Projects

To perform the following projects, you will use *Outlook*® to provide practice in integrating journaling and note-taking to describe the instructional process or coordinate professional activities. After completing the projects, close *Outlook*®.

1 **Recording Information about Microsoft® *Office* Files in Journal:** (**NOTE:** This is a feature of computers that uses the Windows® operating system.) You can use Journal to locate information about a file based on when you performed actions on that file. For example, you can quickly look up a *Word, Excel,* or *PowerPoint*® document you recently worked on if you set these documents to be automatically recorded in Journal. You can open a journal entry and review details about the activity, or you can use the Journal as a shortcut to go directly to the file to which the journal entry refers. To automatically record a document in Journal, select **Tools | Options** select the **Preferences** tab, and click **Journal Options.** Select the check boxes beside **Microsoft Excel, Microsoft PowerPoint,** and **Microsoft Word.**

2 **Using Journal for Reflection about Teaching:** (**NOTE:** This is a feature of computers that uses the Windows® operating system.) Use Journal to record your observations and reflections about classroom behavior and as a platform for discussion during the teaching/mentoring process.

3 **Save a Note as a File:** You may want to save the contents of notes in a file to process with another program, such as Microsoft® *Word.* You can save a note as a file and open it in Microsoft® *Word.* You can save a note as a simple text file or in rich text format to retain some of the original formatting, such as fonts. Select the **Notes** icon to select the **Notes folder** and click a note to highlight it. On the File menu, click **Save As** and in the **Save in** list click the location where you want to save the file. In the **File name** box, type a name for the file, and in the **Save as type** box, select **Text Only** or **Rich Text Format.** After you have saved the note as a file, open it from *Word.*

Exercises to Review and Expand Your Skills

Set 1: **Reviewing Terms and Concepts**—For each question below, provide a term on the blank that matches the description.

_____ **1.** Activities that are scheduled in Calendar that do not involve inviting other people or reserving resources.

_____ **2.** A personal or work-related activity that can be tracked through completion.

_____ **3.** The electronic equivalent of paper sticky notes.

_____ **4.** Automatically create a new item by dragging an item of one type into a folder of items of another type.

_____ **5.** A Calendar activity that lasts twenty-four hours or more and allows you to display your time as either free or busy.

Set 2: **Expanding Your Skills**—Expand on the skills you learned in this chapter with these activities. Send an e-mail to your own e-mail address. Attach different types of files and then practice opening and saving the attachments.

1. **Open an E-mail Attachment.** Send a message to your own e-mail address and attach a Microsoft® *Word* and a Microsoft® *Excel* file to the message. When you receive the message, open an attachment by double-clicking on it.

2. **Save the Contents of an E-mail Attachment.** Save the contents of each attachment in your My Documents folder or other folder. After you save the documents in a folder, close *Outlook*® and then open each of the saved files to determine that each of the files is saved correctly.

Set 3: Use Microsoft® Help—Look up the following features to get further information and tips, and then test each of these features with one or more of the learning activities you used in this chapter.

- Look up **Task** and find **Assign a task to someone else** to learn to use collaboration features of *Outlook*® to assign tasks.
- Look up **Form** to get information on built-in forms for sending messages and for storing contact information.
- Look up **Collaboration** to get information on putting your calendar online, scheduling meetings online, and conducting meetings online.

Set 4: Create Your Own Lesson—After reviewing the lessons in this chapter, develop and describe a lesson targeted for the grade level you teach or plan to teach that makes effective use of each of the following *Outlook*® features. Describe the procedure you or the students would need to create to complete the lesson. Enter your lesson idea or plan into the **Lesson Plans ePortfolio**.

- Students are presented with a problem on a topic or subject related to the curriculum requiring students to use critical thinking including problem solving or decision making. Students conduct a series of online problem-solving or decision-making discussions with students in another classroom, create a journal of their discussions, and prepare a written report of their solution using Microsoft® *Word*.
- Students keep an electronic journal of their ideas, observations, or reflections about a specific subject or issue. The electronic journal entries are then synthesized into a poem, story, or report.
- Students organize into teams and identify and research a specific topic or subject related to the curriculum (e.g., social studies, literature, earth science). Each team presents periodic progress reports to the teacher via e-mail and the teacher provides feedback. Students prepare a final report based on their research and teacher feedback and send it as an attachment to the teacher.
- Students brainstorm to develop ideas for a story, science experiment, history project, or research topic and use Notes to record brainstorming ideas and Categories to classify and prioritize ideas.
- Students use Tasks to maintain homework assignments and prepare a custom view to print a weekly homework completion report.

REFERENCES

Baugh, I., & Baugh, J. (1997). Global classrooms: E-mail learning communities. *Learning and Leading with Technology, 25*(3), 38–41.

Boehm, D. (1997). I lost my tooth! *Learning and Leading with Technology, 24*(7), 17–19.

Forcier, R. C., & Descy, D.E. (2002). *The computer as an educational tool: Productivity and problem solving.* Upper Saddle River, NJ: Prentice-Hall, Inc.

Harris, J. (1994). Information collection activities. *The Computing Teacher, 21*(6), 32–33.

Harriss, S. (1992). Let's build our science vocabularies. *The Florida Technology in Education Quarterly, 4*(2), 71–72.

International Society for Technology in Education (2001). [Web site] (http://www.iste.org)

Jonassen, D. H. (2000). *Computers as mindtools for schools: Engaging critical thinking.* Upper Saddle River, NJ: Prentice-Hall, Inc.

Justice, B. (1996). Eating right? Fat chance! Teaching math and nutrition with spreadsheets. *Learning and Leading with Technology, 23*(8), 16–19.

Morrison, G. R., Lowther, D.L., & DeMeulle, L. (1999). *Integrating computer technology into the classroom.* Upper Saddle River, NJ: Prentice-Hall, Inc.

Roblyer, M. D. (2003). *Integrating educational technology into teaching.* (3rd ed.) Upper Saddle River, NJ: Prentice-Hall, Inc.

Roblyer, M. D., & Edwards, J. (2000). *Integrating educational technology into teaching.* (2nd ed.) Upper Saddle River, NJ: Prentice-Hall, Inc.

Wresch, W. (1990). Collaborative writing projects: Lesson plans for the computer age. *The Computing Teacher, 18*(2), 19–21.

MICROSOFT® *OFFICE* FEATURES

OFFICE® MENUS AND TOOLBARS

All Microsoft® *Office* programs operate from a common user interface. A menu located at the top of the display screen or application window called the Menu Bar displays a list of commands. Some of these menu commands have images next to them so you can easily associate the command with the image. Toolbars can contain buttons, menus, or a combination of both. The buttons on the toolbars provide shortcuts for performing menu commands rather than selecting the command from the menu.

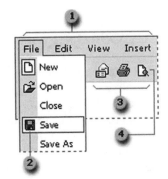

1. Menu Bar
2. Menu command
3. Toolbar
4. Button

DISPLAYING COMMANDS AND BUTTONS USED MOST OFTEN

Microsoft® *Office* automatically customizes menus and toolbars based on how often you use various commands. When you first start an *Office*® program, only the most basic commands appear. As you work with the program, the menus and toolbars adapt to your command selections so that only the commands and toolbar buttons you use most often appear on the drop-down menu.

DISPLAYING ADDITIONAL COMMANDS ON A MENU

To look for a command that you do not use very often or have never used before, click the double-arrows (❤) at the bottom of the menu to show all the commands. You can also double-click the menu to expand it. When you expand one menu, all of the menus are expanded until you choose a command or perform another action.

When you click a command on the expanded menu, the command is immediately added to the short version of the menu. If you do not use the command often, it is dropped from the short version of the menu.

POSITIONING TOOLBARS

Toolbars can be positioned next to each other in the same row or above and below each other in different rows. For example, to place the **Standard Toolbar** above the **Formatting Toolbar**, select **Tools | Customize**, select the **Options** tab, and uncheck the **Standard and Formatting toolbars share one row** check box. Then click **Close.**

You can also drag toolbars. Point at a toolbar's left side until the cursor changes to a four-headed arrow. Click and drag the toolbar to a new location and drop it there. Generally, the toolbars you want displayed are the **Standard Toolbar** and the **Formatting Toolbar**.

DISPLAYING HIDDEN TOOLBAR BUTTONS

When you place multiple toolbars in the same row, there may not be enough horizontal space on the program window to display all of the buttons. If enough space is not available, the buttons used most recently are displayed and the others are hidden.

You can resize a toolbar to display more buttons, or you can show all buttons on a toolbar. To see a list of the hidden buttons, click **More Buttons** at the end of the toolbar. When you use a hidden button that is not displayed on the toolbar, that button is moved to the toolbar and a button that has not been used recently is dropped to the hidden list.

CUSTOMIZING MENUS AND TOOLBARS

You can customize menus and toolbars by adding and removing buttons and menus on toolbars, creating your own custom toolbars, hiding or displaying toolbars, and moving toolbars. You can customize the **Menu Bar** the same way you customize any built-in toolbar. For example, you can quickly add and remove buttons and menus on the **Menu Bar**, although you cannot hide the **Menu Bar**.

You cannot add, delete, or reset a menu in _Office_®, but you can modify a command image, rename a command, display an icon and text for a command, or move or copy commands to or from a menu. For example, to add a command to a toolbar, select **Tools | Customize** and select the **Commands** tab. In the **Categories** box click the command category (menu) for the command, and click and drag the graphic button for the command from the **Commands** box onto the toolbar on which you want it to be displayed and then release the mouse (the toolbar must already be displayed in the program window).

CUSTOMIZING THE OPERATING ENVIRONMENT

You can modify the operating environment of any _Office_® program by selecting **Tools | Options**. The **Options Menu** allows you to select or modify default operations of the application. For example, you can select the default location for saving files you create with the _Office_® program: in _Word_ select the **File Locations** tab; in _Excel_ select the **General** tab; and in _PowerPoint_® select the **Save** tab.

When you first use a program, review its options so you can customize the program to meet your operating preferences and maximize your personal use of the program.

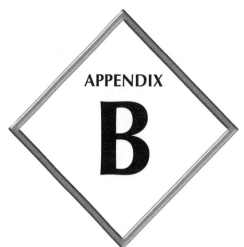
MICROSOFT® OFFICE FAMILY OF PRODUCTIVITY TOOLS

MICROSOFT® OFFICE FAMILY

Microsoft® *Office* is the most widely used suite of productivity software. It helps you complete common business tasks including e-mail, word processing, presentations, data management and analysis, and much more. The Microsoft® *Office* suite includes Microsoft® *Word*, Microsoft® *Excel*, Microsoft® *Outlook*®, Microsoft® *PowerPoint*®, Microsoft® *Access*, Microsoft® *FrontPage*®, and Microsoft® *Publisher*.

MICROSOFT® OFFICE XP NEW FEATURES

Microsoft® *Office* for Windows® has migrated through several updates and versions during its life span. The latest version of Microsoft® *Office* for Windows® is *Office*® *XP*. *Office*® *XP* includes the following new features:

- ***Office*® Task Panes.** The most common tasks in Microsoft® *Office* are organized in panes that display with the *Office*® document. For example, you can continue working with a document while you search for a file using the Search Task Pane or pick from a gallery of items to paste in the *Office*® Clipboard Task Pane. You can create new documents or open files using the Task Pane that appears when you start an *Office*® program. Other Task Panes that are available vary with each *Office*® program.

- **New look.** Microsoft® *Office* XP uses soft colors to contribute to a cleaner, simpler look to its interface.

- **More convenient access to Help.** The full power of the Answer Wizard is available in an unobtrusive package. When you enter a question about an *Office*® program in the Ask a Question box on the Menu Bar, you can see a list of choices and read a Help topic whether or not you are running the Office Assistant.

- **Control paste options and automatic changes with Smart Tags.** New in-place buttons called "Smart Tags" let you adjust how information is pasted or how automatic changes occur in *Office*® programs. For example, when you paste text from a *Word* document into a *PowerPoint*® document, a button appears next to the text. Click the button to see a list of choices for fine-tuning the formatting of the pasted text, or ignore the Smart Tag and continue working and the Smart Tag disappears. Smart Tags and their associated choices vary with each *Office*® program.

- **Updated Clip Art Organizer.** The Clip Art Gallery is now called the Clip Art Organizer in *Office*® *XP*. The Clip Art Organizer contains hundreds of new clips, provides an easy Task Pane interface, and preserves the existing capabilities of the Clip Art Gallery to organize clips and link to new digital art on the Web.

- **Conceptual diagrams.** *Word*, *Excel*, and *PowerPoint*® include a new gallery of conceptual diagrams. You can choose from diagrams such as Pyramid for showing the building blocks of a relationship or Radial for showing items in relation to a core element. Several categories of diagrams are available.

- **Voice commands and dictation.** In addition to mouse and keyboard methods, you can select menu, toolbar, and dialog box items by speaking. After meeting some special hardware requirements, you can also dictate text. This feature is available in the Simplified Chinese, English (U.S.), and Japanese language versions of Microsoft® *Office*.

- **Support for handwriting.** You can use handwriting recognition to enter text into an *Office*® document. You can write by using a handwriting input device, such as a graphics tablet or a tablet-PC, or you can write using your mouse. Your natural handwriting is converted to typed characters. In *Word* and Microsoft® *Outlook*® you can also choose to leave text in handwritten form.

- **Improved fidelity of pictures and drawings.** Microsoft® *Word*, *Excel*, *PowerPoint*®, *FrontPage*®, and *Publisher*® use an improved graphics system in Microsoft® *Office XP*. Under this new graphics system digital pictures stay sharper and clearer when they are resized. Shapes and WordArt have smoother outlines and adjustable levels of transparency with true blending.

- **Accessibility.** *Office*® *XP* programs support technology that makes accessibility aids such as screen readers or screen enlargers more effective.

- **Find printers.** If your computer uses Microsoft® *Windows*® 2000 and the Active Directory service, you can search for printers across your network from the Print dialog box in *Office*® *XP* programs.

- **Storing documents with Microsoft® *Exchange* Server 2000.** You can store Microsoft® *Office* documents on *Exchange* Server 2000 and access them through the File | Open, File | New, and File | Save dialog boxes as you would any other *Office*® document.

- **Digital signatures.** You can apply a digital signature to Microsoft® *Word*, *Excel*, and *PowerPoint*® document files to confirm that the file has not been altered.

- **Increased protection against macro viruses.** Network administrators can remove Microsoft® *Visual Basic* for Applications, the programming language of Microsoft® *Office*, when deploying *Office*®. This can decrease the possibility of viruses spreading via *Office*® documents.

- **Target your Web publishing efforts.** You can save your Microsoft® *Office* documents as Web pages for older versions of various Web browsers to give readers the best possible Web surfing experience.

- **Share your *Office*® documents over the Web.** When you save documents to Web sites on MSN from any *Office*® program, you can have an instant collaboration space where you can share files with other people.

- **Save a Web site as a single file.** A special Web archive file format is available in Microsoft® *Access*, *Excel*, *PowerPoint*®, *Publisher*®, and *Word*. This file format lets you save all the elements of a Web site, including text and graphics, into a single file.

- **Open *Office*® Web pages for editing from the browser.** *Office*® programs recognize the HTML pages that they generate. From Microsoft® *Internet Explorer* you can open an *Office*® document that you have saved as a Web page in the program in which it was created.

- **Document recovery and safer shutdown.** The document file you are working on when an *Office*® program encounters an error or stops responding can be recovered. The document is displayed in the Document Recovery Task Pane the next time you open the program.

- ***Office*® Safe Mode.** Microsoft® *Office XP* programs can detect and isolate startup problems. You can either bypass the problem or run your *Office*® program in safe mode.

- ***Office*® crash reporting tool.** Diagnostic information about program crashes can be collected and sent to an organization's information technology department or to Microsoft®, allowing engineers to correct these problems so they do not cause interruptions again.

System Hardware Requirements—Microsoft® *Office XP*

The latest version of Microsoft® *Office* for Windows® is *Office*® XP. The recommended system configuration to use Microsoft® *Office XP* is Microsoft® Windows® XP on a personal computer with a Pentium III processor and 128 MB of RAM. The following hardware configuration describes the minimum requirements your computer needs to run *Office*® XP:

- **Computer/Processor:** Pentium 133 megahertz (MHz) or higher processor (Pentium III recommended)

- **Memory requirements depend on the operating system used:** Windows® 98 or Windows® 98 Second Edition—24 MB of RAM plus an additional 8 MB of RAM for each *Office*® program running simultaneously; Windows® Me or Microsoft® Windows® NT—32 MB of RAM plus an additional 8 MB of RAM for each *Office*® application running simultaneously; Windows® 2000 Professional—64 MB of RAM plus an additional 8 MB of RAM for each *Office*® application running simultaneously; Windows® XP Professional or Windows® XP Home Edition—128 MB of RAM plus an additional 8 MB of RAM for each *Office*® application running simultaneously

- **Hard Disk requirements will vary depending on configuration:** *Office*® XP *Standard*—210 MB of available hard disk space; *Office*® XP *Professional and Professional Special Edition*—245 MB of available hard disk space; additional 115 MB is required on the hard disk where the operating system is installed (Computers without Windows®XP, Windows® 2000, Windows® Me, or *Office*® 2000 Service Release 1 (SR–1) require an extra 50 MB of hard disk space for System Files Update.)

- **Operating System:** Windows® 98, Windows® 98 Second Edition, Windows® Millennium Edition (Windows® Me), Windows® NT® 4.0 with Service Pack 6 (SP6) or later, Windows® 2000, or Windows® XP or later

- **CD-ROM Drive**

- **Super VGA (800 × 600) or higher-resolution monitor** with 256 colors

- **Peripherals:** Microsoft® Mouse, Microsoft® IntelliMouse®, or compatible pointing device

Some *Office*® XP features have additional hardware, network, or communications requirements. The following additional items or services are required to use certain features:

- **For multimedia and sound:** an accelerated video card or MMX processor for improved graphics rendering

- **For speech recognition:** (available for U.S. English, Japanese, and Simplified Chinese only) a Pentium II 400 MHz or higher processor with 128 MB RAM or more, close-talk microphone and audio output device, and Microsoft® *Internet Explorer* 5.0 or later

- **For e-mail:** Microsoft® *Exchange*, Internet SMTP/POP3, IMAP4, or other MAPI-compliant messaging software

- **For advanced collaboration functionality in *Outlook*®:** a Microsoft® *Exchange* Server

- **For Internet functionality:** Internet access (May require payment of a separate fee to a service provider, and local or long-distance telephone charges may apply.)

- **For dial-up services:** 28.8 Kbps or higher modem

- **For handwriting-input features:** a graphics tablet is recommended

- **To enable multicasts of live broadcasts to more than ten audience members:** Microsoft® Windows® Media encoder-compatible video camera for broadcasts including video, Microsoft® Exchange Chat server for chats during live broadcasts, and Windows® Media Server

- **To install *Office*® XP Media Content on a hard disk:** 100 MB of additional hard disk space

- **For each additional language interface installed:** 50 MB of additional hard disk space

- **To use Microsoft® IntelliMouse® Explorer1 with the scroll wheel and all the programmable buttons:** Microsoft IntelliPoint version 3.0 software, Windows® 95, Windows® 98, or Windows® NT® Workstation 4.0 with SP3 or later operating system, 30 MB of available hard disk space, round mouse port (PS/2-compatible) or USB port (connection using USB port on a PC requires a computer running Windows® 98), and a CD-ROM drive.

More information about Microsoft® *Office XP* is available on the Microsoft® Web site at *www.microsoft.com*.

MICROSOFT® *OFFICE*: MAC V.X NEW FEATURES

Microsoft® *Office* for Macintosh® has migrated through several updates and versions during its life span. The latest version of Microsoft® *Office* for Macintosh® is *Office:mac v.X*. *Office:mac v.X* has been enhanced and improved to run on the Mac OSX operating system and take advantage of Mac OSX technologies.

- **New Aqua user interface.** Each of the *Office*® *v.X* programs features a new Aqua user interface that is consistent with Mac OSX. *Office*® *v.X* programs look, feel, and behave like a Mac OSX program.

- **Stability and responsiveness.** *Office*® *v.X* uses key components of the modern Mac OSX architecture to establish a more stable and responsive suite of programs.

- **Quartz technology.** The Quartz 2-D drawing layer shared by all *Office*® *v.X* programs allows you to create graphics that contain anti-aliased lines and shapes and true transparency.

- **Sheets.** Sheets are a new way of displaying dialog boxes in *Office*® *v.X*. A sheet is attached to only one document, which means that it does not demand attention if you are working in another document. This approach more closely resembles the way you actually work with multiple documents.

- **Compatibility with *Office*® 2001 for Mac, *Office*® 98 Macintosh® Edition, and Windows® *Office*.** You can share files with users of *Office*® 2001 for Mac and *Office® 98* Macintosh® Edition. Since *Office® v.X* uses the same file formats as Windows® *Office XP/2000/97,* you can easily exchange files across platforms.

- **Compatibility with AppleWorks 6.** *Office® v.X* works with *AppleWorks 6.0* documents so you can import documents into *Word X.*

- **Communicating with others.** You can easily send and manage e-mail messages on-line and off-line with *Entourage™ X* through connections to Microsoft® *Exchange* servers, Hotmail, and Mac.com.

- **Keeping your schedule on track.** The *Entourage™* Calendar has been improved to let you easily organize your schedule, invite others to events and meetings, and set reminders for important events and projects. It displays your schedule by month, week, or day and includes a Tasks pane that shows tasks for the current day without switching windows.

- **Improved Address Book.** Store information about your contacts and view contact information at a glance in the Preview pane. You can easily locate an address on a map by using Expedia.com, visit a contact's Web page, and more.

- **Office Notifications.** Office Notifications helps you manage your *Office® v.X* calendar events, tasks, and Microsoft .NET Alerts from MSN® Messenger 2.1 for Mac in a single window. Notifications appear on top of any open programs.

- **Project Gallery.** You can access customizable templates for resumes, catalogs, newsletters, calendars, and more from the Project Gallery. The Clip Art Gallery includes hundreds of images and provides tools to work with graphics.

- **Formatting palette.** All formatting tools throughout *Office® v.X* are centralized on a single, improved, context-sensitive palette so it is not necessary to search for commands on toolbars and drop-down menus.

- **Full-text search engine for Help.** You can perform a full-text search for the Help topics in each *Office® v.X* program by simply typing a word or two in either the Office Assistant balloon or the Help Viewer. You can also print Help topics.

- **Office Tools on the Web.** Tools on the Web allows you to link to free updates, templates, downloads, clip art, and third-party offerings for *Office® v.X* for Mac. To access Tools on the Web, click **Tools | Tools on the Web** in any *Office® v.X* program.

System Hardware Requirements—Microsoft® *Office*: mac v.X

The following hardware configuration describes the minimum requirements your computer needs to run *Office® v.X for Mac.*

- **Computer/Processor:** G3 that is Mac OSX compatible
- **Operating system:** Mac OSX version 10.1 or later
- **Memory:** 128 MB of RAM
- **Hard Disk:** 196 MB of available hard disk space for a default installation although the hard disk space requirement varies according to the components you choose to install and the amount of data you store in *Office;* installation of Value Pack components requires additional hard disk space; 80 MB are required for drag-and-drop installation of the individual programs (*Word, Excel, PowerPoint®*)
- **CD-ROM Drive** or a connection to a network if you are installing *Office* from a network volume

- **Monitor that can display 256** colors and a resolution of 800×600 or higher (a monitor that can display thousands or millions of colors and a resolution of 1024×768 or higher is recommended)

Some *Office*® *v.X* features have additional hardware, network, or communications requirements. The following additional items or services are recommended to use certain features:

- For Internet functionality: Internet access (May require payment of a separate fee to a service provider, and local or long-distance telephone charges may apply.)
- For dial-up services: a 14.4 Kbps modem or higher.

More information about Microsoft® *Office v.X* is available on the Microsoft® Web site at *www.microsoft.com.*

OFFICE PRODUCTIVITY TOOLS

Word—The *Office*® Word Processor

Word processing is a software tool that facilitates written communication. Microsoft® *Word* is currently one of the most widely used applications for creating text documents such as letters or reports. *Word* can also be used to create Web pages. The newest version of *Word*, version 2002, provides tools that streamline the process of creating, sharing, reviewing, and publishing documents.

Excel—The *Office*® Spreadsheet

Electronic spreadsheets are computerized ledger sheets organized in rows and columns that automatically perform calculations or other operations on numeric or text data. Microsoft® *Excel* is a productivity tool that enables users to access, process, analyze, share, and display information used to run businesses or perform tasks at work. *Excel* version 2002 was designed to make it easier than before to access, analyze, and share critical business data and provide everyday users with the tools they need to get the most out of their data.

Outlook®—The *Office*® Personal Information Manager and Communication Solution

Microsoft ®*Outlook* version 2002 is designed to help users manage their time and information more effectively. Outlook helps computer users to send and receive e-mail and maintain and organize e-mail information, appointments, contacts, tasks, and documents. *Outlook*® also enables a computer to function as a client to a Microsoft® Exchange Server to more effectively collaborate and share personal information.

PowerPoint®—The *Office*® Presentation Program

Presentation software provides the capability to combine and present instructional or informational content. Additionally, movies, sounds, music, graphics, animation, and hyperlinks can be added to the presentation to create a multimedia presentation. Microsoft® *PowerPoint*® provides a set of easy-to-use tools to create professional-looking slides and multimedia presentations. *PowerPoint*® version 2002 provides new and improved tools that make it easier to share and collaborate on presentations over the Web.

Access—The Office® Database Solution

Microsoft® *Access* is one of the most versatile applications in the *Office®* suite. *Access* is a database management system that contains a rich set of tools useful to both beginning and experienced database users. *Access* version 2002 extends this versatility by giving developers and more experienced users new functionality for building powerful database solutions as well as enabling beginning users to discover and use more of the existing application. *Access* is not available on the Macintosh® platform.

FrontPage®—The Office® Web Site Creation and Management Solution

Microsoft® *FrontPage* is a Web page authoring and publishing tool. It enables users to create and manage Web sites. With *FrontPage®* Web page authors can import, edit, and format HTML the way they want using the familiar Microsoft® *Office* interface. Microsoft® *FrontPage®* version 2002 enables you to add dynamic content with the new Photo Gallery component, *PowerPoint®*-like Drawing Tools, and Automatic Web Content from Microsoft® MSN, MSNBC, Expedia, and bCentral. Since *FrontPage®* looks and works like a Microsoft® *Office* application, users can get started quickly and work in a familiar environment.

Publisher—The Office® Desktop Publishing Solution

Microsoft® *Publisher* is an easy-to-use desktop publishing program designed for users who are serious about creating their own materials without the help of a professional designer. *Publisher®* provides support for commercial printing functionality. The latest version of *Publisher®* includes additional print and Web enhancements and a complete set of sales and marketing tools.

Entourage™—The Macintosh® Personal Information Manager and E-mail Solution

Microsoft® *Entourage™* is a complete e-mail and personal information management program designed specifically for Macintosh®. *Entourage™* is integrated with the other *Office®* programs and combines e-mail with a calendar, address book, task list, reminders, and notes. Although *Entourage™* is similar in function to *Outlook®* for Windows®, if a Macintosh® computer is a client on a Microsoft® Exchange Server network, *Outlook:mac* should be used rather than *Entourage.™*

OFFICE® XP SUITES

Microsoft® has created several *Office® XP* suites that are designed for different purposes. These suites include *Office® XP Professional Special Edition*, *Office® XP Professional*, *Office® XP Standard*, *Office® XP Standard for Students and Teachers*, and *Office® XP Developer*.

- **Office® XP Professional Special Edition** provides the ultimate set of productivity and business tools. In addition to the core set of Microsoft® *Office XP* programs, you get a database management system, a Web site creation and management tool, a desktop publishing solution, and a Microsoft® IntelliMouse for *Office® XP* users. This suite is available only to upgrade customers from authorized resellers.

***Office*® *XP Professional Special Edition* contains:**
Microsoft® *Word* version 2002
Microsoft® *Excel* version 2002
Microsoft® *Outlook*® version 2002
Microsoft® *PowerPoint*® version 2002
Microsoft® *Access* version 2002
Microsoft® *FrontPage*® version 2002
Microsoft® *Publisher* version 2002
SharePoint Team Services from Microsoft®
Microsoft® IntelliMouse Explorer

- ***Office*® *XP Professional*** provides a set of productivity tools to create documents, spreadsheets, and presentations. You can manage personal information and communications and manage data with a desktop database management system.

***Office*® *XP Professional* contains:**
Microsoft® *Word* 2002
Microsoft® *Excel* 2002
Microsoft® *Outlook*® 2002
Microsoft® *PowerPoint*® 2002
Microsoft® *Access* 2002

Microsoft® *Office XP Professional* is also available preinstalled from personal computer manufacturers with *Publisher*. This suite includes Microsoft® *Word, Excel, Outlook*®, *PowerPoint*®, *Access*, and *Publisher*®.

- ***Office*® *XP Standard*** is designed for users who require only the core desktop productivity tools. It includes word processing, presentation, and spreadsheet programs as well as the *Outlook*® e-mail and desktop information management tool.

***Office*® *XP Standard* contains:**
Microsoft® *Word* 2002
Microsoft® *Excel* 2002
Microsoft® *Outlook*® 2002
Microsoft® *PowerPoint*® 2002

- ***Office*® *XP Standard for Students and Teachers*** is available to qualifying students and teachers at a significant discount and provides the core set of *Office*® productivity tools they use at school.

***Office*® *XP Standard for Students and Teachers* contains:**
Microsoft® *Word* 2002
Microsoft® *Excel* 2002
Microsoft ®*Outlook*® 2002
Microsoft® *PowerPoint*® 2002

- ***Office*® *XP Developer*** is designed to help professional software developers build custom *Office*® solutions. *Office*® *XP Developer* includes the *Office*® *XP* Professional suite, as well as tools and documentation for building, managing, and deploying *Office*®-based solutions. It also gives you the *FrontPage*® 2002 Web site creation and management program.

***Office XP Developer* contains:**
Microsoft® *Word* 2002
Microsoft® *Excel* 2002
Microsoft® *Outlook*® 2002
Microsoft® *PowerPoint*® 2002
Microsoft® *Access* 2002

Microsoft® *FrontPage*® 2002
SharePoint Team Services from Microsoft®
Developer Tools
Documentation

- *Office® XP Small Business* is only available preinstalled from a computer manufacturer, not as a full-packaged product. *Office® XP Small Business* includes the *Office®* programs that small businesses use most.

Office® XP Small Business contains:
Microsoft® *Word* 2002
Microsoft® *Excel* 2002
Microsoft® *Outlook*® 2002
Microsoft® *Publisher*® 2002

- *Office:mac v.X* is the *Office®* productivity suite designed for the Macintosh®® platform. It includes the software programs you need to manage your personal information and communications and create documents, spreadsheets, and presentations. It also provides a set of documentation and tools to help you deploy, configure, and support *Office®: mac v.X.*

Office:mac v.X contains:
Microsoft® *Word* X
Microsoft® *Excel* X
Microsoft® *Entourage*™ X
Microsoft® *PowerPoint*® X

INDEX